Building Resilience

Building Resilience

Social Capital in Post-Disaster Recovery

DANIEL P. ALDRICH

The University of Chicago Press
Chicago and London

Daniel P. Aldrich is associate professor of political science at Purdue University. He is the author of *Site Fights: Divisive Facilities and Civil Society in Japan and the West.*

The University of Chicago Press, Chicago 60637
The University of Chicago Press, Ltd., London
© 2012 by The University of Chicago
All rights reserved. Published 2012.
Printed in the United States of America

21 20 19 18 17 16 15 14 13 12   1 2 3 4 5

ISBN-13: 978-0-226-01287-2 (cloth)
ISBN-13: 978-0-226-01288-9 (paper)
ISBN-13: 978-0-226-01289-6 (e-book)
ISBN-10: 0-226-01287-5 (cloth)
ISBN-10: 0-226-01288-3 (paper)
ISBN-10: 0-226-01289-1 (e-book)

Library of Congress Cataloging-in-Publication Data

Aldrich, Daniel P.
    Building resilience : social capital in post-disaster recovery / Daniel P. Aldrich.
        pages ; cm
    Includes bibliographical references and index.
    ISBN-13: 978-0-226-01287-2 (cloth : alkaline paper)
    ISBN-10: 0-226-01287-5 (cloth : alkaline paper)
    ISBN-13: 978-0-226-01288-9 (paperback : alkaline paper)
    ISBN-10: 0-226-01288-3 (paperback : alkaline paper)
    [etc.]
        1. Disaster relief—Social aspects. 2. Disaster relief—Citizen participation.
3. Disaster victims—Social networks. 4. Social capital (Sociology). 5. Social action.
I. Title.
    HV553.A45 2012
    363.34'8—dc23

                                                                    2011050821

♾ This paper meets the requirements of ANSI/NISO Z39.48-1992 (Permanence of Paper).

Contents

Preface

Whereas some scholarship might be dry, written from a distant position in a detached ivy-covered tower, this book was written "wet"—figuratively and literally. In mid-July 2005 my family moved to New Orleans, where I was to begin an assistant professorship at Tulane University. Only six weeks later, at 4:00 a.m. on Sunday, 28 August, my wife and I packed our two small children into our van and drove west to Houston to seek shelter as the rains of Hurricane Katrina began to fall. Heeding the warning of a concerned neighbor who realized we had no experience with the realities of life on the Gulf Coast, we had crammed three days' clothing into a suitcase, snatched up our slow cooker and some photographs, and left behind our rented house filled with new furniture, books, clothes, computers, and records, as well as our second car (a gift from my parents). By noon on Monday, we and other evacuees who were crowded into a motel at the edge of Houston were transfixed by the grainy television images of broken levees. Thereafter, the eleven feet of water that rushed into our New Orleans neighborhood of Lakeview from the nearby Seventeenth Street Canal sat stagnant for almost three weeks, destroying all our possessions and ripping apart the community that had so recently become part of our daily lives.

Although we immediately applied to the Federal Emergency Management Agency for assistance, our initial applications were denied, and we received essentially nothing until our multiple appeals were finally answered in March 2006. Because we had so recently arrived in the Big Easy, we had not had time to activate flood insurance or renters' insurance; hence we had no coverage for our possessions or property. During that period I had a chance to reflect on the course of recovery—as individuals, as a family, and as a community; I started to read the work of disaster experts to examine their analyses of past crises. There was little agreement on what conditions promote a more effective and efficient recovery. Given this lack of consensus, I concurred with other scholars who argued that it was "extremely important to determine what factors impact the recovery process" (Rodriguez et al. 2006, 171). After Hurricane Katrina, I had a chance to see firsthand exactly how individuals, neighborhoods, and cities do—or do not—recover after natural disasters. In my own family's experience, it was friends, friends of friends, acquaintances, and family who did the most for us; subsequently I have found that disaster survivors around the world tell stories remarkably similar to ours. Then, as I completed the first draft of this book, a tremendous earthquake and tsunami struck northeastern Japan on 11 March 2011, and I heard the same narrative from friends and colleagues in Tokyo and around the country.

A great deal of academic work has focused on disasters (Oliver-Smith and Hoffman 1999; Vale and Campanella 2005; Chamlee-Wright 2010; Kage 2011; see Valelly 2004; Tierney 2007; and Aldrich 2011 for overviews). Another tremendous body of literature has focused on social capital—the ties that bind people together (Cohen and Arato 1992; Putnam 1993, 1995, 2000; Castiglione, van Deth, and Wolleb 2008) even in the contentious processes of nonviolent conflict (Chenoweth and Stephan 2011). All of us recognize the role that networks and personal contacts have in our professional and personal lives, but scholarship on disasters and government decision makers has been slow to integrate this concept into its theoretical frameworks. This book brings these two critical concepts together to understand how social resources influence post-disaster recovery. Using extensive studies of four major disasters in the twentieth century, it uncovers how social networks and connections form the core engine of recovery after even the most devastating of events.

While many government disaster mitigation and recovery programs are predicated on the idea that the amount of aid provided and the amount of damage caused by the disaster are important, I bring quantitative and qualitative evidence demonstrating that social resources, at least as much as material ones, prove to be the foundation for resilience and recovery. Some scholars have suggested that social resources are important for recovery (Nakagawa and Shaw 2004; Dynes 2005), but Koh and Cadigan have called for an investigation that "should verify and extend these concepts, offer more quantitative assessments of social capital as applied to disasters, [and] demonstrate their utility through more rigorous analyses" (2008, 283). Others have argued more pointedly that "no empirical studies demonstrate that building social connectedness among community resident results in community resilience" (Chandra et al. 2010, 23). This book responds to these challenges, applying cutting-edge methodologies to new data. I show that neighborhoods with higher levels of social capital work together more effectively to guide resources to where they are needed. Individuals who are connected to extralocal organizations and decision makers prove more resilient because those networks remain robust even after a local crisis. Survivors borrow tools from each other, use their connections to learn about new bureaucratic requirements and procedures, and collaborate to organize community watch organizations.

These results have profound implications not only for future research on social capital and disasters, but also for nongovernmental organizations (NGOs), bureaucrats, and politicians in guiding resource allocation. Today, common approaches to disaster recovery still remain rooted in a 1950s paradigm of physical infrastructure, focusing on the rebuilding of bridges, power lines, homes, roads, and shops. While material-based assistance is important—and certainly saves lives in the short run—alone it will not contribute to long-term resilience in communities subject to past or future crises. Social capital, like other resources, can be nurtured through both local initiatives and foreign interventions. In the future, disaster mitigation programs (such as those analyzed by Swaroop 1992) will need to better integrate physical infrastructure and social infrastructure.

In reading hundreds of disaster case studies, I noticed that many built their conclusions on a single event; many others had been written without even one visit to the affected community. Determined to avoid these pitfalls, I conducted one year of fieldwork in Japan and India, creating four new data sets describing 225 neighborhoods and hamlets across space and time that were affected (to varying degrees) by a disaster. They include information on forty neighborhoods in 1920s Tokyo, nine wards in 1990s Kobe, sixty hamlets and villages, along with an additional 1,600 survey respondents in southeast India in the early twenty-first century, and 115 zip codes in post-Katrina New Orleans. For some urban sites I have more than a decade of information on how neighborhoods responded to catastrophe. To gather materials for this book, in addition to archival work in libraries in three countries, I interviewed close to eighty people, including survivors, NGO members, neighborhood activists, and civil servants in Japan, India, and the United States, and drew on the transcribed interviews of many more. I visited villages across Tamil Nadu, India, and spent time in disaster-struck neighborhoods of Tokyo, Kobe, and New Orleans.

To analyze data for each chapter in the book, I used a combination of quantitative and qualitative methods, including process tracing, time series, cross-sectional maximum likelihood models, and propensity score matching. Given that no single approach is appropriate for analyzing all types of data, many of the chapters are built on "mixed" or "hybrid" approaches that draw on the strengths of both large-N data analysis and detailed historical research. Further, while many scholars continue to provide extended lists of coefficients marked by asterisks to indicate "significant" findings from their research, here I use confidence intervals and simulations to provide more nuanced interpretations of my findings. Each chapter includes graphs and figures that provide predictions based on the empirical findings (although scholars looking for tables of numbers can find them in appendix 1). These figures also indicate the degree of uncertainty about the predictions, illuminating the 95 percent confidence interval around forecasts (Tomz and Wittenberg 1999; King, Tomz, and Wittenberg 2000).

Finally, scholars have repeatedly stressed the importance of replication and transparency in the provision of data; researchers cannot build on past results unless they themselves can reproduce them independently (King 1995). Social science follows the scientific tradition in requiring that both the data and the procedures used to analyze them be made public (King, Keohane, and Verba 1994, 8). To meet these standards, all the data analyzed here are available for free download from my website and from such online data storage sites as the Harvard University DataVerse project and the Interuniversity Consortium for Political and Social Research. I hope these data will provide the foundation for future investigations on disaster recovery.

All books are the work of networks, and never the product solely of the author. First, I am *makir tov* to the Borei Olam for all I have received. The Abe Fellowship administered by the Social Science Research Council and the Center for Global Partnership provided funding for a year of field research in Japan and India. The Law Faculty and the International Center for Comparative Law and Politics at Tokyo University hosted me during my time in Tokyo, and the Jamsetji Tata Centre for Disaster Management within the Tata Institute of Social Sciences in Mumbai hosted me during my fieldwork in India. The Abe Fellowship and the Center for Global Partnership also sponsored a retreat in January 2009 that provided helpful feedback at an early stage of the project. The Mansfield Foundation under the direction of Paige Cottingham-Streater and Sara Seavey provided multiple opportunities for broadening my connections to the academic and policy worlds while I was writing the manuscript through the United States–Japan Network for the Future program. The Purdue Research Foundation and the Purdue Alumni Association provided funds for additional fieldwork in New Orleans.

Suggestions from colleagues at the Public Policy and Political Theory workshop at Purdue University—in particular Pat Boling, Aaron Hoffman,

Jay McCann, Leigh Raymond, Laurel Weldon, and Dwayne Woods—improved my arguments. The East-West Center in Honolulu provided a tranquil yet intellectually stimulating environment in the summer of 2011 for editing the final manuscript. A big *mahalo* to Allen Clark, Carolyn Eguchi, Roland Fuchs, Karl Kim, and Nancy Lewis.

I had the opportunity to present sections of my research at the annual conferences of the Association for Asian Studies and the American Political Science Association, and also at the German Institute for Japanese Studies, Japan International Cooperation Systems, the Contemporary Japan Group at the Institute of Social Sciences of Tokyo University, and the Tata Institute of Social Science conference on disaster in January 2008. A book conference in March 2010 sponsored by the Center for Global Partnership, the Purdue Climate Change Research Center, and Purdue University's Discovery Park allowed me to hear feedback from five world-class scholars: Rieko Kage, Sudarshan Rodriguez, Yasuyuki Sawada, Shigeo Tatsuki, and Rick Weil. I appreciate their thoughts and comments.

Special thanks to Joie Acosta, Simon Avenell, Gomathy Balasubramanian, Arjen Boin, Anita Chandra, Stephanie Chang, Lane Conaway, Emily Chamlee-Wright, Susan Cutter, Paul Danyi, Christina Davis, Cindy Fate, Rose Filley, Carolyn Fleisher, Cary Friedman, Mary Alice Haddad, Ken Hartman, Travis Henry, Jacques Hyman, Gary Isaac, Jeff Kingston, Anirudh Krishna, Howard Kunreuther, Jennifer Lind, Irfan Nooruddin, Sadaaki Numata, Rob Olshansky, Charles Perrow, Susan Pharr, Barry Rabe, Nicole Restrick, Ian Rinehart, Rafe Sagarin, Paul Scalise, Len Schoppa, Miranda Schreurs, Hideaki Shiroyama, John Sides, Gavin Smith, Pat Steinhoff, Ezra Suleiman, Kathleen Tierney, and Rick Valelly. They provided guidance, feedback, and support throughout the process. Marion Pratt took the time to work completely through an early version of the manuscript, and her suggestions greatly improved it. Christian Brunelli deserves special mention because of his suggestion that I excavate Tokyo's past by digging in the archives of the Tokyo Metropolitan Police (Keishichō) from nearly a century ago to better understand how neighborhoods there recovered after the 1923 earthquake.

Eric Berndt, Erik Cleven, Kevin Crook, Eric Nguyen, Elli Reuland, Ross Schoofs, Takahiro Yamamoto, and Laura Young provided excellent research assistance. The hard work of Janki Andharia, Hari Ayyappan, Lokesh Gowda, Jacquleen Joseph, Sunil Santha, and V. Vivekanandan made my research in India possible, as did Annie George and her staff at the Nagapattinam Coordination and Resource Centre. I appreciate their help. Two anonymous reviewers for the University of Chicago Press provided constructive, detailed comments that have improved the manuscript tremendously. Bert Rockman, my chair at Purdue University, has been a pillar of support and encouragement, as has Dean Irwin Weiser.

When we fled to Houston as the rain came down in New Orleans, several families opened their homes and their hearts. Craig Aldrich, Wesley Ashendorf, Sheldon Bootin, and their families, along with the United Orthodox Synagogue in Houston, turned what could have been a traumatic week into an almost comfortable one, and for that we are grateful. In Brighton, Massachusetts, the Blumberg, Miller, Moskovitz, Sadetsky, and Shanske families went out of their way to help us restore our home and our lives, and Ellie Levi and her community in New York worked to help us rebuild our destroyed library. Thanks to Sterling Chen, Asuka Imaizumi, and Chana Odem for their excellent graphics work and to David Pervin and Shenny Wu of the University of Chicago Press for their help and Alice Bennett and Deborah Gray for their editing.

This book is dedicated to the members of my immediate and extended family, who have given me all that matters. My parents, Howard and Penny Aldrich, my brother Steven and sister-in-law Allison Aldrich, my parents-in-law Louis and Sun Cha McCoy, my aunt Dalia Carmel, and my grandmother Dorotha Aldrich have provided love, assistance, and advice beyond measure. A number of my relatives are no longer here to share their lives with us, but the memories of my grandfather Jack (Yaakov) Daum, my grandmother Fifi (Freida Yehudis Goldstein) Daum, my great uncle Herb (Dov Ber) Goldstein, and my grandfather Howard Aldrich continue to be a blessing. My wife, Yael, has fulfilled the words of our sages as both the foundation stone and a source of spiritual growth for our family. Through her dedication to our well-being and her work with our four wonderful children—Gavriel Tzvi, Yaakov, Yehudis, and Dov Ber—she is my *aishes chayil*.

Social Capital: Its Role in Post-Disaster Recovery

Within two years of Hurricane Katrina, the neighborhood of Mary Queen of Vietnam within Village de L'Est in the northeast corner of New Orleans had rebuilt many of its heavily damaged homes and restored most of its shops. Census tract data from the year 2000 show that income in the area was lower than the state and national averages, and there is no evidence that government agencies provided special assistance to local residents after the flooding (author interviews, 2010). Yet two years after the levees broke, while much of the rest of the city stood empty, surveys reported a 90 percent repopulation rate and a 90 percent business recovery rate in this section of the Big Easy (LaRose 2006; Faciane 2007). More than five years after floodwaters as high as eleven feet surged through the area, though, much of New Orleans's Lower Ninth Ward—approximately twelve miles to the southeast—looks as damaged as the day the levees broke. Poverty rates in the Village de L'Est area are close to those of the Ninth Ward (Chamlee-Wright 2010), yet across the Ninth Ward, less than 35 percent of the original population has returned, and many houses sit empty, with visible water lines on their walls (*New York Times*, 27 August 2010).

Thousands of miles away and a year earlier in Tamil Nadu, India, the 2004 Indian Ocean tsunami devastated hundreds of villages and killed thousands of residents along the sandy southeast coast. Within a year of the catastrophe, some villages put fishermen back to work, built new housing for the community, and brought in aid from both domestic and foreign organizations. Other hamlets—similarly devastated by the tsunami—seemed to be off the map of aid relief (*Hindu*, 17 March 2007). After disasters, some communities bounce back quickly, while others struggle to meet basic needs for food, water, shelter, and employment (Fletcher 2010). Certain neighborhoods draw their survivors back and attract new residents, while other areas in the same city become ghost towns, emptied of people.

This book seeks to explain the variation in post-disaster recovery by focusing on the role of social capital—the networks and resources available to people through their connections to others. I argue that higher levels of social capital—more than such factors as greater economic resources, assistance from the government or outside agencies, and low levels of damage—facilitate recovery and help survivors coordinate for more effective reconstruction.[1] Even highly damaged communities with low income and little outside aid benefit from denser social networks and tighter bonds with relatives, neighbors, and extralocal acquaintances. Alternatively, neighborhoods with lower levels of social resources can find themselves unable to organize collectively to deter looting and garbage dumping, to communicate necessary requests to the authorities, and to work together to rebuild their community. Deeper reservoirs of social capital serve as informal insurance[2] and mutual assistance for survivors, help them overcome collective action constraints, and increase the likelihood that they will stay and work to rebuild (as opposed to moving elsewhere) (Simile 1995).

However, social capital can be a double-edged sword, helping in-groups recover more effectively but at the same time slowing or halting rebuilding for those with fewer social resources who sit outside the mainstream. Neighborhoods and groups with fewer social resources face negative outcomes, both inadvertent and deliberate. The absence of social capital can stall a community's recovery, short-circuiting attempts to overcome collective action problems (Chamlee-Wright 2010). Further, strong bonding social capital can reinforce existing systems of discrimination and justify programs that provide benefits only locally, not regionwide or citywide, harming those on the margins of society. I explore the "Janus-faced" nature of social capital (Szreter 2002) through studies of four disasters that took place between 1923 and 2005.

Defining Disasters and Their Impact

Sociologists define disasters broadly as failures of social systems (cf. Girard and Peacock 2000, 203; Erikson 1976, 154) or as occasions "when extraordinary efforts are taken to protect and defend some social resource whose existence is perceived as threatened" (Dynes 1989, 9). Here I use the word *disasters* to refer to collective events that—at least temporarily, and often for years afterward—suspend normal daily life routines owing to widespread damage (Fischer 1998, 3). Speaking broadly, disasters are events that overwhelm capacity in multiple ways (cf. Sawada 2010).[3] Turner (1976, 755-756) saw a disaster as "an event, concentrated in time and space, which threatens a society or a relatively self-sufficient subdivision of a society with major unwanted consequences." For this book a disaster is *an event that suspends normal activities and threatens or causes severe, communitywide damage.* This open-ended definition of disasters excludes traffic jams, plane delays, and fender benders but includes earthquakes, tsunamis, nuclear meltdowns, tornadoes, fires, and floods. Such events take lives, destroy homes and businesses, disrupt the standard flow of goods and services, put standard operating procedures on hold, and damage critical infrastructure. The four main events I discuss in this book fall into the category of *megacatastrophes* in that each killed more than one thousand people and destroyed thousands of residential and commercial structures. Some of the cases involved the devastation of half of the affected city (the 1923 Tokyo earthquake; cf. Aldrich 2008c) or the flooding of four-fifths of the area (Hurricane Katrina).

Attempts to further subcategorize disasters as "natural" or "man-made" are increasingly problematic given that much of the destruction from a disaster like Hurricane Katrina[4] occurred precisely because of human attempts to subvert or artificially control nature (Steinberg 2000). Some have called this resulting vulnerability *endogenous* in that the outcome is at least in part the result of human actions (Auerswald et al. 2006, 5). Societies regularly build houses and provide insurance for residents in floodplains and flood-prone coastal areas; planners construct cities below sea level, while developers destroy the components of natural ecosystems such as mangroves, marshes, and wetlands that would protect such areas from flooding (Kolbert 2006). By centralizing and concentrating energy, population, and economic power into smaller areas, we have made the consequences for emergencies and disasters all the more intense (Perrow 2007).

Scholars of disaster continue to debate whether catastrophes have long-term structural impacts on localities and nations—that is, whether crises serve as a mechanism for Schumpeter's vision of "creative destruction." Some see crises as bringing economic opportunity, while others see either no long-term effects or negative outcomes for disaster-struck areas. For example, Douglas Dacy and Howard Kunreuther suggested that "a community may benefit economically from a disaster through a rapid inflow of capital for rebuilding purposes" (1969, 181).[5] J. M. Albala-Bertrand (1993) studied the aftereffects of twenty-eight disasters in twenty-six Central and South American countries and found that despite varying levels of damage and pre-disaster economic development, even the worst disasters rarely had long-term, measurable economic impact. In their study of the population of Japanese cities bombed during the Second World War, Donald Davis and David Weinstein (2002, 1283) argued that "even very strong temporary shocks have virtually no permanent impact on the size of cities."

Taiji Hagiwara and Toshiki Jinushi (2005) studied the Kobe earthquake and argued that by 2001—some six years after the event—any effects of the quake on the economy were negligible. Gary Becker (2005) argued that "lasting economic effects are similarly small for most other natural disasters that have occurred during the past couple of centuries." Stephanie Chang (2000), on the contrary, posited that severe disasters, including the Kobe earthquake, did have a long-term structural impact on the economy; Eduardo Cavallo, Andrew Powell, and Oscar Becerra (2010b) estimated that a decade after a major disaster, national output per capita may remain one-third below normal. Furthermore, quantitative studies have shown that disasters may dampen the technological transfer between developed and developing countries, with major catastrophes reducing the spillover of knowledge (Cuaresma, Hlouskova, and Obersteiner 2008, 225).

Regardless of their measurable effect on the economies of cities and regions, disasters remain among the most critical events affecting residents and their neighborhoods around the world. Sociologists have underscored that the individual-level course of post-disaster recovery cannot be captured through simple economic measures; instead, recovery for many survivors involves an associational, mental transition from victim to citizen (Tatsuki et al. 2005, 3). For communities at large, recovery involves both population recovery and the (re)creation of bonds among neighbors; surveys have confirmed that after disasters, most survivors see social connections and community as critical for their recovery (Tatsuki and Hayashi 2002, 3; Tatsuki et al. 2004). Understanding what factors speed or impede disaster recovery is critical both for survivors and for decision makers who must allocate scarce resources after a crisis.

According to the Emergency Events Database, over the past three decades "natural" disasters killed close to three million people and inflicted billions of dollars in property damage. The 2004 Indian Ocean tsunami devastated the southeast Indian coast of Tamil Nadu; floodwater inundated New Orleans after Hurricane Katrina in 2005; and the 2010 Haiti earthquake may have killed 300,000 people. The 9.0 magnitude earthquake off Japan's northeast shore on 11 March 2011 set off a massive tsunami that killed close to 20,000 people in Aomori, Fukushima, Miyagi, and Akita Prefectures and triggered a terrifying nuclear crisis in that country.[6] While large-scale crises such as the 1991 Bangladesh cyclone, the 2008 Cyclone Nargis in Myanmar, Marmara earthquakes, and Italy's 2009 earthquake captured media attention, numerous smaller-scale floods, typhoons, earthquakes, and mudslides killed hundreds of thousands of victims around the world and affected far more. Researchers have confirmed an upward trend in the number of disasters, individuals affected by them, and their economic costs over the past two decades (Hoyois et al. 2007). Scientists predict that the global cost of disaster, in both lives and property damage, will only increase with the progression of climate change.

Scholars recognize that the negative effects of disasters are concentrated in the most socially vulnerable populations, which include the poor, minorities, women, and the elderly (Steinberg 2000, 194; Morrow 2005; Cutter and Emrich 2006; Gill 2007; Cutter and Finch 2008).[7] We know much about common flaws in disaster responses, such as the ways communications networks are likely to break down (Kweit and Kweit 2006), how intergovernmental relations impede effective coordination (Rubin and Barbee 1985; Schneider 1990), and the fundamentally rhetorical "fantasy documents" prepared by disaster planners that play little role in actual disaster responses (Clarke 1999). However, researchers know little about what has gone right (cf. Valelly 2004). Specifically, scholars and disaster planners often overlook the fact that within disaster-affected regions, certain neighborhoods and towns recover from catastrophe more quickly than others (Edgington 2010, xv). Some areas display remarkable resilience after a crisis, while others seem unable to recover (*Gulf Times,* 25 June 2006). A clearer understanding of post-disaster resilience along with the factors that promote recovery will provide policy makers and victims alike with "usable knowledge"—knowledge that is both accurate and politically tractable (Haas 2004, 572).

Resilience and Recovery

Throughout this volume, I focus on the recovery of disaster-struck communities and the presence (or absence) of a capacity I call resilience. There are thousands of ways to define recovery after catastrophe, including economic (Albala-Bertrand 1993), demographic, infrastructure, and transportation-focused metrics (Liu, Fellowes, and Mabanta 2006; Karatani et al. 2000).[8] The simplest definition of recovery—and perhaps the one least likely to occur—is one in which the community or city restores itself to its pre-disaster condition (Albala-Bertrand 1993, 173). But recovery is not a static point or a single moment in time: it is an extended process. Based on past studies, I define community recovery as *the process of repopulation by survivors—who may have fled or been evacuated—and new residents along with the gradual resumption of normal daily routines for those occupants.*[9] In the case studies, I use

various proxies to capture this concept, including yearly measures of population change, household and village access to and receipt of aid packages,
and the construction and occupation of temporary housing.[10] Some of these
measures, such as temporary housing and access to assistance, encapsulate
earlier stages of recovery, while others, such as population return, immigra-
tion, and growth, capture events that take place over years and even decades.
Whereas popular press accounts hope to see results within weeks or months,
an actual return to normality may take far longer, and population levels may
never reach pre-disaster points. New Orleans, for example, will likely remain
a smaller city than it was before Katrina.

For the studies of the 1923 Tokyo and 1995 Kobe earthquakes, I focus on
population change because, as others have argued, "the numerical resilience
of the population may be a reasonable proxy for recovery. For cities that have
lost huge percentages of their populations, the restoration of the city as a
place of habitation is itself a signal achievement" (Vale and Campanella 2005,
12). Population growth demonstrates whether survivors and newcomers are
repopulating what may otherwise be a ghost town. The importance of monitoring how many residents and newcomers return to a city after a disaster
can be seen in the efforts of United States government officials to capture this
quantity of interest after Hurricane Katrina (Russell 2006). Authorities used
creative measuring techniques, such as monitoring the US Postal Service's
change of address form filings, to measure population return to New Orleans
after the storm (Lang 2006; Warner 2006). Weil (2010) has tied repopulation levels to various indicators of social capital and civic engagement in
post-Katrina New Orleans. Similarly, in their study of the resilience of Japanese cities from 1925 to 1965—a period during which many of those areas in
the study were bombed by Allied Forces—Davis and Weinstein (2002) used
population measures to track overall trends in development. Observers
pointed out that after the tragic 1972 Managua earthquake in Nicaragua,
many citizens chose to flee to neighboring nations rather than attempt to
return home and rebuild in a culture poisoned by civil war and corruption
(Garvin 2010). David Edgington followed the population recovery for more
than a decade after the 1995 Kobe earthquake to understand patterns of recovery in the city (2010, 206). Etsuko Yasui (2007, 319) argued that population recovery has proved to be an essential part of disaster recovery.

Beyond the process of recovery, scholars and decision makers alike have
recently focused on resilience (Smith 2011). President Barack Obama praised
New Orleans in the fall of 2010 as a "symbol of resilience," primarily because
of the return of people and businesses to the area in the five years following the
citywide floods (Bowman 2010). International disaster planners at the 2005

World Conference on Disaster Reduction adopted the Hyogo Framework for Action, focused on "building the resilience of nations and communities to disasters" (United Nations International Strategy for Disaster Reduction 2005).[11] George Galster, Jackie Cutsinger, and Up Lim investigated the ways urban neighborhoods demonstrate what they call stability: outcomes are stable "if, upon being upset by some transient external force, the indicator tends to return to its original state" (2007, 169). The word resilience derives from the Latin word *resilire,* meaning "to jump back" or "to recoil," and it generally describes "the capacity of a material or system to return to equilibrium after a displacement" (Norris et al. 2008, 127; cf. Adger et al. 2005). Across social science and biological science research, resilience indicates the "capacity for successful adaptation in the face of disturbance, stress, or adversity" (Norris et al. 2008, 129).

Broadly speaking, there are at least five dimensions to resilience after disaster, including "1) personal and familial socio-psychological well being; 2) organizational and institutional restoration; 3) economic and commercial resumption of services and productivity; 4) restoring infrastructural systems integrity; and 5) operational regularity of public safety and government" (McCreight 2010, 4-5). In this book I define resilience at the communal, not individual, level, focusing on the ability of a neighborhood, ward, or area to engage in positive, networked adaptation after a crisis. Resilience is a neighborhood's capacity to weather crises such as disasters and engage in effective and efficient recovery through coordinated efforts and cooperative activities. Neighborhoods demonstrating less resilience fail to mobilize collectively and often must wait for recovery guidance and assistance from private or public sectors (Chamlee-Wright 2010). It is possible to use public policy programs and local initiatives to build resilience—that is, to increase a neighborhood's capacity to recover effectively—as I discuss throughout this volume and at length in the conclusions and concrete policy recommendations in chapter 7.

Standard Theories of Recovery

Researchers have proposed hypotheses that link the ability of a region, town, or neighborhood to recover to a variety of factors, but few have carried out replicable empirical analyses to test them. Standard analyses envision quality of governance, aid, damage from the disaster, socioeconomic and demographic conditions, and population density as among the most important factors used to determine recovery rates. More recently, some studies have added social resources to the list of potential factors.

As a result, many observers assume that the quality of governance—whether local or regional—best determines how resilient disaster-struck areas will be. After disasters, affected people and commentators rush to judge the effectiveness of the government response. Following Hurricane Katrina, for example, pundits argued that the Bush administration had underestimated the damage from the broken levees and was unprepared for the scale of tragedy that followed (Murray 2006). Critics argued that Federal Emergency Management Agency (FEMA) director Michael Brown seemed unaware that people were sheltering in the New Orleans Superdome and had little experience in handling disasters; many claimed that bureaucrats and low-level personnel within FEMA were the weak link in the recovery system.[12] Others were quick to blame Mayor Ray Nagin, while some believed Louisiana governor Kathleen Blanco had been too slow to bring in the National Guard. Some residents of the Big Easy argued that the city of New Orleans itself was "autocratic, incompetent, [and] corrupt" (quoted in Baum 2006, 63) and that its police force lacked moral fiber (see Maggi 2006 for details). North Americans are not alone in their desire to play the blame game (Boin, McConnell, and 'T Hart 2008; see Roberts 2007 for an alternative perspective).

After the Kobe earthquake, for example, residents and Japanese editorial pages criticized the central government for failing to immediately order the Self-Defense Forces stationed nearby to assist in fire fighting, search and rescue, and recovery efforts (Edgington 2010, 51). Following the earthquake, Prime Minister Tomiichi Murayama, after visiting the city of Kobe, first told survivors to "cheer up and fight the hardships," but he soon told Parliament that his "government's first response to the quake may have been 'confused' " (quoted in Begley and McKillop 1995). Furthermore, the central government's prioritizing housing for the elderly had perverse effects: the rush to place senior citizens in temporary housing after the Kobe earthquake separated them from their friends and support networks and may have caused "lonely deaths" (*Mainichi Shinbun*, 17 January 1997, 4; Suga 2007).[13] Indian activists angrily pointed out that the government of India had used the Indian Ocean tsunami as a chance to force many fishermen back from their traditional locations directly along the seashore while allowing commercial businesses such as tourist hotels to maintain those same spots (Menon, Rodriguez, and Sridhar 2007). After the March 2010 Chilean earthquake observers claimed that the government seemed slow to react (*Economist*, 4 March 2010).

While it is easy to lay the blame for poor or unsteady recovery on politicians, bureaucrats, or cultures of corruption, empirical data from disasters show that regardless of the quality of governance, different neighborhoods under the same leadership come back at different rates over the medium to long term. While a poor decision immediately following a catastrophe may delay the arrival of food, water, medical assistance, and supplies, in the long term other factors matter more. If an incompetent mayor or a slow-acting governor alone determined the rate of recovery, all neighborhoods within the affected area would stagnate or recover at the same rate. Empirical evidence at the neighborhood level does not support this belief. As such, we can dismiss claims that the local mayor, state governor, or overall governance best explains variation within disaster-struck cities.

Folk wisdom also postulates that the amount of aid received by the affected area will always influence recovery. The more money, proponents argue, the faster the area will rebuild. One official working in post-Katrina Louisiana stated, "First this is about cash, and getting money to people. It's about getting dollars on the ground as quickly as possible" (quoted in Caputo 2010). Scholars have argued that "the resilience of cities depends on political and financial influences exercised from well outside the city limits" (Vale and Campanella 2005, 342). When President Jimmy Carter asked Governor Dixie Lee Ray of Washington State what he could do to assist in the aftermath of the eruption of Mount St. Helens, she spelled out "m-o-n-e-y" (quoted in May 1985, 71). Some experts have argued that if government support is not forthcoming quickly after a disaster, "confidence rapidly flags, businesses are not reopened, and residents leave the region" (Zandi et al. 2006, 107). Observers tracking the recovery after Hurricane Andrew argued that household recovery depended on both private funds and federal and state public assistance programs (Dash, Peacock, and Morrow 2000, 221).[14] While aid can certainly assist in the immediate post-disaster period and medical assistance and food can save lives, "the large outpouring of aid from rich nations will help only in the very near term" (Becker 2005).

Empirical studies of the effect of aid and government expenditure have failed to provide evidence of a causal link between more aid money and enhanced recovery.[15] After the 1972 Managua earthquake in Nicaragua, the tremendous amount of aid that poured in engendered massive corruption and triggered a revolution and a counterrevolution, not rapid recovery (Garvin 2010). Research on post–World War II recovery in Europe has found no connection between the amount of US aid, provided through such programs as the Marshall Plan, and recoveries in the areas of industrial production or electricity production (Kage 2010b). Taiji Hagiwara and Toshiki Junishi (2005) looked at a sample of 417 observations from thirty towns, villages, and hamlets after the Kobe earthquake and found no statistically significant relationship between aid and various proxies for recovery, including job growth and freight output, and no correlation between aid and added value in manufacturing. Gary Webb, Kathleen Tierney, and James Dahlhamer (2002, 55) used data from the Loma Prieta earthquake and Hurricane Andrew to argue that factors such as external sources of aid did not significantly affect the long-term viability of firms in disaster-affected areas. Similarly, evidence from post-quake 1923 Tokyo in chapter 3 shows that each ward across the city received the same amount of compensation—but neighborhoods showed varying trajectories of recovery. Had money been the core factor in recovery, all areas within Tokyo should have come back at the same speed.

Little systematic evidence connects greater levels of aid and assistance to better long-term recoveries. In fact, there is much evidence that significant amounts of aid can be counterproductive (see Cohen and Werker 2008, 810, for a model of how this might work). In India following the 2004 tsunami, large amounts of financial assistance broke up existing social relationships in fishing villages, pushed many young, undereducated girls[16] to marry early (because they were orphans who received large compensation packages from NGOs and the government, and hence became more attractive to the "marriage market"). The aid also reduced fishing catches (the overprovision of fishing boats led to a decrease in fish stock) (Alexander 2006).[17] Furthermore, the state recovery policies in coastal India emphasized nuclear families, not extended ones, undermining traditional social practices in the area (Rodriguez et al. 2008).[18]

Another factor thought to determine the pace of recovery is damage levels from the catastrophe. Robert Kates and David Pijawka (1977, 12) posited that "the rate of recovery is directly related to the magnitude of the damage," and Dacy and Kunreuther (1969, 72) argued that "it just seems reasonable to assume that the speed of recovery following a disaster will be determined primarily by the magnitude of the physical damage." In writing about Hurricane Katrina recovery in New Orleans, one observer postulated that "New Orleans neighborhoods that suffered the most severe flooding after Hurricane Katrina . . . lost the largest proportion of residents in the decade ending last year" (Krupa 2011). Similarly, Eugene Haas, Robert Kates, and Martyn Bowden (1977) and Yasui (2007, 29) argued that more damaged areas will recover more slowly, while those that escaped devastation and suffered only minor devastation will require less time. More devastated areas take longer to recover because more repairs are necessary, housing is in shorter supply, and injuries and casualties are higher.

Others have argued the opposite: the more damage, they believe, the quicker the recovery. After World War II, for example, the countries that suffered great damage during the war—Taiwan, Japan, and Greece, for example—tended to recover fastest (Kage 2010b). This may be because of the economic advantage of backwardness, in which manufacturers could leap past the standard linear evolution of capital and acquire the newest types of manufacturing equipment and technology. However, empirical evidence supporting arguments about damage has been mixed at best. Scholars such as Murosaki (1973, 55) and Shigeo Tatsuki (2008, 24) have challenged this logic, arguing that the scale of damage and loss do not correlate well with recovery rates. All the case studies here take into account the amount of damage caused by the disaster through investigations of the number of casualties and wounded residents along with measures such as the percentage of the population in the community who are negatively affected by the crisis.

Other researchers, rather than looking at such external characteristics as governance, aid, and damage, have sought to connect internal characteristics of damaged neighborhoods with their recovery pace. A great deal of research has sought to link socioeconomic and demographic conditions to the pace of rebuilding (Donner and Rodriguez 2008). One study of the 1906 San Francisco earthquake (Bowden et al. 1977, 79) argued that "at one end of the spectrum, upper-class districts and individuals stabilized rapidly, whereas unskilled workers at the low end of the spectrum were still in motion five years after the disaster. . . . the high white-collar group had a very high persistence rate of 92%, indicating that early in the second year after the disaster the upper-income residential district had been established." Their research showed that unskilled workers—the lower classes—moved more often and farther than the upper classes, and that this forced migration did not end even several years after the disaster. In a similar argument, Eugene Haas et al. (1977, 30) believed that "the lower socioeconomic rank of the individual, the more frequent post disaster moves will be, the longer the period of deferral of residential stability will be, the fewer the housing alternatives will be, and the greater the chance that the family will be forced to leave the city permanently."

Debate still continues on the role of socioeconomic status in recovery. Yasuyuki Sawada and Satoshi Shimizutani (2008, 465) analyzed household survey data after the Kobe earthquake and found that those families that did not lose their "collateralizable assets" such as equity in their houses, savings, and jewelry were better able to maintain their pre-disaster consumption patterns than families with less financial capital. Aggregating these results to the neighborhood level, communities devastated by disaster require bridge loans and grants as a buffer against these often unexpected shocks (United States Small Business Administration 2006). At such moments, neighborhoods without access to capital will be forced to draw on personal savings; few communities will have sufficient private financial resources to undertake broader recovery schemes. In a study of resilience after the 1995 Kobe earthquake, Shigeo Tatsuki and Haruo Hayashi (2002) used survey data to show that business owners struggled to find capital to rebuild after both homes and businesses were damaged. One recent study of the Kobe earthquake argued that a "neighborhood's relative wealth or poverty is a good predictor of its ability to rebound" (Edgington 2010, 225). Bruce Katz (2006), focusing on the socioeconomic conditions in New Orleans, emphasized that "of the 131,000 poor people in the city in 2000, nearly 50,000 (38 percent) lived in those neighborhoods of extreme poverty." Scholars underscored that "the child poverty rate for the New Orleans metropolitan statistical area was the highest in the nation in 2005" (Webb 2009, 141). In an overview of post-tsunami recovery, one observer argued that "it is a proven fact that richer people are better equipped to face disasters due to better infrastructure, shelter, equipment, knowledge, skill, and the existence of alternatives including insurance" (Siromony 2006, 184).

Conversely, some see a "politics of disposability" where African Americans and other minorities are deliberately neglected by North American authorities after disasters (Giroux 2006), whereas others have argued that government agencies respond differently to the wealthy than to the poor. Some research has supported the argument that race mattered in the disaster recovery, particularly since "black workers from New Orleans were four times more likely than white counterparts to lose their jobs after the storm, all else equal" (Elliott and Pais 2006, 317). As a result, "minorities and the poor suffer a much slower recovery because of lethargic responses by agencies whose participation is critical to their recovery" (Bullard and Wright 2009, xx). Brinkley (2007, 617) similarly postulated that in post-Katrina New Orleans, "wealthier neighborhoods flickered back to life first" presumably because of their greater resources. However, empirical research on post-Katrina recovery has demonstrated that affluence alone is not a strong predictor of recovery after crisis (Chamlee-Wright 2010), as has research on Hurricane Andrew, which used data from one thousand survivors to show that income does not have an effect on rebuilding (Morrow 2000, 146). A study of counties affected by large-scale flooding in North America found no relation between recovery time and socioeconomic status (Eoh 1998). This book regularly tests the role of socioeconomic conditions on recovery and uses statistics on race (and caste) wherever possible.

Scholarship has linked one final internal characteristic with the pace of recovery: population density. Haque (2003), for example, sought to connect population density with the number of deaths and injuries resulting from disasters. Higher-density areas tend to be metropolitan, and such areas, if damaged, require more time for recovery (Donner and Rodriguez 2008). Areas with greater densities may recover more slowly because of the difficulty in providing temporary and permanent housing during the post-disaster period (Tobin and Montz 1997, 14).[19] High-density slums in India have proved a difficult policy challenge for Indian authorities looking to relocate internally displaced people (Tandon and Mohanty 2000), while the destruction of high-density housing projects in post-Katrina New Orleans triggered strong criticism at home and abroad (Nossiter and Eaton 2007; UN News Service, 28 February 2008). As with other potential factors, the cases under study here take into account the population density of the disaster-affected area.

Social Capital: An Underexamined Factor

Outside the field of disaster recovery, research in the social sciences on social capital exploded following the early work of Pierre Bourdieu (1986), James Coleman (1988, 1990), and Robert Putnam (1993, 1995, 2000). According to Nan Lin, social capital is composed of the resources embedded in one's social networks (2008, 51). Chapter 2 fully elaborates on the mechanisms of social networks and resources, but, put briefly, stronger social capital results in building new norms about compliance and participation among network members; providing information and knowledge to individuals in the group; and creating trustworthiness.[20] (Throughout the book, I use the phrases *social capital* and *social networks* nearly interchangeably.) As a result, areas with greater levels of social capital can overcome obstacles to collective action that often prevent groups from accomplishing their goals (Olson 1965; Chamlee-Wright 2010). Scholarship has linked higher levels of social capital to superior health outcomes, stronger governance, and better economic growth. Drawing on this foundational research, a number of disaster scholars have suggested that social capital may play a role in post-disaster resilience (Buckland and Rahman 1999; Nakagawa and Shaw 2004; Dynes 2005; Kage 2010a).[21] Other empirical studies have connected individual recoveries after disasters to self-reported levels of trustworthiness and civic participation (Tatsuki and Hayashi 2002). For example, richer social capital, civic involvement, and active citizenship helped survivors of the Kobe earthquake to see themselves as recovered from the tragedy (Tatsuki 2008). Studies of post-Katrina resilience have indicated strong connections between civic engagement, such as involvement in associations and clubs, trust, and repopulation levels (Weil 2010, 5).

Although many scholars have looked into the internal characteristics of neighborhoods such as race and socioeconomic status to predict their recovery rates, neighborhood-level studies of recovery have rarely included explicit measures for social capital (Rovai 1994; Kamel and Loukaitou-Sideris 2004; Cutter and Finch 2008; Pais and Elliott 2008). This book adds to our knowledge of disaster recovery by both specifying theoretically how social capital operates after a crisis and quantitatively measuring its effects in multiple settings and time periods at the microlevel of analysis. Measuring social capital using the best available historically and culturally sensitive proxies,[22] I argue that social resources can assist in recovery by serving as informal insurance after a disaster, overcoming collective action problems that stymie recovery and rehabilitation, and strengthening "voice" and decreasing the probability of "exit."[23]

One unexpected finding emerging from this research is that social capital does not always function solely as a public good, distributing benefits to all (Berman 1997; Chambers and Kopstein 2001). Instead, as research in other fields has uncovered, it can be seen as a double-edged sword (Aldrich and Crook 2008) or a Janus-faced resource (Szreter 2002), in that in certain circumstances it benefits many survivors, but not all. Stronger social networks indeed benefit the majority of survivors, but when layered on top of existing prejudices, social relationships across certain groups can slow down the recovery of out-groups (see Nagar and Rethemeyer 2007). More specifically, peripheral or marginalized groups within society that hold less social capital benefit little and often are harmed by the groups holding stronger social capital after a disaster.[24] In Tamil Nadu, India, for example, while villages with institutionalized social capital in the form of *uur panchayats* (caste/tribal councils)[25] effectively connected to outside aid, survivors in those villages who were not members and had no connections received little if any help (Gill 2007). Many Dalits (often referred to as "untouchables" or outcastes), women, and Muslims reported active discrimination during the recovery period as organized and connected ethnic groups blocked their progress (Louis 2005; Mercks 2007).

In 1923 Tokyo, after the devastating earthquake that destroyed nearly half of Japan's capital city, thousands of Koreans—an out-group living in Japan—were targeted and killed by mobs acting on false rumors. After Hurricane Katrina, many New Orleans communities recognized the need for temporary housing and FEMA trailers but stigmatized these facilities and sought to exclude them from their neighborhoods (Davis and Bali 2008). In the end, well-organized communities pushed away mobile homes and slowed down recovery by forcing planners to find alternative sites, often in neighborhoods

TABLE 1. Six explanations for the pace of disaster recovery

Variable	Hypotheses and assumptions	Operationalization
Quality of governance	Better-informed, more competent decision makers speed up recovery	Competence of leaders; presence of rent seeking and corruption
External aid	The larger the amount of aid, the faster the recovery	Amount of aid, supplies, and experts provided to the area by the government and NGOs
Amount of damage	The greater the damage, the longer the recovery	Number of dead, wounded, homeless; infrastructure condition and fiscal losses
Population density	Denser areas are slower to recover because of difficulties in replacing housing stock	People per square kilometer
Demographics/ socioeconomic conditions	Wealthier, younger, majority ethnicity, educated, communities recover more quickly	Income, education, race, average age, homeownership, economic inequality
Social capital	Areas with greater volunteerism, membership in voluntary groups, and trustworthiness overcome collective action problems and recover more quickly; can simultaneously slow recovery for out-groups on the periphery	Number of local voluntary organizations; voting rates; levels of trust and volunteerism; membership in uur panchayats; participation in local events and festivals

with fewer social resources (Aldrich and Crook 2008). This book builds on the recognition that strong social capital contains a paradox: it can bring both benefits and costs (Foley and Edwards 1996). Table 1 lays out these six approaches to disaster recovery.

The Argument in Brief

The fundamental question concerning which factors facilitate or impede recovery after floods, hurricanes, earthquakes, and similar events remains largely unanswered. I argue that *high levels of social capital—more than such commonly referenced factors as socioeconomic conditions, population density, amount of damage or aid—serve as the core engine of recovery.* Survivors with strong social networks experience faster recoveries and have access to needed information, tools, and assistance. Communities and neighborhoods with little social capital may find themselves unable to keep up with their counterparts with these deep networks. More pernicious is that for those already on the periphery of society, who lack strong network ties to translocal authorities, other groups with strong social capital can further marginalize them, pushing these less-connected survivors out of the rehabilitation process and slowing down their recovery (cf. Elliott, Haney, and Sams-Abiodun 2010). For some this might mean bearing the burdens of unwanted facilities such as FEMA trailers, while for others it may mean further stigmatizing and even being targets of expulsion, riots, or other violence.

Although the newest generation of disaster scholarship includes social capital on its agenda, most studies investigating social resources and catastrophe have relied on qualitative and impressionistic evidence from a few cases (Buckland and Rahman 1999; Nakagawa and Shaw 2004; Dynes 2005) or quantitative evidence from individual-level surveys (Tatsuki and Hayashi 2002; Tatsuki 2008). Only recently have scholars integrated measures of social capital into quantitative studies of rehabilitation (Kage 2010a, 2011). For many scholars, it has become something of a self-evident truth (Ostrom 2000) that social capital functions as a public good (Coleman 1988; Cohen and Arato 1992; Putnam 1993; Cohen and Rogers 1995)—a resource that provides nonexcludable benefits, so that all residents of a high social capital neighborhood enjoy its positive effects (Adger et al. 2005). This book challenges this view and argues that social capital can bring intended and unintended negative externalities as well.

Much work on disasters has treated cities or regions as the unit of analysis; observers often ask how long it will take for a city or society to rebuild after a crisis. However, evidence has shown that recovery after disasters is not constant across neighborhoods within a given city (Rovai 1994; Kamel and Loukaitou-Sideris 2004; Aldrich and Crook 2008; Pais and Elliott 2008; Wood, Burton, and Cutter 2010), and therefore macrolevel data (at the national, regional, or even city level) may mask patterns at the meso- and microlevels. As a result, this book illuminates the role of social capital alongside other factors that might influence rates of disaster recovery at the ward or neighborhood level. Through complex methodologies, I untangle the effects of social capital from confounding factors such as socioeconomic conditions, damage, and population density.

Understanding post-disaster recovery is vital not only for survivors, relief organizations, and governments but also for social scientists. Catastrophes can change participation venues for survivors (Sinclair, Hall, and Alvarez 2009), alter legislative priorities (Birkland 2006), increase the likelihood of regime changes in developing nations (Albala-Bertrand 1993), and act as focal points for broader discussions of social and welfare policy. Crises—whether "natural" such as a tsunami, or human-caused such as terrorism—can bring down previously popular governments (Boin, McConnell, and 'T Hart 2008), create political casualties among politicians (Waugh 2006), and trigger conflict in unstable nations (Enia 2008; Nel and Righarts 2008). Broadly, understanding disaster recovery is important because "work that unravels the logics of avoidable catastrophes could prove extraordinarily useful to policy makers and government officials" (Valelly 2004, B6).

Scholars have demonstrated the vital role of social capital in lowering rates of interethnic violence (Varshney 2001), promoting economic growth (Knack 2002), improving governance (Putnam 1993), and providing important policy feedback to governments (Aldrich 2008b). This book adds to the literature on civil society by revealing how social networks can both assist and harm affected populations as they seek to rebuild their lives after disasters. If social resources prove critical in rebuilding, policy makers should reallocate such resources to at least maintain, if not deepen, social networks among vulnerable populations. Here I envision "vulnerable" populations not solely in terms of their age or income (cf. Cutter and Emrich 2006; Cutter and Finch 2008) but in terms of their lack of connections and embeddedness in social networks. Given that existing disaster responses can actually damage social capital, this book can help bureaucrats and scholars reenvision the recovery process.

Selection of Case Studies

Scholars generate robust results by examining multiple cases of a phenomenon, often looking at similar constellations of occurrences over time and space. While historians and journalists are often satisfied with "letting the facts speak for themselves" or providing a compelling narrative, the broader goal of social science is causal inference (King, Keohane, and Verba 1994). That is, social scientists seek to understand what factors or conditions brought about a certain measurable outcome. We risk erroneous conclusions or overly sweeping predictions if we generalize from a single case or archetype; imagine if we studied market systems by looking solely at the United States. Drawing conclusions about how governments and markets interact based only on the North American experience would ignore a fantastic amount of variety in other systems; we can more clearly see the broad spectrum of systems, from market to coordinated liberal economies, thanks to the comparative research in the literature on varieties of capitalism. Much of the strongest work in social science takes an explicitly or implicitly comparative approach to the subject (Tocqueville [1835] 2000; Weber [1904] 1958; Skocpol 1979; Vogel 1996; Putnam 2000).

Students of disaster have begun to recognize the need for comparative research (Özerdem and Jacoby 2006). Russell Dynes (1989), for example,

explicitly argued for "the advantages of cross-national and comparative research" because it "provides the opportunity to understand the consequences
of differences" in government structure, the resource capabilities of various
units, and so on. He also noted the pitfall of "read[ing] too much uniqueness
and discontinuity into social life which the word 'disaster' usually evokes."
Lawrence Vale and Thomas Campanella's (2005) edited volume *The Resilient
City* continues in the comparative vein. By examining Mexico's 1985 earthquake alongside China's 1976 Tangshan earthquake, and Tokyo's multiple
recoveries (from natural disasters and from war) with man-made disasters
such as the Oklahoma City bombing and 9/11, the volume demonstrates the
essential congruity across space and time. While each crisis is unique to its
culture and time, the processes of recovery, reconstruction, and mitigation
reveal important similarities that demand examination and analysis.

Because all the cases studied here involve the deaths of thousands of residents and a tremendous amount of destruction of infrastructure, they are
all "tough cases" for testing the role of social capital in the recovery process
(George and Bennett 2004, 120). It would be easy to claim that social capital
plays an important role in the case of a small-scale crisis, such as an automo-
bile accident, corruption of hard-drive data, or a lost child. In such events, we
would naturally assume that family members, friends, and networks of acquaintances would help resolve the problem. In these catastrophes, though,
with widespread loss of life and millions—if not billions—of dollars in damage to homes and businesses, we cannot simply assume that social resources
are critical in predictable ways. Observers might infer that the disaster itself
damages existing stock of social capital by scattering residents and eliminating opportunities to stay connected, making the use of social networks all but
impossible. If quantitative and qualitative analysis of these disasters reveals
that—despite controlling for factors such as damage, wealth, and so on, and
understanding that existing networks may have been damaged by the crisis
itself—social capital indeed matters, we have a far more robust framework
both for evaluating disaster recovery and for designing new policies and disaster recovery schemes.

The four megadisasters used in this book differ according to several
variables, allowing me to draw stronger and broader conclusions about the
power of social resources in a variety of environments. By choosing cases
from different eras, I hope to avoid erroneous conclusions that would come
about because of data analysis based only on recent events involving modern technologies and correspondingly higher citizen expectations.[26] Through
cases taken from different nations with different cultures, norms, and local
conditions, I hope to push aside arguments that would have us believe that

the "culture" of a particular nation, city, or neighborhood drives recovery in a particular way. S. Hayden Lesbirel's study of the siting of power plants in Japan challenged often-heard claims about "Japanese" styles of negotiations along with references to indigenous, cultural traits. As he pointed out when assessing why certain processes of siting for power plants took longer than others, "Cultural explanations are not necessary to account for observed variations, even assuming some cultural diversity at the regional level" (1998, 20). Here, too, what might erroneously be seen as "cultural response"—such as the resilience of the primarily Vietnamese and Vietnamese American Village de L'Est community in New Orleans—can be found in other milieus, such as 1920s Tokyo and twenty-first-century southeastern India (see Weil, n.d.).

Another axis for investigating recovery is time; some past studies have followed communities and cities for a few weeks after catastrophes, while others have followed up on their status for years and even decades. Experts on disaster often divide recoveries into phases, such as search and rescue, rehabilitation, and long-term recovery; others separate the process into emergency, restoration, and reconstruction phases (May 1985). One classical model of post-disaster rebuilding sets the stages as emergency, restoration, replacement reconstruction, and developmental reconstruction and even predicts how long each will take (Kates and Pijawka 1977). While it may be easy to differentiate between emergency response (when medical personnel, police officers, and other responders are present and assisting survivors) and recovery periods (when the situation has stabilized to the point that professional responders are no longer necessary), many have pointed out that restoration, reconstruction, and recovery often blend into each other (Dynes and Quarantelli 2008). Furthermore, "different social groups, even within the same community, can experience the sequence quite differently" (Kates et al. 2006, 14655). More important than distinguishing among the phases of reconstruction is that in all stages of post-disaster recovery, social capital should be of interest to social scientists, especially because different stakeholders may be affected differently at different times.

Immediately following the Indian Ocean tsunami, for example, direct stakeholders—boat owners, fishermen, and extended families living along the coast—lost both lives and assets. However, within a month, even indirect stakeholders, such as salt panners, shrimp workers, boat hands, and diesel fuel suppliers who were connected financially to boat owners and fishermen, suffered financially as a result of the tsunami (Sudarshan Rodriguez, pers. comm., 25 March 2010). Other scholars have documented what they call the "cascading consequences of extreme events," in which immediate failures, such as the collapse of bridges, infrastructure, and hospitals, lead to later problems such as the inability of businesses to restart owing to lack of clients and poor service at remaining hospitals overburdened by patients (Alesch, Arendt, and Holly 2009, chap. 3). In post-Katrina New Orleans, scholars have documented the catch-22 where local residents waited to hear about local businesses reopening before committing to return to their homes, while at the same time business owners needed a confirmed client base before reopening their stores (Chalmee-Wright 2010). Coordination and mobilization problems differ among disaster-affected communities over time. Therefore, to better understand social capital's role over time, I use four extended case studies to look at recoveries in the short, medium, and long term. The Tokyo and Kobe cases follow population recovery for more than a decade after those two earthquakes; hence both cases illuminate the medium and long term. The cases of New Orleans and India focus on the short and medium term, looking at questions of temporary housing and access to aid immediately after Hurricane Katrina and the Indian Ocean tsunami. By illuminating how social capital drives recovery in all four cases, I stress its role in every post-crisis phase.

A different variable for comparison is the strength (and competence) of the government. In these case studies, the national government was weakest in the case of the Indian Ocean tsunami and most effective in the 1995 Kobe earthquake. Somewhere in the middle of these two extremes were the responses from the United States federal government and the New Orleans city government in Katrina and those of the Japanese government in the 1923 Tokyo earthquake. Although governments may be competently organized and honest or disorganized and corrupt, civil society's role remains critical across the spectrum of institutional capacity. In some cases, disaster recovery took place primarily in rural areas, such as the villages in Tamil Nadu, India, while in others it occurred in urban settings, such as Kobe, Tokyo, and New Orleans. In some of the investigations—such as those of Kobe and Tokyo— survivors received no special funds from the central government (owing to the Japanese government's "no personal compensation" policy, although the regional Hyogo government did create a recovery fund for survivors of the 1995 earthquake),[27] whereas FEMA provided more than $16 billion to survivors of the New Orleans hurricane and the government of India made $2.1 billion available to victims of the tsunami. Most obviously, these cases involve different types of disasters—earthquake, tsunami, and flood—along with varying levels of ethnic homogeneity.[28] Tamil Nadu and New Orleans in the twenty-first century and Tokyo in the early twentieth century all had large concentrations of multiple ethnic groups and minorities; Kobe in the late twentieth century was perhaps the most homogeneous.

Within each case and city, different neighborhoods recovered at different speeds. In 1920s Tokyo, for example, in some wards population grew rapidly after the disaster, while in others a portion of the population that fled after the quake never returned. Across post-Katrina New Orleans, certain neighborhoods like Village de L'Est recovered rapidly while others, such as the Lower Ninth Ward, have languished (Weil 2010). In some coastal villages in India, all eligible families received the aid packages provided by the government, while in others close to one-quarter of the families did not. Furthermore, some tsunami survivors received almost twice as much as others, holding constant levels of damage, education, and other potentially confounding factors. Using this microlevel variation in resilience as a starting point (Bates and Green 2009, 235), the book illuminates how strong social resources assist (and weak ties impede) post-disaster recovery.

Overview of the Book

This book begins with an investigation of the resource of social capital. Chapter 2 details the mechanisms through which social capital creates trustworthiness, diffuses information, and encourages the creation of new cooperative and civic norms. It uses examples from a variety of cases in addition to the four main disasters studied here to suggest how social networks influence post-crisis recovery. It underscores that social networks bring both positive benefits and deliberate and incidental negative externalities. Communities that have both strong ties to each other and connections to decision makers in the government or in NGOs experience better recoveries than those without either resource or those holding only horizontal bonding connections.

Having established the potential of social capital as a critical resource in post-disaster recovery, I then provide detailed evidence to describe its role in actual post-crisis situations. Chapter 3 focuses on recovery following the 1923 Tokyo earthquake, which measured 7.9 on the Richter scale and whose shocks and resulting fires leveled nearly half of the capital city. Using detailed neighborhood-level data drawn from the archives of the Tokyo Metropolitan Police (Keishichō), I track how each area recovered, maintained, or lost population in the decade that followed. Annual population growth rates in Tokyo varied from a loss of more than half the jurisdiction's population in one precinct to a gain of nearly 100 percent in another. After the quake, most

of the forty or so jurisdictions had growth rates hovering around zero, meaning they neither gained new residents nor had existing citizens migrate elsewhere. However, some jurisdictions showed positive annual growth through
the recovery period. Two measures of social capital at the communal level—
voter turnout in municipal elections (universal male suffrage had been intro-
duced just before these two electoral races) and the number of political demonstrations per year—led to improved population recovery. Chapter 3 also
underscores the tragic externalities of strong levels of bonding social capital
through the race riots and murders of non-Japanese minorities immediately
after the disaster.

Chapter 4 focuses on a second megadisaster in Japan, the 1995 Kobe earthquake, known in Japanese as the Hanshin Awaji Daishinsai. This quake killed
more than six thousand residents and destroyed more than 100,000 buildings
across the densely populated urban landscape. Using case studies of two pairs
of neighborhoods in Kobe along with quantitative data on all nine wards
over fifteen years, this chapter shows how higher levels of social capital led to
greater population growth after the quake. Here I use a measure of social capital that captures the number of nonprofit organizations created per capita
by ward and control for such confounding factors as damage, socioeconomic
resources, population density, and socioeconomic inequality. As expected,
neighborhoods with more welfare-dependent households showed less success in recovering population, but once again the proxy for social capital had
a large and statistically significant effect on population growth. Wards in
Kobe that organized to create their own community assistance organizations
proved more adept at recovery than ones that did not.

Chapter 5 uses multiple types of data from the 2004 Indian Ocean tsunami
to show both the positive benefits and the negative externalities of strong social capital after crisis. The chapter begins with qualitative case studies of six
villages in Tamil Nadu that had varying levels of social resources. Some had
both bonding and bridging social capital—connecting them strongly to each
other and to outside agencies—while others had either only bonding social
capital or weak levels of both. Those villages with higher levels of both types
of networks had the best overall recoveries except for the Dalits, women, and
other minorities in the villages. Then the chapter uses a quantitative analysis
of sixty villages in the area to illuminate which ones were able to attract more
assistance in the post-tsunami period. Using three dependent variables—the
length of time (measured in days) spent in the relief camps, the percentage
of eligible families receiving the initial bundle of relief supplies, and the percentage of eligible families receiving 4,000 rupees in assistance—this analysis shows that caste was the strongest predictor of poor recovery across the

board. The final part of chapter 5 uses a large-N analysis of responses from 1,600 survivors of the tsunami to show that individuals with more bonding and bridging capital (measured through participation in such local rituals as funerals and weddings and through connections to extralocal organizations, respectively) received more assistance from the government and NGOs than those with fewer translocal connections.

Chapter 6 turns to a recent disaster in the United States to track how social capital influenced the distribution of temporary housing. Tracking the siting of FEMA trailers and temporary homes across zip codes in New Orleans after Hurricane Katrina in 2005, I show that communities with strong levels of social capital—measured using voter turnout rates—mobilized quickly to block what they saw as a "public bad" from being placed in their backyard. Decision makers kept trailers and low-income housing out of these better-coordinated neighborhoods, pleasing local residents but forcing both FEMA and the city of New Orleans to expend more resources and find amenable locations for the temporary housing. In short, stronger social capital benefited mobilized groups with more social capital but pushed unwanted facilities into the backyards of less cohesive networks of residents.

The seventh and last chapter provides policy recommendations and concrete examples of ways to apply the theories and data in the book to future disaster recoveries. Drawing on the investigations of the four megacatastrophes and building on new field evidence that social capital can be created both through indigenous efforts and through foreign intervention, Chapter 7 provides a series of policy tools that can improve resilience and mitigate future disasters. It may be that the most effective—and perhaps least expensive—way to mitigate disasters is to create stronger bonds between individuals in vulnerable populations. With building resilience as the goal, I now examine the resource of social capital.

Social Capital: A Janus-Faced Resource for Recovery

On 12 January 2010, a 7.0 magnitude earthquake struck Haiti just before 5:00 p.m., collapsing homes, office buildings, and hospitals in the capital of Port-au-Prince and around the country (Taft-Morales and Margesson 2010). Damage from the quake has been estimated at more than $8 billion (Cavallo, Powell, and Becerra 2010a), and a year after the disaster more than a million people remained in tent cities. After the catastrophic temblor, which claimed more than 300,000 lives, freed prisoners from jails, and brought commerce and industry to a standstill, local residents spontaneously formed committees to watch over sleeping residents and protect their belongings from thieves.

On Rue Clairveau, Petionville, outside the capital, cooks prepared food for survivors while neighbors talked and sang together to pass the time (Burnett 2010). Despite the grim circumstances and the threat of additional aftershocks, many residents bonded with each other and worked together in their communities to get by. Because the delivery of relief supplies from international donors was sporadic and inconsistent, sharing food became a powerful norm for survivors, who could otherwise go days without anything to eat. Neighbors in Port-au-Prince pulled together to start impromptu soup kitchens, and many people fed and sheltered homeless neighbors in their own surviving dwellings (Cave 2010). Research on the hastily formed networks in post-earthquake Haiti has shown that levels of trust, relationship norms, and mutuality influenced the response time and quality of outputs from these groups (Nolte and Boenigk 2011). However, the drive to work together for survival and recovery brought serious consequences for those suspected of violating either the law or post-quake norms. In one grim reminder of the seriousness of these expectations, a crowd beat a suspected thief to death and dragged his body through the streets in front of cameras and media representatives from around the world (*Daily Mail*, 17 January 2010). The social ties that bind catastrophe survivors to each other can also be the barriers that exclude lawbreakers and norm violators from the recovery or punish nonconforming outsiders.

This chapter provides details about social capital, a critical component in governance, economic growth, development, and, as I argue, disaster recovery. I will define the term through a brief intellectual history and lay out how it can affect policy outcomes, then I will investigate how to measure this often vague concept, demonstrate that social capital brings both positive benefits and negative externalities, and conclude with a discussion of social capital's role in disaster recovery.

Most of us recognize that our networks of acquaintances and whom we know strongly affect our daily lives. Inside details of otherwise private events travel quickly through our networks and alter our decision making. New house listings and information about mortgage deals may be shared among a select circle of friends before going public (Pittman 2008); real estate agents use new information technologies to broaden their social connections and reach potential clients (Wigand et al. 2001). Job searches regularly begin with an informal discussion, a short list circulated among colleagues, or private e-mails sent among acquaintances. Besides vocations and purchases, individual gym attendance and healthier eating, along with happiness and life satisfaction more generally, are functions not only of individual decisions, but of the decisions made by friends and colleagues. Studies have shown that if a person's friends gain weight, that individual also gets heavier (Christakis and Fowler 2007); if your friends show up to vote on Election Day, it is likely that you will vote as well (Liu et al. 2009). Those planning new vaccination programs hope to quiz potential vaccine recipients about their nearest contacts to figure out likely vectors of contagion and inoculate them as well (Curtis et al. 2010).

It is also intuitive that working in a group almost inevitably creates more of an impact than working alone, whether people seek to influence a politician through a letter-writing campaign or demonstrate in front of a facility they find objectionable. In Japan, for example, better-connected rural communities were less likely to be targeted as hosts for controversial and unwanted projects as developers recognized their stronger potential for resistance (Aldrich 2008b). In rural Fiji, informal risk-sharing institutions helped residents recover from illness and disasters through ritual gifts, group lending, religious donations, and transfers of materials (Takasaki 2010). Through parent-teacher associations (PTAs), bowling clubs, fraternities, synagogues, political parties, and Workmen's Circles many individuals join with friends and casual acquaintances both for recreation and for common cause (Putnam 2000). Social networking technologies such as MySpace, Facebook, Plaxo, LinkedIn, and Twitter connect individuals with others who share similar interests and can, for example, suggest new book and movie purchases and potential areas of interest (*Economist*, 28 January 2010). Over the past two decades, social science has begun to take more seriously these networks of connections, known as "social capital." Joseph Stiglitz (2000, 59) has argued that social capital is "a concept with a short and already confused history," while Krishan Kumar (1993, 376) has argued that it has a "perplexing history." An overview of its nearly two-century intellectual history, however, reveals several consistent themes that underscore its value as an analytical tool for post-disaster situations.

A Brief Intellectual History of Social Capital

Scholars since the early nineteenth century have focused on how social networks, groups, and norms of reciprocity and trustworthiness interact with political and economic outcomes. Among the first was Alexis de Tocqueville, a French aristocrat, politician, and writer who traveled to the United States in 1831 and 1832. The first volume of his chronicles, published in 1835 as *Democracy in America*, praised the young nation for its passion and lauded its citizens' penchant for "forever forming associations." In these books—which would become classics read by students and presidents alike and cited by many later scholars of social capital—he recognized that groups of American citizens working together tempered the potential tyranny of the majority and prevented decision makers from enacting ill-fitting policies (Tocqueville [1835] 2000, 183). Modern social scientists would call these organizations voluntary associations, that is, groups composed of individuals with analogous interests dedicated to shared values and goals. Tocqueville also understood the importance of networks of people working together; he warned later in the same work that "all fall into impotence if they do not learn to aid each other freely" (490). His contributions to social science are many, but most important is that almost two hundred years ago a keen observer of human nature understood that individuals working as a group achieved their goals more effectively and created improved policy outcomes for governance as a whole.

More than half a century later, Lyda J. Hanifan, a school superintendent in West Virginia, became one of the first to use the term "social capital." In 1916 he envisioned it as "those tangible substances [that] count for most in the daily lives of people: namely good will, fellowship, sympathy, and social

intercourse among the individuals and families who make up a social unit"
(quoted in Woolcock and Narayan 2000, 228; see also Farr 2004). Hanifan's
writing focused on kinship ties and close friends, recognizing that these relationships could be seen as a form of capital, that is, something that can
be accumulated, dispersed, and used in day-to-day life. Especially in rural
West Virginia, far removed from official government institutions, ties between friends, family, and neighbors could improve the community in ways
that solely material resources could not. However, later research in sociology
would emphasize that even ties between casual acquaintances bring access to
both information and resources.

Mark Granovetter's (1973) work on weak ties underscored that information—such as insights into new professional, managerial, or technical job opportunities—often flows through "weak ties," that is, through relationships
that were not based on daily or even regular contact between the parties.
Rather than looking to close ties between kin, family, and friends as Hanifan
had specified, Granovetter emphasized that occasional and often informal
connections would connect different groups of individuals. Because individuals tend to contact close friends more often than less well known colleagues,
and those close ties usually hold the same type of information, individuals
from outside the close-knit inner circle are best suited to provide new perspectives and resources. His observations about weak ties—which he called
only a "fragment of a theory"—invigorated a new field of research known
today as social network analysis (see Breiger 2004 for an overview).

The mid-1980s brought several new books and articles on the topic of
social capital and civic norms. Robert Bellah and his colleagues (1985) traced
the intellectual roots of their best-selling book *Habits of the Heart* back to
Tocqueville, focusing in their research on the balance between the individual
and the community, and on the "way in which citizens do, or do not, participate in the public sphere" (vii). Interviewing over two hundred middle-class
white Americans across the nation, the team collected narratives from individuals who often found themselves materially successful but emotionally
and psychically unsatisfied. The team argued that too many Americans "have
put our own good, as individuals, as groups, as a nation, ahead of the common good" (285) and suggested that one remedy would be to recognize that
"civic friendship toward our fellow citizens [is] preferable to restless competition and anxious self-defense" (295). Bellah and his team normatively
appealed to collectivism and group activity during an era when individual ca-
reer advancement seemed like the best metric for success, and this approach
would be picked up by Robert Putnam in the 1990s.

Pierre Bourdieu's (1986) article "Forms of Capital" revisited a number of issues raised by earlier observers and scholars. Bourdieu, in searching for an explanation for unequal scholastic achievement among children, illuminated an inheritable resource he called social capital that could magnify the effect of education. He believed that membership in a group provided its members with legitimacy and "credentials" that could be drawn on in exchanges with others. He saw that people often surround well-known individuals in cliques because of the credibility and legitimacy it gives them. Bourdieu saw one's own stock of social capital as dependent on one's location within the social order (such as rank within a military agency or bureaucracy, family name, or membership in the dominant class). He also believed that social capital itself rested on economic capital, since wealth played a key role in societal achievement and reputation (DeFilippis 2001). In that sense, Bourdieu's vision of social capital portrayed society as one in which individuals who already have fame and fortune continue to dominate society through connections to other elites, while those without these resources have little chance of "breaking in" (Field 2003).

James Coleman's 1988 article similarly raised parallels between financial, physical, human, and social capital. He defined social capital as a variety of entities that "all consist of some aspect of social structures, and . . . facilitate certain actions of actors—whether persons or corporate actors—within the structure" (1998, S98). Coleman illustrated the concept with the example of wholesale diamond dealers who regularly trust each other in transactions involving tens of thousands of dollars of merchandise, which could easily be stolen or swapped for counterfeits. Within the closed community of Orthodox Jewish Brooklyn, "the strength of these ties makes possible transactions in which trustworthiness is taken for granted and trade can occur with ease" (S99). Expectations about future interactions guide behaviors that would be risky outside this specific context. While both Bourdieu and Coleman saw strong parallels between social and other forms of capital (financial, human, etc.), Kenneth Arrow (1999, 4) urged researchers to stop using "social capital" because he felt it was inappropriate to apply the term to something that seemed to lack the economic properties of other recognized forms of capital. At the other end of the spectrum, Ben Fine (2001) also criticized the term, because he believed that all forms of capital—even financial and human capital—are inherently social.

Despite such warnings, Robert Putnam popularized the concept of social capital in his 1993 book *Making Democracy Work*. This book sought to explain why northern and southern Italy ended up with different qualities of governance structures and different levels of economic development. Empirical evidence demonstrated that northern Italy had "strong, responsive, effective representative institutions" (Putnam 1993, 6) while the southern part of the country had poorly run governments. To illuminate why these two regions ended up with measurably different regimes, Putnam looked to *civic virtue*, a concept he traced back to Tocqueville's idea of self-interest embedded in a broader civic context. From this perspective, individuals ideally seek to advance themselves in the context of communal and national obligations (88). Putnam found the origins of "civic communities" in Italy in the medieval period around 1100 CE, arguing that the norms of reciprocity developed early in the north were reinforced by leadership and governance structures, while in the south norms of opportunism and distrust became standard. Hence the same regions that had cooperatives, mutual aid societies, and guilds in the twelfth century had mutual aid societies and cultural associations in the nineteenth century, and then high levels of citizen involvement in the twentieth century (162). Putnam also put forward his own definition of social capital, arguing that it is "trust, norms, and networks that can improve the efficiency of society by facilitating coordinated actions" (167).

Putnam's definition involves three aspects of social capital: trustworthiness (how people anticipate that others will behave in the future), norms (the informal laws that govern exchanges and daily life), and networks (the connections between individuals). Because this definition may involve both cause and effect—for example, trust and networks may be the source of norms—other scholars have sought to pin down the concept more tightly. Putnam soon expanded on his book on Italy's civic culture through an article titled "Bowling Alone" (1995) and then a book of the same title (2000), both focusing on social capital and its decline in the United States. Putnam provided empirical evidence that membership in associations, neighborliness, voting rates, social trust, and other forms and outcomes of social capital were in decline in the United States for a variety of reasons, including generational change, women's working outside the home, greater television and Internet use, and increasing suburban sprawl. Although his work has been challenged on a number of levels by other scholars (Foley and Edwards 1996; Tarrow 1996; Jackman and Miller 1998; DeFilippis 2001; Sobel 2002; McLaren and Baird 2006; Portes and Vickstrom 2011), it remains among the best known and widely read works on the topic.

Since the flowering of research on social networks, researchers have struggled to clarify whether social capital comprises the data about, reputations of, and information flowing between members of a group or if it *is* the network of relationships and connections itself. Simon Szreter and Michael Woolcock (2004, 654) see work by scholars like Putnam defining social capital as the "wires" through which information and resources run; hence the networks

and relationships are its core components. Other scholars, however, see social capital as the "electricity" running through those wires, that is, the information and resources that are passed back and forth. Nan Lin (2008, 51),
for example, sits squarely in the latter category, defining social capital as "resources embedded in one's social networks, resources that can be accessed or
mobilized through ties in the networks." Lin envisions social relationships in
three layers—the topmost (and least interactive) involves membership and
identity, the middle level comprises shared information and sources, and the
bottom is made up of intense interaction and reciprocity (2008, 59). Szreter
and Woolcock (2004, 655) follow Lin to posit that "if social capital is not a
property of individuals, per se, it is, however, a property of their relations
with each other, occupying the abstract socio-cultural space of relationships
between individuals."

Other scholars define social capital in ways that link back to the foundational research in the field. In a nod back to Hanifan's 1916 essay, Lindon
Robison, Allan Schmid, and Marcelo Siles (2002), for example, define social
capital as "a person's or group's sympathy toward another person or group
that may produce a potential benefit, advantage, and preferential treatment
for another person or group of persons beyond that expected in an exchange
relationship." Anirudh Krishna (2008, 442) bases his approach to social capital on Putnam, explicitly arguing that "at the community level, social capital is regarded, following Putnam, as an asset, a functioning propensity for
mutually beneficial collective action, with which different communities are
endowed to diverse extents." Michael Woolcock and Deepa Narayan (2000,
226) believe that "social capital refers to the norms and networks that enable
people to act collectively," leaving out Putnam's third, attitudinal concept of
trust(worthiness).

While Putnam and other scholars have usually discussed it as a factor that
influences state decision makers, many scholars see social capital as endogenously tied to political and formal institutions. William Maloney, Graham
Smith, and Gerry Stoker (2000), for example, use data from Birmingham,
England, to argue that political institutions shape the context of associational activity and the creation of social capital. Similarly, Wendy Rahn and
Thomas Rudolph (2005) argue that city-level factors such as political institutions shape levels of trust in local government. Mark Schneider and his
colleagues (1997) argue that government institutions delivering local public
goods—such as schools—can create incentives that increase social capital in
parents. Mario Small (2009, 122) takes an "organizational embeddedness"
perspective on social capital and argues that institutions such as day care pro-

vide emotional support, informational support, material support, and companionship to members, even in poor neighborhoods. Hence, taking one's children to a local kindergarten or play group can provide a caregiver with new connections and necessary information.

One useful way to map the tremendous amount of scholarship on social capital is to use Woolcock and Narayan's (2000) typology of communitarian, network, institutional, and synergy views. Communitarian perspectives—such as those of Putnam (1993, 1995, 2000), Tocqueville ([1835] 2000), and Bellah et al. (1985)—focus on horizontal associations and civic groups and champion citizen engagement in the public sphere. Network views—such as the work of Granovetter (1973), Lin (2008), and Siegel (2009)—focus on the horizontal and vertical aspects of social connections. The institutional view focuses on the political and private organizations that shape local networks and can be found in the work of scholars like Szreter (2002), Maloney, Smith, and Stoker (2000), Kenneth Newton (2001), Rahn and Rudolph (2005), and Small (2009). The synergy view—adopted by Woolcock and Narayan (2000) and further seen in Regina Birner and Heidi Wittmer (2003)—is premised on the idea that economic development requires cooperation between the state and local civil societies and recognizes the need for bridging connections between the two.

Beyond communitarian, network, institutional, and synergy views, scholarship traces social capital in three dimensions: bonding, bridging, and linking. In Kai Erikson's fascinating interviews with survivors of a flood in Appalachian country in West Virginia (1976, 187–188), he asked local residents to define "neighbor." One interviewee told him, "What's a neighbor? Well, when I went to my neighbor's house on a Saturday or Sunday if I wanted a cup of coffee I never waited until the lady of the house asked me. I just went into the dish cabinet and got me a cup of coffee or a glass of juice just like it was my own home. They come to my house, they done the same. See?" These sorts of bonds within and between community members—where they can bypass social niceties and operate as if they were members of the same family—epitomize *bonding social capital*. Many observers may see such connections as intrusive and "premodern" in that they assume high levels of familiarity and involve a willingness to forgo some degree of privacy. Putnam (2000, 22) sees bonding social capital as "undergirding specific reciprocity and mobilizing solidarity" among homogeneous individuals. Woolcock (2002, 26) similarly defines it in terms of relations between "family members, close friends, and neighbors." This form of network centers on horizontal ties between individuals who are quite similar to each other and may live within walking distance. Bonding social capital can at times produce negative externalities, as is documented through several of the case studies of disaster recovery in this book. A strong sense of belonging to a group, tribe, or nation can create indifference or even hostility to nonmembers. Nationalism, patriotism, and even xenophobia are potential outcomes for populations that feel strongly committed to their group identity (see Kohnert 2009 for a review of literature on these forces in Africa). Residents with deeply felt connections to their group can engage in deliberate polarization, isolation, and even violence toward out-group individuals.

Further, bonding social capital by itself may not be a panacea for social and economic ills. Szreter (2002, 577) pointed out that among lower-class, poorer residents, social capital "primarily manifests itself as bonding social capital only." What, then, are they missing? Thomas Ohlemacher (1996) described individuals who acted as "social relays," that is, people whose connections and interactions span multiple groups and bridge or link otherwise disconnected networks.[1] These individuals are critical for the remaining two dimensions of social capital.

Bridging social capital connects members of the group or network to extralocal networks, crossing ethnic, racial, and religious cleavages. Where bonding social capital facilitates cooperation among members of a family or neighborhood, bridging social capital involves "linkage to external assets" and generates "broader identities" (Putnam 2000, 23). Bridging activities and organizations bring together individuals from different locations, identities, and language groups (Schuller, Baron, and Field 2000). In Ashutosh Varshney's (2001) work on ethnic violence in India, for example, he discovered that Hindu-Muslim riots between 1950 and 1995 were least likely to occur in villages with cross-ethnic associations. Varshney argued that groups that brought together members from the Muslim and Hindu communities—such as business councils, reading rooms, the Federation of Traders Association, and peace committees—dampened potential violence (although see Bhavnani and Backer 2007 for more ambiguous results in their study of Africa). Following the 1992–1993 riots in Mumbai, which killed more than a thousand people, many citizens sought to defuse future tensions by regularly meeting with other members of the "peace committees" and "Mohalla committees" (Kaur 2003). Through monthly meetings, these groups seek to proactively dispel rumors and tension and keep lines of communication open between ethnic groups and individuals who may rarely meet face to face (Thakkar 2004). In Singapore, for example, the government has mandated that certain percentages of public housing be given to specified ethnicities; here the state has intervened to manufacture social ties (Simon Avenell, pers. comm.,

March 2008). Such networks and living spaces epitomize bridging social capital.

The third form of social capital is *linking social capital*, made up of "networks of trusting relationships between people who are interacting across explicit, formal or institutionalized power or authority gradients in society" (Szreter and Woolcock 2004, 655). Whereas bonding and bridging social capital primarily connect individuals of the same status—whether neighbors and kin with bonding social capital or out-of-town acquaintances from another ethnic group with bridging social capital—this form takes into account vertical distance as well. "It takes on a democratic and empowering character where those involved are endeavoring to achieve a mutually agreed beneficial goal (or set of goals) on a basis of mutual respect, trust, and equality of status, despite the manifest inequalities in their respective positions" (Szreter 2002, 579). Elso DaCosta and Sarah Turner (2007, 195) point out that for developing or underdeveloped communities, linking networks are particularly important for economic development because they provide resources and information to cities and towns that are otherwise off the grid or under the radar. In rural southeastern India, for example, most villagers never come into direct contact with government representatives or NGOs; linking social capital would provide them with a pipeline to external resources and information. Figure 1 illustrates these three types of social capital along axes of horizontal and vertical distance.

Each circle represents an individual within a network who is tied to friends, kin, and neighbors (through bonding social capital), to other ethnic, demographic, or religious groups (with bridging social capital), or to authorities and decision makers who sit some vertical distance away in positions of power (through linking social capital).

To define social capital, I build on Lin's (2008) network view of social capital and envision it as the resources available through bonding, bridging, and linking social networks along with the norms and information transmitted through those connections (cf. Chamlee-Wright 2010, 21–22). This approach revolves around the information, data, expectations, reputations, and other goods that flow through the connections between people and communities. I focus on the ways horizontal and vertical ties between members of social networks transmit information and provide access to resources at critical times. Rather than emphasizing how government activities alter social networks, I illuminate the ways social capital accesses or alters public policies. Some, such as Bourdieu, have envisioned social capital as "a societal, not an individual property [which] should be studied as a social or collective phenomenon" (Newton 2001, 207), while others have argued that it is a

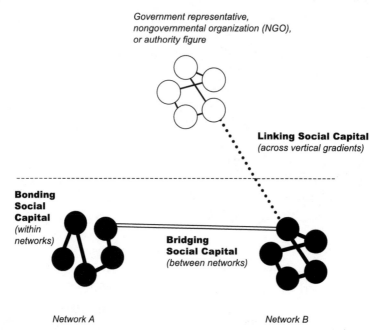

FIGURE 1. Bonding, bridging, and linking social capital.

process and hence "not located at any one level of analysis" (Bankston and Zhou 2002, 285). This book investigates social capital as an asset held by both individuals *and* communities; individuals benefit both from their personal social networks and from their presence in neighborhoods rich in local and extralocal connections (cf. Poortinga 2006). Some individuals have many e-mail and Facebook contacts and broader social networks, while others are more isolated and independent. Similarly, certain neighborhoods have developed deep connections across their population both to each other and to out-of-town organizations and decision makers, while other areas remain fragmented and disconnected.

In most of the case studies—those of the Tokyo and Kobe earthquakes and post-Katrina New Orleans—I measure social capital at the community level, while for the study of Indian Ocean tsunami-affected villages, I measure social resources at both the individual and village levels. Further, rather than seeing social capital as an exogenous, national-level variable that functions like a durable civic or regional political culture (Almond and Verba 1963; Putnam 1993), this book envisions it as a local, endogenous one, which can vary at the regional and city level (Aldrich 2008b; Aldrich and Crook 2008) and, more important, from neighborhood to neighborhood (cf. Jackman and Miller 1998).

Causal Mechanisms: Overcoming Collective Action Problems

Given its makeup, exactly how does social capital work? Mobilizing people to work collectively is difficult, as Thomas Hobbes expressed it in 1651 when he argued that life was "*solitary*, poor, nasty, brutish, and short" (emphasis added). Mancur Olson (1965) underscored this pessimism through his widely cited work on cooperation (and its absence). Olson argued that even when people agree that a problem exists and share ideas about how to solve it, most large groups fail to take the final and necessary step of broader participation. Olson named this difficulty the "collective action problem," positing that "rational, self-interested individuals will not act to achieve their common or group interest" (1965, 2). Because people in the group—whether a university club, roller skating association, autoworkers' union, or PTA—recognize that their own lack of participation will likely not be noticed and they will still benefit from the final product of the rest of the group's work, they have little incentive to spend the time, effort, or money to participate in group activities. The impulse to refrain from work and coast on the labor of others is labeled free riding, and it can be seen in many areas. The gap between those who watch public television or listen to public radio and those who contribute money to these organizations exemplifies this problem.

Observers pointed out two other problems that thwart coordinated activity: the tragedy of the commons and the prisoner's dilemma. The prototypical setting for a tragedy of the commons involves farmers who all have access to a green pasture held by the village as a whole (that is, the pasture is not privately owned, but rather is public land). Each farmer has little reason to hold his or her cows back from grazing, even though ultimately the grass is completely depleted for all actual and potential users. The cost of each cow's meal is difficult to calculate (even if the farmers wanted to "repay" the commons), the damage to the grass is incremental (and hence difficult to see even by conscientious farmers), and there are no barriers to entering the commons itself (such as a charge per cow or a license to graze there). Garrett Hardin (1968) and others pessimistically predicted that ultimately, without some coercive mechanisms to alter behavior, people tend to overuse common resources such as clean air and oceans. Global warming and air pollution are two all too familiar examples of the tragedy of the commons; corporations have strong incentives to pollute, recognizing the difficulty of enforcing existing regulations and of tracing environmental damage back to people's actions, known as "agency slack."

A similar problem occurs when two hypothetical criminals are arrested and brought in for questioning by law enforcement officers; each is told that confessing and turning in the partner will reduce his sentence (and yield a longer one for the partner). If each stays quiet, however, there will be insufficient evidence, and overall both sentences will be short; if each turns the partner in, both will serve long sentences (because with two confessions available the district attorney does not need to cut a deal). Each prisoner realizes that by staying quiet while the partner confesses, he will be in jail longer. Rational choice theorists predict that the "dominant strategy" is for both to confess, resulting in longer prison terms for both than if each had stayed quiet (Ordeshook 1995, 207). As Axelrod (1984, 9) wrote, "Individual rationality leads to a worse outcome for both than is possible"; most observers predict that both criminals will turn in their partners because they cannot trust them to keep quiet.

In all three scenarios, economists assume that people engage in behaviors that have poor outcomes for themselves and for society because of shortsightedness, a lack of trust, and low motivation to cooperate. Economists would argue that to counteract this trend, groups must employ selective incentives (rewards), social pressure (criticism and ostracism), and surveillance (visible oversight of members); these social control mechanisms allow the large group to ensure broader participation. Forming a smaller group would also at least partially solve many of these problems because it would be easier to monitor and control behavior than in a larger group, as Olson (1965) suggests. Thus, town councils and legislatures publish rosters of participants and attendees, sports teams fine athletes who miss team practice, and fraternities call out members who have skipped social events. Similarly, public radio stations and universities publicly praise listeners and alumni who have donated their time or financial resources. In Japan, members of the Japanese mafia known as the Yakuza demonstrate their loyalty to the group and unwillingness to confess or turn others in through self-mutilation (see Hill 2003 for an overview). Through these activities, all these groups and organizations seek to reward compliance and participation and punish noncompliance and shirking.

However, high levels of social capital might be another way of solving these collective action problems. Strong social connections among members of a social organization—such as *kendo* (Japanese fencing) club participants who practice, travel to kendo tournaments, eat, and raise club funds together—make collective action more likely than in a group whose members share few activities and have little in common. Asking for help from such a tightly knit group would produce more enthusiastic volunteers than in an organization that meets only occasionally and does little to build connections between its participants. Similarly, regular interaction among house-owning neighbors at block parties, garage sales, and informal meetings on the street builds trust in a way that short-term renters bumping into each other in a large condominium or student dormitory cannot attain. Given the common criticism that scholarship invoking social capital often suffers from a "weak specification of causal relationships" (Farrell and Knight 2003), this section seeks to lay these connections out clearly. Social capital has three main mechanisms that can help overcome collective action problems, the tragedy of the commons, and the prisoner's dilemma: building new norms about compliance and participation among network members; providing information and knowledge to individuals in the group; and creating trustworthiness.

First, social capital can shape the expectations citizens have about the behavior of others (Boix and Posner 1998, 691). The group or network can develop and disseminate expectations about issues and responsibilities and thereby alter its members' actions and preferences. For example, if every family in a neighborhood is socialized to believe they have a responsibility to take part in walking patrols, attend local watch meetings, and call the authorities should suspicious characters show up, they will more consistently participate in these activities and there will be fewer gaps in neighborhood surveillance.

Alternatively, a neighborhood where residents believe crime is someone else's problem or that someone else will call the authorities should violence break out is likely to be less safe. Coleman (1988, S104) mentions that "effective norms that inhibit crime make it possible to walk freely outside at night." Quantitative research has demonstrated that areas with higher levels of social capital have fewer murders and other crimes and opportunistic behaviors (Lee and Bartkowski 2004). Scholars have also shown that strong social bonds create high costs for individuals within the network who would break from expected patterns of behavior. Mary Alice Haddad's work on volunteer firefighters in Japan (2007, 2010) underscored how ties create strong expectations that are enforced through social control mechanisms.

A consequence of shared norms about responsibility and compliance is that fewer resources are necessary to generate agreement with the law or norms through extended contracts, government coercion, or third-party intervention. Hence, governments in regions with high levels of social capital need devote fewer resources to the "costly and complex mechanisms of enforcement" (Boix and Posner 1998, 691), since shared norms and expectations "reduce the transaction costs associated with formal coordination mechanisms like contracts, hierarchies, bureaucratic rules, and the like" (Fukuyama 1999). Another consequence of strong social bonds is the development of civic virtue—citizens' belief that participating in government and community affairs is important—and the creation of a virtuous cycle where active citizens press government to become more transparent and respon-sive. Citizens will turn out to express their opinions at public forums, wait in line on Election Day, and respond to census questions if they believe the government pays attention to their needs. Once governments demonstrate their responsiveness to the citizenry, this in turn induces expectations about stronger and better governance from citizens who see evidence of their own efficacy (Putnam 1995). Alternatively, governments can seek to manipulate existing social networks to induce cooperation and manage difficult and con-tentious social issues where government and societal approaches may diverge (Nordlinger 1981; Aldrich 2008b).

In the second mechanism, social networks provide information and knowledge about the environment, business conditions, trends, and other important issues to members of the network or group. Social networks hold and diffuse information that central or local governments cannot replace or substitute for; these "signals" from members of the network, in fact, can be drowned out by official pronouncements that provide little new or useful information (Chamlee-Wright and Rothschild 2007). Given that acquisi-tion of knowledge is both costly and time consuming (Coleman 1988, S103), networks can provide critical information free or at a low cost. Granovetter (1973) underscored that more blue-collar American workers found out about job openings through personal connections than through other methods (such as job announcements in newspapers, industry newsletters, and radio advertisements) and that this proved true for professional and managerial positions as well. Some scholars have suggested that people seek out informa-tion from members of their networks rather than expending energy and time on records or documents because other individuals are "typically easier and more readily accessible than the most authoritative printed sources" (Case 2002, 142). Communicating rumors or up-to-date information—such as the best prices for a short-lived commodity such as fresh fish or ways to navigate complex bureaucracies—ties network or group members to each other as they come to recognize the value of these data (*Economist*, 10 May 2007). Further, through repeated interactions over time with others in networks, members with high levels of social capital move beyond single-shot games (such as the prisoner's dilemma described above) to long-term relationships. By remaining in contact over the long term, people build up trust and de-velop cooperation as they recognize that they will have future dealings with the other parties and cannot free ride or shirk without repercussions (Axel-rod 1984).

Finally, social capital builds trust by transmitting data about levels of trustworthiness. This third mechanism involves the diffusion of information about reputation and trust, not just data about jobs, prices, and so forth as in the second mechanism detailed above. Coleman (1988, S102) brings the example of rotating credit associations in Southeast Asia, where each month individuals pay into a pot, which is given to a different member until each member has had a turn at drawing out the capital.[2] High levels of trust combined with future expectations keep these institutions functioning, since a less than scrupulous member could simply take the payoff early in the rotation and not pay in again. Similarly, Farrell and Knight (2003, 541–542) analyze data on a manufacturing district of Bologna, Italy, in which informal and formal institutions provide information about the trustworthiness of others in the area. By learning of others' reputations for honesty, members are more likely to carry out transactions and business with them and hence are more productive than similar businesses in areas with less social capital. If a friend tells us an acquaintance has defaulted on past contracts or delayed returning a borrowed tool, we are less likely to engage in risky interactions with that individual.

With these three mechanisms, higher levels of social capital reduce transaction costs, increase the probability of collective action, and make cooperation among individuals more likely. In the language of economics, social capital reduces shirking (not doing one's job well), free riding (relying on others to get the work done), and agency slack (underperforming, knowing that one's output cannot be continuously monitored). As Putnam (2000) put it more colloquially, social capital "greases the wheels that allow communities to advance smoothly." Strong relationships in networks create beliefs about complex and critical concepts, such as compliance with the law and civic virtue and expectations about future interactions. With these mechanisms defined, I now turn to the difficult task of capturing social capital through proxies and indicators.

Measurement

Pinning down accurate measures of social capital has been an elusive goal for social science. Researchers have regularly criticized the concept itself as being "elastic" or "fuzzy" (Portes 1998), perhaps because of conceptual confusion between social capital and its effects (Robison, Schmid, and Siles 2002). Many have pointed out that attempts to measure it rely heavily on macrolevel data, often at the national level, and have demonstrated the difficulties of consistently measuring associational membership cross-nationally (Diez de Ulzurrun 2002). Such broad attempts to capture social resources are hard to implement successfully, given that just as socioeconomic conditions vary among and within cities (Wood, Burton, and Cutter 2010), so too levels of social capital vary from city to city and neighborhood to neighborhood. Furthermore, because social capital involves both structural aspects (such as participation in horizontal associations and civil society groups) and cognitive characteristics (levels of trust in neighbors and others) (Brune and Bossert 2009), the only point of agreement among scholars is that there is no single ideal measure for it. Grootaert and van Bastelaer (2002, 11) argue that "like human capital, social capital is difficult, if not impossible, to measure directly; for empirical purposes the use of proxy indicators is necessary."

Broadly speaking, there are four ways to quantitatively capture social capital. The first, focused on attitudes, uses surveys covering large numbers of individuals—such as the General Social Survey in North America, the World Values Survey and Eurobarometer in Europe, and the Afrobarometer for Africa—to measure subjective levels of trust. Questions may ask, "Generally speaking, would you say that most people can be trusted, or that you cannot be too careful in dealing with people?" Such questions seek to understand respondents' expectations about others' behavior. Experts have determined that belief in the trustworthiness of others is one of a number of signs that individuals—and their communities—have high levels of social capital.

The second approach to capturing social capital also uses surveys but instead focuses on behavior. For example, behavioral questionnaires may ask respondents to indicate if they leave their doors unlocked, often lend money to friends, or regularly invite newcomers to their house for a meal. Those who regularly demonstrate other-focused practices—whether opening their house for a card game, donating blood, or providing interest-free loans to those in need—show through their actions that they have higher levels of social capital. One interesting study of the links between social capital and corruption in India used social conflict—measured through the number of riots per year—as an indicator of levels of trust and social capital (Kingston 2005).

The third approach looks at participation in activities such as voting, voluntary associations, community events such as weddings and funerals, and involvement in political demonstrations. This approach seeks to capture both civic norms (whether citizens in a community, zip code, or region take the time and energy to volunteer or to express their opinion) and their connectedness to others in the area (whether they engage in festivals, communities, PTA membership, and so on). The fourth approach uses field experiments, such as the trust game,[3] to capture social preferences. Recognizing that in most of these experiments the observed behavior deviates from the predicted Nash equilibrium—a set of self-serving decisions, based on the decisions

SOCIAL CAPITAL: A JANUS-FACED RESOURCE

of others, made to maximize one's personal payoff—researchers see social capital, belief in reciprocity, and norms as factors strongly influencing tactics (Karlan 2005; Cardinas and Carpenter 2008; Levitt and List 2009).

Within these four categories, the types of proxies for social capital have varied tremendously. Coffé and Geys (2005) used electoral turnout, crime rates, and associational life in their study, while Aldrich (2008b) used membership in horizontal associations. Hamilton (1993), Putnam (2000), and Aldrich and Crook (2008) have also used voter turnout as a way of measuring social capital; this may measure a created norm (civic virtue), but it does not directly capture participation in other forms of communal life. Weil (2010) looked at various measures of civic engagement, including civic leadership, attendance at club meetings, performance of service, and involvement in neighborhood associations. Breaking social capital into individual and collective features in terms of networks/contacts, trust/confidence, and civic norms/values, Jan Van Deth (2008, 162) listed more than forty major measures of social capital, including "crime rates, voting turnout, associational density, the amount of blood donated, or even the number of lawyers." Joep de Hart and Paul Dekker argued for the importance of local civil society data such as municipal and police statistics as well as information from observational studies, in-depth interviews, and focus groups (de Hart and Dekker 2003, 166).

Given that social capital does not manifest itself in the same form across time and societies, its measurement must be sensitive to the historical period and cultural environment under investigation (Krishna 2007, 944–945). Serra (2001), for example, argued that standard Western measures of social capital, such as those Putnam used in his 1993 study of northern and southern Italy—including literacy, voter turnout, and membership in associations—did not map well onto the empirical realities of Indian states. Krishna (2003, 9) similarly argued that measures that capture the "density of formal organizations" would be "particularly inappropriate for Rajasthan villages." Instead, Serra (2001, 699) posited that in India, "kinship ties or . . . caste and religion, which provide vital support to individuals" best reflect social resources. In studies of India, scholars like Krishna have looked closely at informal—and not formal—networks and organizations. For my case study of India in chapter 5, I use measures of connections to extralocal organizations, participation in local village functions such as marriages and funerals, and membership in village *uur panchayats*[4] to capture these networks.

With broader disagreements in the field of social science on how to capture social capital empirically, and with a variety of historical and cultural contexts under study in this book, I have sought to use the best data available for measuring this resource over time and space. I used these aforementioned accessible proxies—voter turnout rates, participation in political activities, involvement in communal festivals, connections to extralocal organizations, and the like—both because many scholars have previously used similar measures in their studies of these societies and because of the paucity of other forms of information. Some may disagree about whether these best capture social capital, and I recognize their concerns as potentially valid. In the quantitative study of post-earthquake Tokyo in the 1920s, for example, I measure both voter turnout among the eligible population and the number of political demonstrations and rallies per precinct. No doubt some observers will envision these activities as better measures of political, not social, connections. Yet Japanese historians have underscored the ways civic engagement, antigovernment networks, and neighborhood affairs flourished during this period known as "Taisho democracy" (Large 1972; Yamada 1973; Smethurst 1986; Lewis 1990; Matsuo 1990; Kimbara 1994; Tamanoi 2009). Networks of mobilization in 1920s Tokyo may have had political goals, but at their core they remained platforms for bonding and linking relationships.

Similarly, in the case study of post-Katrina New Orleans, I use voter turnout as a way of capturing connections between citizens in the neighborhood (bonding and bridging capital) and to decision makers outside it (linking social capital). A number of scholars, including Putnam (1995, 2000), Stephen Knack (2002), Ken'ichi Ikeda and Sean Richey (2005), and Luke Keele (2007) saw social capital as creating or reinforcing the norm of civic engagement (although some few disagree; cf. Atkinson and Fowler 2010). In his study of public policy choices after Hurricane Katrina, John Logan connected electoral participation with better outcomes: "Neighborhoods with the highest electoral participation have likely strengthened their hands in the battles over public investment and development planning that are sure to be a major feature of local politics in the next several years" (2009, 258). The underlying assumption that social capital encourages communitywide political participation through the mechanism of voting has a great deal of empirical support, but alternative explanations may be no less plausible. As one scholar emphasized, "Clearly, no measure of social capital will be entirely satisfactory" (Kingston 2005, 20). Until social scientists can agree on ways to effectively evaluate social capital during different periods and in different nations and can implement new, consistent surveys or experiments to collect these data, we must do our best with the records and information available to us.

Until now, the most obvious consequences of higher levels of social capital have primarily been positive ones—increasing trust, decreasing shirking, ensuring superior cooperation, and so on. I now turn to the potential dark side of social capital.

Social Capital as Liability and Asset

Much scholarship has identified a number of primarily positive effects that come with stronger social capital at the individual and the national levels. Beginning at the microlevel, Granovetter (1973) posited that even weak ties improved job acquisition for both blue-collar and white-collar workers. Naoki Kondo et al. (2007) showed that Japanese senior citizens who participated in rotating credit unions—that is, who were active members of social networks—had greater functional capacity than their less connected counterparts. Szreter and Woolcock (2004, 651) pointed out that higher levels of social capital are linked to "improved child development and adolescent well-being, increased mental health, lower violent crime rates and youth delinquency, reduced mortality, lower susceptibility to binge drinking, to depression, and to loneliness, sustained participation in anti-smoking programmes, and higher perceptions of well-being and self-rated health." North American neighborhoods with higher levels of social capital have lower mortality rates overall and for heart diseases for whites and blacks (Lochner et al. 2003).

At the national level, Coffé and Geys (2005, 497) argued that it "leads to a better quality of the government's financial management, even after controlling for various socioeconomic and political differences between the municipalities." Jonah Levy's (1999) study of French local governments and civil society showed that, without strong civil society, the central government found itself unable to implement plans because it lacked administrative capacity; organizations throughout the country proved to be vital ingredients in undertaking effective public policy. Knack (2002) argued that higher levels of social trust, volunteering, and census response bring about better government performance, and Hirokazu Ishise and Yasuyuki Sawada (2006) provided strong empirical evidence that social capital positively affects economic growth. Ashutosh Varshney (2001) used evidence from India to show that bridging social capital suppressed ethnic violence that claimed lives in other towns.

However, much recent scholarship has recognized that social capital is not a panacea for all economic, governance, and health difficulties and that it cannot function as a magic wand for eliminating such problems. Sheri Berman (1997, 402) underscored that high levels of bonding social capital do not necessarily lead to improved societal outcomes, since "high levels of

associationalism, absent strong and responsive national government and political parties, served to fragment rather than unite German society" during
the Nazi rise to power (although see Reiter 2009 for a criticism of her approach). William Callahan (2005, 500) posited counterintuitively that "the
circulation and accumulation of social capital by "good groups" like the Thai
political reform movement has negatively affected society in an environment
where corruption has become the norm. Recent research also uncovered the
institutionalized gender differences in social capital acquisition that lead men
to gain more from it than women (Djupe, Sokhey, and Gilbert 2007).

Initially, it was something of a self-evident truth (Ostrom 2000) that social capital functions as a public good (Coleman 1988; Cohen and Arato 1992;
Putnam 1993; Cohen and Rogers 1995), that is, a resource that provides nonexcludable benefits so that all residents of a high social capital neighborhood
enjoy its positive effects. More recent studies underscore that it has elements
of both public good and quasi-private good (Adger 2003). That is, the benefits
of social capital do not affect all individuals the same way; certain groups or
people gain more from strong social networks than others do. Scholars now
take seriously the "possibility that these outcomes may be attained at another
group's expense" (Woolcock and Narayan 2000, 231), since "many groups
achieve internal cohesion at the expense of outsiders" (Fukuyama 2001, 8).
Simone Chambers and Jeffrey Kopstein (2001) and Na'ama Nagar and Karl
Rethemeyer (2007) focus on associational life in organizations such as the
Nation of Islam, the Church of the World Creator, and anti-Arab groups that
espouse worldviews anathema to liberal democracy and to outsiders. While
PTAs, synagogues, and fraternities are examples of groups held together by
bonding social capital, so are skinheads, the Ku Klux Klan, Hamas, and other
organizations dedicated to hate. Olson himself pointed out that lobby groups
and trade unions have positive private returns that do not necessarily generate
aggregate benefits for society (1965). T. K. Ahn and Elinor Ostrom (2008, 73)
underscored that the "externalities of the use of social capital may be positive
(when a group of neighbors clean up a neighborhood) or negative to the outsiders (when a gang of youth protect their turf)." Rather than a naive conception of social capital as a public good, Michael Foley and Bob Edwards (1996)
urged researchers to recognize the inherent "paradox" accompanying it.

Applications to Disaster Recovery

Much research on disaster recovery seeks to connect the demographic characteristics of survivors—their socioeconomic status, race, gender, and age—
with their success in rebuilding homes and lives. Susan Cutter and Chris-

topher Emrich (2006), for example, used geographic information systems (GIS) data in combination with census information to literally map out locations within the United States that have a higher "social vulnerability" to disaster (see also Clark 2001; Donner and Rodriguez 2008). While many authors mention "complex constructs" such as provision of health care, social capital, and access to lifelines that correlate with outcomes such as being homeless, jobless, or sick after a disaster, their data typically reflect only the influence of socioeconomic status (Cutter, Boruff, and Shirley 2003). When scholars recently sought to create an updated nationwide social vulnerability index, its greatest variance was explained by socioeconomic status, followed by age, education, and race (Cutter and Finch 2008); again, there was no mention of data on levels of social capital in these widely cited papers (Flanagan et al. 2011).

Given the positive benefits and negative externalities that accompany social capital, research has begun to uncover its role in pre-disaster mitigation and post-disaster recovery. In the same way that other resources such as financial savings are assets, Woolcock and Narayan (2000, 226) argued that social capital is similarly an asset "that can be called on in a crisis." In an extended overview of the concept, Dynes (2005, 7) suggested that "during the emergency period, it is the form of capital that serves as the primary base for a community response." Survivors regularly argue that social infrastructure problems, not economic or disaster-related obstacles, delay their crisis recovery (Hyōgoken Kendo Seiribu Fukkōkyoku Fukkō Suishinka 2007, 9). By providing norms, information, and trust, denser social networks can implement a faster recovery. Table 2 builds on the three mechanisms identified above to show how social capital applies in disaster recovery.

First, social ties can serve as informal insurance, providing victims with information, financial help, and physical assistance. Rather than a type of formal, market-based insurance in which members pay premiums to a corporation in exchange for health or life insurance (which reimburses them in case of loss), informal insurance or mutual assistance involves friends and neighbors providing each other with information, tools, living space, and other help (Chamlee-Wright 2010, 46). Some researchers label these "collective coping behaviors," and they include turning to other homeowners in the neighborhood for support (Paruchuri 2011). Studying the responses of close to six hundred survivors of Hurricane Andrew, scholars argued that "being embedded in a network of higher kin composition, greater density, larger size, and lower diversity increased the probability that a respondent received informal recovery support" (Beggs, Haines, and Hurlbert 1996a, 216). In nonroutine situations, routine support—such as housing help, child care

TABLE 2. Mechanisms of social capital in noncrisis events and in disasters

Broad mechanism	Post-disaster application
Strong social capital provides information, knowledge, and access to members of the network	Social resources serve as informal insurance and mutual assistance after a disaster
Strong ties create trust among network members	Strong social capital helps by overcoming collective action problems that stymie recovery and rehabilitation
Social capital builds new norms about compliance and participation	Networks strengthen voice and decrease the probability of exit

assistance, short-term loans, and information—is readily available from core network members at a time when it may not be accessible from standard sources such as the local government, professional child care services, and other critical institutions (Hurlbert, Haines, and Beggs 2000).

For example, because of the lack of systematic assistance from government and NGOs, neighbors and community groups are best positioned to undertake efficient initial emergency aid after a disaster (Tsuji 2001). Since "friends, family, or coworkers of victims and also passerbys are always the first and most effective responders," we should recognize their role on the front line of disasters (Perrow 2007, 4). After the 1995 Kobe earthquake in Japan, many survivors initially went to live with family and friends who provided a spare bedroom or cleaned out unoccupied space for their new boarders. Most survivors initially preferred the company of kin and friends rather than seeking anonymous and potentially isolating long-term shelter in government-provided housing; only after more than four days in the houses of relations did survivors start searching for alternative housing (Kimura 2007). Survivors of tornadoes in the American Midwest may need to borrow water, chainsaws, generators, and other supplies or equipment that they do not own and that are not available because stores in town are closed. In one study of local responses to a catastrophic oil spill, Dow (1999, 87) argued that "among the fishers, coping capabilities that lessened vulnerability came from existing local supports." During the disaster and right after the crisis, neighbors and friends—not private firms, government agencies, or NGOs—provide the necessary resources for resilience.

While many social ties that provide post-disaster assistance may be local, "actors who have connections outside their immediate community are likely to be better off, as they can draw on these links when local resources are insufficient or unavailable" (Wetterberg 2004, 7). For example, after the 1985 typhoon in Tam Giang Lagoon, Vietnam, which caused six hundred deaths, the government sought to resettle the sampan dwellers to reduce their vulnerability to future events. This resettlement forced boat dwellers away from their nomadic lifestyle and encouraged them to form new networks and join organizations such as the Vietnam National Farmers' Union and the Women's Union. This new linking capital provided access to "resources, ideas and information . . . from formal institutions beyond the immediate community" (DaCosta and Turner 2007, 202). These new extralocal ties allowed the former boat dwellers to develop their new community economically. In a study of survivors of the 1995 Kobe earthquake, Shigeo Tatsuki and Haruo Hayashi demonstrated a correlation between survivors who had ties to more than one network and improved recovery compared with those who had access to only a single set of acquaintances. "Those who were resistant to and resilient from disaster damage utilized multiplex social ties, while those who were vulnerable tended to rely on a single network" (2002, 4).

Information and signals from network members—such as who is coming back when and what services will be provided—are critical to the decision making of survivors and cannot be replaced by government pronouncements (Chamlee-Wright and Rothschild 2007, 2). In many interviews, survivors described post-disaster situations in which contradictory information dominated and they were uncertain of the actual conditions and pertinent laws. More specifically, local community members—more than outsiders—know where they should be digging for survivors and what supplies will be useful for rebuilding. After the search and rescue phase, social capital still matters, providing important data to displaced people. Survivors of the 2005 post-Katrina flooding in New Orleans, for example, did not want to return to be the only household on the block; the alternation of well-maintained homes with empty lots has been labeled the "jack-o'-lantern syndrome" in the Big Easy (*New Orleans City Business,* 24 June 2010; Joiner 2010). While New Orleans city officials could regularly update the status of electrical and gas utilities, schools, and other facilities after the storm, such top-down memos and press releases about broader "Building Back Plans" held little useful information for homeowners, who were more interested in hearing whether their neighbors also planned on returning. In an interview, one survivor of Katrina described attending a number of city-level planning meetings: "All I get is mixed signals and question marks. And no one seems to know what the actual rules are" (quoted in Chamlee-Wright 2010, 136). Instead, survivors wanted to hear from neighbors, store owners, and friends about their plans—this information was critical to their own decision making (Chamlee-Wright 2008, 618). Similarly, one study used data on forty-six prefectures in Japan after World War II to demonstrate how regional social capital and civil society worked with the national government to speed up reconstruction. "By generating greater amounts of information, a strong civil society helps to identify the areas of most acute need, facilitate implementation, and provide effective monitoring" (Kage 2010a, 164). Social networks thus provide essential information, support, and guidance through strong and weak ties (Granovetter 1973).

Second, organized communities can effectively mobilize and overcome barriers to collective action (Olson 1965). With high levels of social capital, "meetings can be planned [and] events can be organized" (Paxton 2002, 257). As DeFilippis (2001) has argued, social capital can help individuals attract and control resources, since well-organized and mobilized regions can more successfully access the loans, supplies, and other resources (Dow 1999). After the 1995 Kobe earthquake, for example, local residents in some neighborhoods organized to plan cooperative, fireproof housing while other areas waited for guidance from city officials (Olshansky, Johnson, and Topping 2005). Survivors of the 2010 Haiti earthquake spontaneously organized watch committees to guard belongings from theft and protect individuals from harm (Burnett 2010). Buckland and Rahman's (1999) study of the Red River Flood, which forced 25,000 to flee their houses Manitoba, Canada, showed that coordinated communities reacted more efficiently when the disaster struck. That is, "communities with higher levels and more community-oriented patterns of development . . . generally responded more effectively to the flood" (188) by engaging in active mitigation and evacuation strategies. Similarly, after the 1985 Mexico earthquake, thousands of survivors who called themselves *los damnificados* (the victims) banded together neighborhood by neighborhood to pressure the government to build more permanent housing (Ovalle 2010). In New Orleans, census tracts across the city with "greater associational involvement, civic leadership, performing service, attendance at club meetings, and social trust correlate significantly ($p < 0.01$) with stronger repopulation and less damage, blight, and violent crime" (Weil 2010, 4). Levels of individual and family evacuation ahead of Hurricane Rita in Houston were highly connected with neighborhood-level decisions. If one's neighbors evacuated, one was far more likely to evacuate before the storm (Stein, Dueñas-Osorio, and Subramanian 2010, 827; Dueñas-Osorio et al. 2011, 21).

Neighbors with higher levels of social capital share information about bureaucratic procedures and upcoming deadlines, monitor public space to prevent dumping, and deter looting in their community. In Shigeyoshi Tanaka's (2007) study of survivors and villages after the Banda Aceh earthquake, he illuminated the role of the local community in rehabilitation. "The community served as a bridge between the NGO and the individual survivors, in which the community would bring in the resources provided by the NGOs. The community would guide the rich resources from outside into the hands of survivors" (Tanaka 2007, 242). In New Orleans, when five hundred signatures were needed to prompt Entergy—the local utility—to restore electrical power to the neighborhood, more than a thousand residents of Village de L'Est were able to sign on by the end of the day. While survivors may agree that housing, clearing of debris, and reconnection to utilities are critical, they may not be able to coordinate their efforts to bring about these outcomes. After the earthquake, the neighborhood of Mikura in Kobe was unable to coordinate its recovery; free debris removal sponsored by the city government required written agreement from the property owners, but no one volunteered to organize its signing (Yasui 2007, 227).

Finally, social networks raise the cost of exit from a community and increase the probability that residents will use "voice" (Hirschman 1970).[5] The term *exit* represents the chance to migrate elsewhere, and after a disaster that has destroyed lives, housing, and infrastructure, many survivors must make the difficult decision about what to do next. They could relocate themselves and their families to other communities, taking advantage of housing and jobs that may no longer be available in their old neighborhoods. Alternatively, and perhaps at steep costs, they could seek to rebuild their damaged or destroyed homes and communities. Senator Mary Landrieu, then chairman of the Ad Hoc Subcommittee on Disaster Recovery of the Senate Committee on Homeland Security and Government Affairs, recognized this when she spoke on 23 September 2008, saying, "I want to speak directly to the people of Louisiana and Texas who are going through the trouble of figuring out what to do, trying to find some sense of direction during a very confusing, frustrating, and difficult time" (quoted in Committee on Homeland Security and Governmental Affairs 2008).

Given better conditions and job availability, after Hurricane Katrina a number of displaced people from New Orleans ended up settling in communities such as Houston and Dallas in the "largest mass movement of people within the United States since the Dust Bowl migrations of the 1920s and 1930s" (Appleseed 2006, 1; Nigg, Barnshaw, and Torres 2006, 113). Some observers have estimated that as many as 100,000 people have stayed in Texas since their initial evacuation to that state (Benning 2010). One survivor told her interviewer that departing from New Orleans after Hurricane Katrina was "like a bird leaving a cage. . . . I'm in Texas because there's opportunity for me to grow. Home is still suffering" (Mildenberg 2011). One survivor said that the lack of community near her old home made her feel alienated, since "all that was gone—community, friends—scattered. You feel like, when you go [to New Orleans], you're walking into a strange country" (quoted in Nossiter 2007). Deeper social ties act as a barrier to exit and make it more likely that residents who are embedded in the community will work for a solution. Strong bonding ties created through a sense of connection to place motivate survivors to invest their energy and money in recovery even in the most damaged areas (Chamlee-Wright and Storr 2009b). In interviews with survivors of the 1995 Kobe earthquake, for example, many expressed a strong desire to return to rebuild the ruined neighborhoods in which they had lived before the disaster (Takahashi 2001, 57). Similarly, after the 2004 Chuetsu earthquake in Japan, "residents who had negative feelings toward their original communities were more likely to decide for relocation, while residents with pride and contentment toward their communities were more likely to decide to return" (Iuchi 2010, 213). Areas with more social capital can turn social resources into political capital, as seen in studies of tightly connected communities in Thailand that lobbied, staged rallies, and contacted politicians to alter natural resource management practices (Birner and Wittmer 2003).

Given that "private citizens with a stake in the outcome are best situated to lead their own recovery" (Chamlee-Wright and Rothschild 2007, iii), members of neighborhoods with low reservoirs of social capital are less likely to express their voice and work as leaders in rebuilding. In their study of the aftermath of the devastating floods that hit the American Upper Midwest in 1997, Kweit and Kweit (2004) showed that citizens in Minnesota who actively participated in the recovery reported greater satisfaction and displayed more political stability after the disaster, while a similar town in North Dakota with less civic engagement had greater dissatisfaction and higher government turnover. Similarly, in their comparative study of post-earthquake rebuilding in Gujarat, India, and Kobe, Japan, Yuko Nakagawa and Rajib Shaw (2004, 17) argued that individuals living in areas with higher levels of social capital were more satisfied with post-disaster planning. Areas with softer voices—those plagued by weak community ties—rebuild more slowly, if they rebuild at all (Kamel and Loukaitou-Sideris 2004). In fact, citizens with fewer ties to their neighbors are more likely to engage in illegal and disruptive acts, which can impede recovery efforts (Varshney 2001; Lee and Bartkowski 2004).

While much research has emphasized the potential benefits of strong social capital in post-disaster recovery (Tatsuki et al. 2005), newer studies have underscored the negative externalities that can accompany it. Adger (2003, 396) pointed out that under pressure from extreme climate and natural hazards, social networks can reinforce previously existing inequalities. Aldrich and Crook, in their (2008) study of post-Katrina FEMA trailer siting, demonstrated that neighborhoods within New Orleans that had measurably higher levels of civic norms (as seen through their turning out to vote in elections) were the same neighborhoods that did not receive temporary housing after the disaster. Social capital allowed these neighborhoods to coordinate their resistance to what were seen as "public bads"; things the general public recognizes as necessary for modern life but that are often unwanted in one's own backyard. While these neighborhoods in the Big Easy were pleased that they had excluded mobile homes and FEMA trailers, this resistance slowed down the overall recovery, since planners had to expend resources and energy to find more amenable neighborhoods—ones that often had lower levels of social resources and resistance. In Tamil Nadu, Dalits, women, and members of other marginalized groups who lacked both bonding and linking social capital found themselves excluded from much of the aid and assistance flowing in after the tsunami. These peripheral groups—whether the poorly organized neighborhoods in New Orleans or the socially excluded Dalits in India[6]—had their attempts at rebuilding slowed or impeded by groups with strong social capital that dominated the recovery process.

Do Disasters Alter Social Capital?

One remaining question is the relation between social capital and disasters; some have suggested that disasters alter existing levels of social capital. For example, Rebecca Solnit's A *Paradise Built in Hell* (2009) popularized the notion that after a disaster, local residents work together and avoid the "elite panic" that grips decision makers but not survivors in the street. That is, despite—or perhaps because of—horrendous conditions after a crisis, survivors work together to solve their problems; Solnit's argument is that the amount of (bonding) social capital seems to increase under difficult conditions. On the other hand, scholarship on Hurricane Andrew argued that after the disaster, social infrastructure was heavily damaged (Dash, Peacock, and Morrow 2000, 217) and that residents no longer kept up their previous communication and interaction. Their study and others (such as Tootle 2007) implied that disasters damaged rather than improved social networks (see also Foner 2005 for a study of how the terrorist events on 9/11 altered social and occupational realms in New York City).

Much research on disasters has long supported the concept that most victims and survivors act rationally and cooperatively after disasters, with enhanced levels of bonding. Fischer (1998, xv), for example, labels the idea that "widespread irrational, antisocial and dysfunctional behavior" occurs after crises as a "disaster mythology." His review of a number of disasters illuminated that very few survivors rioted or harmed others. Academic research on post-disaster norms and trust show that, at least for a short time, "immediately following a disaster, cooperative behavior increases" (De Allesi 1975, 127). De Allesi cites several examples where stores and corporations either voluntarily lowered prices on critical supplies—such as food, water, and generators—after disasters or were pressured to do so by residents. At the individual or family level, survivors may feel a stronger sense of family duty and connectedness for a short time after the crisis (Knowles, Sasser, and Garrison 2009, 99). Sorensen (2007, 63) observed the same thing almost one hundred years ago after the 1923 Tokyo earthquake: the rapid spread of neighborhood associations that linked Tokyo residents to each other. Crisis may also trigger widespread—if short-lived—volunteerism. For example, after the 1995 Kobe earthquake, authorities estimated that between 630,000 and 1 million volunteers streamed into the area to help rebuild (Tierney and Goltz 1997, 2; Shaw and Goda 2004, 19).

However, scholars have been able to provide empirical examples of widespread dysfunctional behavior through their investigations of various disasters, including the anti-Korean riots that followed the 1923 Tokyo earthquake.[7] After the 1755 earthquake and tsunami that decimated Lisbon, authorities had to deal with "pillage, arson, and murder" (Shrady 2008, 33). Looters ransacked stores throughout New Orleans after Hurricane Katrina, carrying away expensive consumer items such as television sets and power tools (Brinkley 2007), although other observers argued that "what was striking was not how many stores were ransacked but how few" (Baum 2006, 58). More recently, looting in Chile after its March 2010 earthquake forced government authorities toward more coercive attempts to control unrest (*Economist*, 6 March 2010).

Although some research has found greater social consciousness and civic mindedness among survivors of disasters even five years after the event (Tatsuki and Hayashi 2000), many studies have shown that any alterations in the social fabric of disaster-affected neighborhoods—whether toward altruistic cooperation or occasionally toward violent dysfunction—are short-lived. Sweet (1998) used interviews with roughly one hundred residents of Potsdam, New York, who had suffered a severe ice storm that cut off power to many for two weeks to measure their levels of social cohesion three years before and one month after the disaster. While there were short-term changes—social cohesion increased for less than a month—the effects quickly dissipated: there was no "long-lasting effect of the solidarity generated in response to the disaster" (330). As Kobe earthquake survivors regained a sense of normality in their lives, their likelihood of expressing communitarian worldviews[8] in which they actively sought to participate in citizenship and civic activities decreased (Tatsuki et al. 2005, 8). In fact, more than a decade after the 1995 Kobe earthquake, survivors expressed concern that manners and morals had worsened in their communities and that many had lost faith in the government (Tatsuki 2010). Scholars have similarly understood that disasters can motivate survivors to participate in civil society organizations and governance structures for only short periods (Tatsuki and Hayashi 2002, 2; Tatsuki 2008, 14). After disasters in Florida, for example, the number of homeowners' associations initially increased, but then it gradually decreased as time went on (Paruchuri 2011). This book builds on the evidence that any changes to pre-disaster social capital are limited in time and effect; hence post-disaster social networks are likely to tightly mirror pre-disaster conditions. This is important because in the case study of New Orleans after Hurricane Katrina, I rely on social capital measures taken before the storm and argue that these data continued to reflect immediate post-disaster conditions as well.

3

Tokyo Earthquake, 1923

In the fall of 1923, a tremendous earthquake struck Japan's capital city of Tokyo,[1] and the quake, along with the fires it started, destroyed nearly half of the highly modernized city.[2] The disaster deeply affected the Honjo ward on the eastern side of the downtown area: "The earthquake killed approximately one-sixth of the residents of the ward. . . . Fire swept over 95 percent of the surface of the ward, and 220,018 people lost their homes" (Hastings 1995, 57). Many observers, such as Edward Seidensticker (1991), believed the quake brought about a shift of people and businesses away from the Low City (Shitamachi, or the downtown, eastern parts of Tokyo) to the High City (Yamanote, the western area), implying that the recovery of the downtown area was slow or halting. However, even poorer, working-class neighborhoods in the Shitamachi area, such as Honjo, displayed resilience after the fires. Local neighborhood associations and nonprofit organizations (NPOs)—which embodied local connections and social networks—quickly resumed their activities in the area. "In Honjo, reservists fought fires, cared for the wounded, facilitated communication, patrolled the area, distributed food and water, repaired roads, and directed traffic" (Hastings 1995, 102). At the municipal elections that followed the enactment of universal male suffrage in 1925, this same poor area had higher voting rates than wealthier wards. Honjo was not the only heavily damaged area that displayed both strong social capital and efficient recovery.

Neighborhoods such as Atago, Kojimachi, and Tsukiji, all of which suffered greatly from the earthquake (with more than three in a thousand of their residents wounded or killed) nonetheless demonstrated higher population growth over the following decade—meaning they brought back residents and attracted new migrants—than areas that were equally or less damaged. This chapter argues that these resilient communities avoided becoming depopulated ghost towns because of greater solidarity, as seen through their higher participation in civic activities. Specifically, residents of tightly bonded areas turned out to vote in elections at higher rates (above 70 percent for these three neighborhoods) and held more political demonstrations (more than 160 a year in each); both required expending energy and time on costly undertakings and overcoming collective action problems. Strong connections between residents brought about better recoveries, tempering exit among survivors and reinforcing voice. Similar-sized but less damaged neighborhoods such as Toriizaka and Horidome had lower levels of civic engagement and, accordingly, lower population growth: they were unable to bring back residents or attract newcomers. These more fragmented neighborhoods had almost no political gatherings each year, and only 50 percent of the eligible population voted.

Rapid recoveries across Tokyo came about through cooperation and coordination. Even poorer residents worked together to build barracks—temporary shelters made of wood and other available materials—and to set up stalls on the sites of their old streetside shops. Images from the time show wooden huts being haphazardly built in public spaces and parks throughout Tokyo, often with a wagon or cart parked outside (Taiheiyō Sensō Kenkyūkai 2003, 106). More than five hundred barracks were set up in a temporary village in Ueno Park; those residents organized their own police force to ensure their safety and to keep thieves away (Tanaka 2006, 306). Pharmacists and doctors across the city coordinated their efforts and supplies to care for the victims they could reach, and faculty at Tokyo University's Law School put out a Tokyo Disaster Bulletin to provide the latest information (Busch [1962] 2005, 196). "The city burned for some forty hours, and before the last embers were out reconstruction had already begun" (Seidensticker 1991, 8). One observer of the time predicted a strong recovery for the city because the residents "all felt as one people, united in misfortune and united in their efforts for relief. This spirit of solidarity extended over all classes of society and all conditions of people, so that now students are assisting fellow students in distress to continue their studies" (Dahlmann 1924, 129–130).

The Earthquake

At 11:58 a.m. on 1 September 1923, an enormous quake measuring 7.9 on the Richter scale struck the imperial capital along with the nearby city of Yokohama.[3] Tokyo's children had begun school that day, and most had been dismissed to go home for lunch. Many observers theorized that the fires that consumed most of the city came from the gas ranges and coal fires set up to cook lunches in homes and restaurants around the city, which were knocked over by the immense shaking (Dahlmann 1924, 18; Hanes 2000, 125). "Across this tightly packed city of 2 million people, 90 percent of whose half million structures were made of wood, glass vials containing combustible chemicals shattered, charcoal braziers and gas cooking stoves overturned, fuel tanks erupted" (Hammer 2006, 117). The fires in Tokyo burned for three days (Naimushō Shakaikyoku 1926, 10), and the conflagration following the quake was far more powerful than well-known citywide fires abroad.[4] The quake left 350,000 houses damaged or completely destroyed and 60 percent of the population homeless; 60,000 residents were confirmed dead, and 11,000 were listed as missing. Officials believe that more than 1.6 million residents were affected by the quake (Tokyo Municipal Office 1930, 35). Of the sixteen newspaper agencies operating in Tokyo, thirteen had no buildings left to work from, and none of the official national or regional papers were printed at all until 6 September (Yoshimura 2004, 143-144). As one eyewitness mourned, "A few seconds sufficed for an overwhelming calamity to bury in ruins and ashes the results of half a century of unremitting labor" (Dahlmann 1924, xiv).

Home Minister Shinpei Gotō, previously the mayor of Tokyo, was put in charge of reconstruction and proposed an ambitious three-part plan that involved creating various government institutions to make decisions about reconstruction, issuing long-term foreign and domestic loans, and a government purchase of all the affected land in Tokyo (Tokyo Municipal Office 1930, 42). He envisioned rationalizing and widening the often narrow (and therefore unsafe) streets throughout the capital, reorganizing infrastructure and houses to modernize them, and increasing the green space throughout the city. He also intended to fireproof much of Tokyo by eliminating the wooden barracks and houses that commonly popped up around the city after the disaster (Tanaka 2006, chap. 7). "Little of Gotō's grandiose and wildly unrealistic urban plan ever came to fruition, however," according to Charles Schencking (2006, 836). While some have argued that the plan failed primarily because of its top-down, centralized nature, the finance minister worked to scuttle plans that would have raised taxes nationally to help fund the reconstruction of the nation's capital. Because all the money would come from the standard central government budget, other ministries had strong incentives to lobby against any attempts to drain more money from the national treasury. Despite Gotō's repeated attempts to increase the funding to the levels he envisioned (close to 4 billion yen) through impassioned lobbying both to advisory councils and to the Diet, Japan's bicameral legislature, in the end

FIGURE 2. Map of the wards (*ku*) of 1920s Tokyo. Image created by Asuka Imaizumi, reprinted with permission.

the Diet set aside less than 470 million yen for rebuilding Tokyo (Mochizuki 1993, 82-83).

The 1923 Tokyo earthquake remains among the most destructive disasters of the past century in Japan[5]—far more powerful than the Great Nōbi Earthquake, which had struck on 28 October 1891 and killed close to eight thousand people—and many groups saw in it important social and professional lessons. The Japanese government used the Tokyo earthquake as an opportunity to directly influence the "moral order" in Japan by promoting various codified stories about heroism and loyalty to the emperor (Borland 2005, 2006). Japanese engineers and architects used the earthquake as a chance to evaluate the stability of Western and Japanese building styles (Clancey 2006a, 2006b). Tokyo officials envisioned the earthquake as a chance to build up a new imperial capital that would be a modern global symbol of Japan's economic progress (Hanes 2000, 132; Schencking 2006, 835).

For social scientists interested in crises and reconstruction, the Tokyo earthquake provides a tragic test case or "natural experiment" for investigating the pace of post-disaster recovery, since recovery rates varied widely across Tokyo's precincts.[6] One scholar has argued that pockets of the city displayed higher levels of civil society—manifested through neighborhood associations along with voting and other political endeavors (Hastings 1995)—which may have accelerated recovery, while others have argued that the amount of damage determined the pace of rehabilitation (Tanaka 2006). The quake provides an excellent opportunity to test various approaches connecting these and other factors to population recovery.

Figure 2 details the division of 1920s Tokyo into wards (*ku*).

Explanations for Recovery Rates

Past research has focused on six main factors and resources that may determine the pace of recovery after a disaster: aid to survivors, damage, population density, human capital, economic capital, and social capital. Here I test the theories detailed in chapter 1 using data from this historical disaster.

Although we may imagine that fund-raising drives for victims of catastrophe are a modern invention, almost one hundred years ago international agencies and governments sent money to help Japan rebuild. Records from the 1920s indicate that the United States, Cuba, Mexico, Panama, Peru, Chile, Argentina, Brazil, China, Siam, Great Britain, Norway, Germany, Holland, Belgium, France, Italy, Switzerland, Russia, Latvia, Turkey, Poland, Austria, Sweden, Czechoslovakia, Bolivia, Uruguay, Romania, and Portugal provided foreign aid to victims in Tokyo (Naimushō Shakaikyoku 1926, 360-361). The sum of approximately 6 million yen was divided and evenly distributed among the wards of Tokyo. The city of Tokyo itself gave out free boiled rice to victims of the disaster until 30 September and opened medical relief depots throughout the city. While aid received from abroad may have helped victims purchase necessary materials and supplies and get back on their feet, it does not account for the variation in levels of population recovery. Since city authorities gave the same amount to all wards in Tokyo and wards had varying levels of recovery, they are not casually connected. Other scholars have looked elsewhere for potential factors in rebuilding.

A number of researchers, following Douglas Dacy and Howard Kunreuther (1969), have argued that "it just seems reasonable to assume that the speed of recovery following a disaster will be determined primarily by the magnitude of the physical damage" (72). Hence the amount of damage a neighborhood or town suffers may determine the pace of its recovery (Haas,

Kates, and Bowden 1977). For example, when analyzing Tokyo's recovery after the 1923 earthquake and subsequent fires, Tanaka (2006) asserted that downtown areas recovered more slowly than their uptown counterparts because there was greater damage.

Rather than damage, some social scientists have argued that population density—the population per unit area—alters the rate of recovery. Scholars have pointed out that 1920s Tokyo was in fact more densely populated than European capitals (Tanaka 2006, 111). Areas with greater densities may recover more slowly because of difficulty in providing temporary and permanent housing during the post-disaster period (Tobin and Montz 1997, 14). Alternatively, the human capital of a neighborhood—the education, job skills, and employment experience of its residents—may tie directly into its ability to bounce back after tragedy (Wright et al. 1979; Berke, Beatley, and Feagin 1993). Similarly, communities with low human capital that suffer from crime and drug abuse may find it difficult to mobilize their resources for rebuilding (Heath 2006).

Along with physical and human capital, scholars and government administrators alike have pointed to economic capital as essential for recovery. Neighborhoods without access to capital will be forced to draw on personal savings; few communities will have sufficient private financial resources to undertake broader recovery schemes. Even in the 1920s, city officials in post-earthquake Tokyo recognized the urgency of rebuilding pawnbrokers' shops to provide much-needed credit to poor and middle-class residents who lacked jobs after the disaster (Tokyo Municipal Office 1930).

Beyond these standard resource- and damage-based approaches to recovery, a number of qualitative and small-N studies have illuminated the potential role of *social capital*—the resources available to communities that facilitate collective action—in explaining the speed of recovery (for a fuller discussion see chapter 2; Nakagawa and Shaw 2004; Dynes 2005; Tatsuki 2008; Kage 2010a).

Data

This chapter uses a new data set focusing on thirty-nine police precincts within Tokyo over the period 1922—1933 to test these various explanations for population recovery. While politicians and bureaucrats divided the city of Tokyo into wards (as displayed in figure 2), the metropolitan police department further partitioned the metropolis into jurisdictions. I take advantage of the precinct-level data, using as the unit of analysis the police precinct— each with an average area of 1.97 square kilometers. Most of the data on these small neighborhoods come from the yearly statistics of the Tokyo Metropolitan Police Department, known in Japanese as the Keishichō.

These population, crime, and demographic data are not off-the-cuff estimates of law enforcement personnel seeking to map their beat. Instead, these records are highly reliable owing to the nature of their creators: local police observers lived in their neighborhoods around the clock in posts now known as *kōban* and had an acute ideological interest in closely monitoring the activities of civil society (Tipton 1991). Through a centralized command structure, Japanese law enforcement created a broader police state using regular and intrusive surveillance along with "reeducation" for those who were envisioned as disrupting the social order (see Keishichō Shi Hensan Iinkai 1960 for details of their involvement). Even modern Japanese police in Tokyo continue their thorough twice-annual surveys of local residents known as *junkai-ren,* which track occupation, household size, vehicle ownership, and other characteristics (Obinata 2000; Bayley 1991, chap. 5). I supplemented these police records with data from electoral records and notes on earthquake-related damage published by municipal authorities. This data set sheds new light on post-disaster recovery not only because of its scope (with demographic, geographic, socioeconomic, and social capital measures) and because it has multiple neighborhoods within the same metropolis, but also because the data begin just before 1923 and continue a decade beyond.

This data set contains variables that match up well with the core approaches to post-disaster recovery described above. I measure population density as individuals per square kilometer. To investigate the role played by human capital, I use the number of factory workers per capita (on the whole, migrants from the countryside) along with the number of commercial vehicles per capita in the neighborhood. The "working class" in Tokyo shifted from urban poor to these factory workers, who benefited from rising wages but found themselves stigmatized as "lower classes" (Yasuda 1994, 38–40). In the 1920s, most trucks and cars owned by Japanese residents in Tokyo were used for commercial transportation and delivery, and their numbers reflected the capital stock of firms in the area. I also include a measure of the per capita cost of crime in the area, based on evidence that individuals with lower human capital—that is, fewer job skills and less education—more often commit crimes (Williams and Sickles 2002). To measure damage levels, the data set includes the percentage of local residents killed in the earthquake, along with a dummy variable representing location in the Shitamachi or the Yamanote district. I use this variable as a test for Tanaka's (2006) argument that the Yamanote (High City) areas of western Tokyo near Shinjuku recovered more rapidly than the downtown section of Shitamachi (Low City) because they were less damaged by fire; all thirty-nine jurisdictions can be mapped to one of these sections.

As a proxy for economic capital, I include observations of per capita pawn-broker lending rates. While most Westerners today may view pawnshops as odd curios, in 1920s Tokyo they were core financial institutions and thus allow the tracking of highly localized assets. Succinctly, "Pawnshops were to the poor of Tokyo what banks are to the rich: the chief source of credit" (Hastings 1995, 47). The underclass of Tokyo could pawn various household objects—including umbrellas, bedding, kettles, tobacco pipes, and clothes—to gain money for rebuilding a business or home or buying necessities such as food. Pawnshops were seen as such important sources of credit that the Tokyo municipal government sought to rebuild pawnshops destroyed in the quake, and it "set up 7 municipal pawnshops with a view to relieving the suffering of labouring communities and other poorer classes who had been deprived of their only financial institutions" (Tokyo Municipal Office 1930, 85–86). Before the earthquake, all pawnshops had been private enter-prises, but most of these were demolished in the quake.

Given that social capital does not manifest itself in the same form across time and society, measurements of it must be sensitive to the historical pe-riod and cultural environment of the case (Krishna 2007, 944-945). I follow Joep de Hart and Paul Dekker's advice to use municipal and police statistics (2003, 166) to capture social capital, and this chapter builds on their advice. I use two proxies that capture the precinct's ability to overcome collective ac-tion problems (Olson 1965) and to express voice, not exit (Hirschman 1970): voter turnout (as a percentage) from municipal elections on 16 March 1929 and 1933 and the number of political demonstrations per precinct per year.[7]

Scholars beginning with Sidney Verba and N. H. Nie (1972) connected voting with broader engagement in citizen networks, and this approach was confirmed by Edward Walsh and Rex Warland (1983) in their study of antinuclear activists. James Hamilton (1993), Robert Putnam (2000), and Daniel Aldrich and Kevin Crook (2008) used voter turnout in elections as a proxy for the strength of social capital. More specifically, voting in early twentieth-century Japan—especially from 1925, when suffrage was extended to all men[8]—similarly reflects mobilization and engagement in voluntary civic activities that required an expenditure of time for little measurable re-turn (and were therefore "costly") (see Havens 1977 for an extended discus-sion of the national elections in 1928). One prominent historical study of 1920s Tokyo focuses specifically on voter turnout across neighborhoods in the capital as an indicator of higher levels of voluntary efforts among residents (Hastings 1995, 162). These figures are not and need not be representative of the population of Tokyo as a whole—especially since women were excluded from voting—but they capture the motivation of eligible voters in each police jurisdiction to turn out and vote. In some jurisdictions, fewer than half of the eligible voters showed up, while in others more than three-quarters did. This range indicates that even among qualified men, civic norms varied widely across neighborhoods.

The second measure—political demonstrations—also captures the ability of local residents to mobilize collectively. Historians have focused on the political activities of neighborhoods in Tokyo in the 1920s and 1930s, where rallies, marches, and participation in new community social networks indicated broader engagement in the political sphere (Ōoka 2001; Sakurai 2002).[9] Reasons for rallies in Tokyo during that time included labor strikes (Large 1972), tenancy disputes (Smethurst 1986), pro-suffrage marches, spontaneous riots (Lewis 1990), anti-Russo-Japanese settlement movements (Matsuo 1990), and anti-facility demonstrations (Yamada 1973; Tamanoi 2009). During this period, the circulation of national newspapers such as the *Asahi Shinbun* and *Mainichi Shinbun* jumped "from tens and hundreds of thousands to millions" (Yamazaki 1992, 247) as popular interest in political affairs grew dramatically. Scholars have regularly used demonstrations and others forms of political engagement as a proxy for social capital in the late twentieth century (Putnam 2000; Krishna 2002; Grenier and Wright 2004). So, too, historians of Japan have envisioned these extensive forms of public collective action during the period known as Taishō democracy as indications of cooperative undertakings that required coordination and mobilization (Kimbara 1994a; Yasuda 1994). These two proxies measure different aspects of social capital—they have a correlation of less than 0.2 (out of a maximum, perfect correlation of 1.00); hence I will use them alongside each other.

These two proxies have a low level of correlation, I believe, because the measure of protests captures bonding social capital, while voter turnout involves both bridging and linking social capital. Residents who organize protest events and leave their homes to stand across from the often repressive police authorities to express their opinions may do so because they have strong connections to other members of the movement. Through marches, antiwar rallies, and other group demonstrations, these residents cement their ties to each other. In voting, however, local residents seek to connect to elected officials and perhaps members of other demographic and political groups. Table 3 summarizes the data set.

As discussed in the first chapter, I use changes in the per precinct population per year to measure post-disaster recovery. I build on past trends in the literature and measure population recovery through yearly popula-

TABLE 3. Descriptive statistics for 1920s Tokyo data

Variable	Mean	Standard deviation	Minimum	Maximum
Dependent variable				
Population growth rate	0.022	0.187	−0.598	1.088
Area				
Area of the precinct (square km)	1.971	0.926	0.763	4.343
Human capital				
Crime damage (in yen) per capita	6.808	32.293	0.100	401.417
Factory workers per capita	0.063	0.090	0.002	0.723
Number of commercial cars and trucks per capita	0.010	0.047	0.000	0.495
Economic capital				
Pawnbroker lending per capita	10.293	6.292	0.000	47.092
Quake damage				
Percentage of residents killed in the quake	0.029	0.062	0.000	0.209
Shitamachi dummy variable	0.590	0.492	0.000	1.000
Geography and density				
Population density (residents per square km)	29098.280	13104.350	1611.553	64955.900
Total population	49745.9	18783.4	3505.0	97036.0
Social capital				
Voter turnout in municipal elections (1929 and 1933)	67.650	6.884	48.700	75.500
Higher than average numbers of political gatherings per year	0.239	0.428	0.000	1.000

Sources: Fukkōkyoku (1930); Keishichō Kanbō Bunshoka Tōkei Henshū (various years); Naimushō Shakaikyoku (1926); Tōkyō Shi Kansakyoku, Tōkeika (1936); Umeda (2003).

tion change (from the last day of year T to the last day of the following year, $T + 1$) to compare this statistic across precincts and cities. The formula

$$\Delta_{population} = \frac{(Y_{i,t} - Y_{i,t-1})}{Y_{i,t-1}}$$ captures this for each year (t) and for each police precinct.

Between 1922 and the early winter of 1923, the earthquake drove out, on average, 40 percent of residents in Tokyo precincts. The government offered

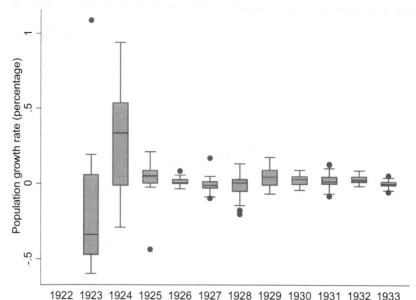

FIGURE 3. Yearly population changes in Tokyo's precincts over the 1920s.

free transportation out of the city to all who wanted it, and many factory owners sent employees home; images of the evacuation show packed trains, some with people sitting on the roofs of the cars clutching small packages (Busch [1962] 2005, 179). Many chose to migrate elsewhere at least temporarily; when schools reopened on 15 October, enrollment was only 26 percent of the previous level (Hastings 1995, 57).

Between 1923 and 1924, the population across Tokyo rebounded from the immediate post-earthquake lows as old residents and newcomers flooded back into the city. Over the next decade or so, the rate of growth stayed close to zero. That is to say, on average, few residents left or immigrated to these precincts in Tokyo. Across Japan, population growth rates during this period hovered between 1 and 2 percent. For example, in the major metropolis of Osaka between 1920 and 1935 the average population growth rate was 1.8 percent, while for Japan as a whole it was 1.4 percent. While overall population growth rates hovered around zero, local government official worked feverishly to rebuild the capital and bring back residents. By 4 September, streetlights were relit and water service resumed to much of the city. Within two weeks, the central post office had reopened in Marunouchi and had resumed delivering lightweight, ordinary mail to survivors. Further, by the second week of September the Bank of Japan, along with thirteen other financial institutions, reopened its doors (Naimushō Shakaikyoku (1926, 70-72). By 1930, city officials felt confident enough to declare the recovery complete. "Seven years have now passed since the great catastrophe of Sept 1st 1923 and the reconstruction of our metropolis, now almost completed, accentuates by contrast the memory of that terrible event . . . and now, 7 years after the fire, it is happy to say, the reconstruction work of the City of Tokyo has reached its final completion" (Tokyo Municipal Office 1930, 99).

However, over the post-earthquake period, the thirty-nine police precincts within Tokyo displayed wide variation in their population growth rates, seen in the length of the vertical bars in figure 3 (with the average growth rate indicated in the center of the vertical box and the black dots indicating extreme outliers beyond the typical minimum and maximum values). For some precincts, annual growth rates regularly reached 1 or 2 percent, while others showed a continual loss of 1 or 2 percent. What accounted for these differences?

Methodology and Results

To begin analyzing the influence on population change of the five factors measurable at the police precinct level—damage, population density, human capital, economic capital, and social capital—I first use a bivariate cross-tabulation to see if voter turnout and demonstrations can be linked to yearly population change. Then, to establish a causal relation between these variables, I use propensity score matching and average treatment effects to generate a preprocessed data set, which compares very similar neighborhoods that differ only in their levels of social capital. Finally, I apply time series cross-sectional models to demonstrate the significance and magnitude of social capital's effects in the context of other potential explanations.

First, using the raw data, I compared the population growth rates for those precincts which had both higher voter turnout and more demonstrations with those having lower levels of both of those proxies in figure 4. The results show a clear gap in population growth rates between neighborhoods with high and low social capital. For police precincts with both low voter turnout and few demonstrations, the average population growth rate was about zero, with a maximum of 7 percent. For those neighborhoods with high voter turnout and more political demonstrations, the average is closer to 7 percent, with a maximum of more than 15 percent. This difference is statistically significant, with a chi-squared value of 0.001. However, this initial analysis does not take into account potential confounding or control variables—for example, whether the jurisdictions had high or low levels of financial capital,

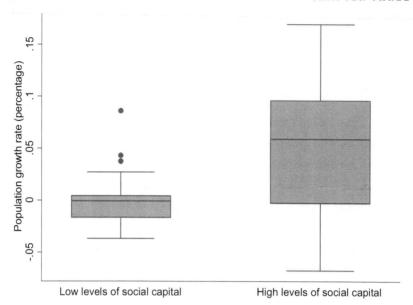

FIGURE 4. Population change in low and high social capital precincts in Tokyo. Precincts labeled "low levels of social capital" had below average voter turnout and numbers of demonstrations, while those labeled "high levels of social capital" had above average voter turnout and numbers of demonstrations. Chi-square value (for a tab test of below average/above average social capital with below average/above average growth rates) = 0.001.

damage, and so on. The next step, then, is to evaluate the impact of these factors using propensity score matching.

Propensity score matching tests causal inference with fewer assumptions than typical regression models, using a smaller, preprocessed data set (see Rosenbaum and Rubin 1983).[10] Matching takes observational data sets—such as the one created here on post-quake Tokyo—and prunes away dissimilar observations to create two groups of data, a control group and a treatment group, which are as alike as possible in all measurable ways except for their exposure to the "treatment." The treatment being investigated in this chapter is the amount of social capital in the precinct—so the data were divided into neighborhoods with higher and lower levels of social capital (using mean-dichotomized measures of voter turnout and number of demonstrations). In essence, this technique builds a "twins study," analogous to testing a new drug through an experiment in which identical twins—alike in all obvious ways—are exposed to different medical treatments. One twin (the control) receives no intervention, while the other (the treated one) receives a vaccine, for example. In such studies, any difference in the health outcome of a twin is assumed to come from the vaccine, since the twins share the same age, body type, genetics, overall health, and so on.

Propensity score matching preprocesses the existing data into a smaller but similarly matched data set split into two groups, simulating a randomized control trial.[11] I used a propensity score—which is the likelihood that the precinct would have high levels of social capital—to match neighborhoods on all the nonsocial capital variables from the time series cross-sectional analysis: area of the precinct (square kilometers), crime damage (in yen) per capita, factory workers per capita, number of commercial cars and trucks per capita, pawnbroker lending per capita, percentage of residents killed in the quake, and Shitamachi dummy variable. In doing so, I dropped observations not on common support—that is, that were statistically unlike the treatment group—to build a smaller, but much more balanced, data set with one group of observations having low levels of voting turnout or demonstrations and the other having high social capital (but similar in all other measurable aspects).

I used five methods of matching on propensity scores, four without replacement (meaning each control is used as a match only once): kernel, radius, nearest neighbor, and Mahalanobis matching techniques, and one with replacement: nearest neighbor with replacement.[12] Matching significantly reduced the bias—that is, the difference between the means for the treated and control groups—for all matched variables but one: 43 percent reduction for the variable measuring area, 97 percent reduction for crime damage, 90 percent for factory workers per capita, 99 percent for the number of commercial cars and trucks per capita, 76 percent for pawnbroker lending per capita, and 85 percent for percentage of residents killed in the quake. For one variable, the Shitamachi dummy variable, matching slightly worsened bias by about 10 percent. The strong reduction in bias indicates that matching created two parallel groups for comparison. Table A1 (in appendix 1) details the reduction in bias through preprocessing.

Once I had assessed the balance using distributions of baseline characteristics and propensity score histograms, I looked at the differences between the two groups using the average treatment effect. The average treatment effect compares the outcome of the control and treated groups to highlight any disparities, which are assumed to result from the treatment (higher levels of social capital). In this case, the outcome of interest is the population growth rate. I found substantial evidence that for both measures of social capital, higher levels of social resources resulted in a stronger population recovery. Neighborhoods that had more political demonstrations than average had—across all five types of matching—2 percent greater population return than very similar neighborhoods (in terms of earthquake damage, economic and human capital, geographic area, and so forth) with fewer rallies, marches, and protests than average. Given that the average growth rate in the city of Tokyo over the post-quake decade was just under zero, this 2 percent increase in population growth is actually quite large. Additionally, this population increase for more mobilized precincts was higher than the national average at the time—approximately 1.4 percent. For precincts with higher than average voter turnout, the results of average treatment effect on the matched data were more impressive: an average—across all five types of matching—of close to 3 percent higher population growth rate than similar neighborhoods with lower than average voter turnout. Table A2 provides details on the outcome of the average treatment effects (ATE) for the two social capital proxies.

With the bivariate analysis and propensity score matching both indicating that social capital and positive growth rates are strongly connected, I now examine time series cross-sectional models. Since the data contain information on both time (they were recorded yearly, when possible, between 1922 and 1933) and location (with thirty-nine precincts), time series cross-sectional approaches capture both the within-precinct and across-precinct influence of the variables under study. I begin with a generalized least-squares model with random effects without including the measure of voter turnout (since it reduces the overall number of observations because municipal elections are infrequent), labeled model 1 in table A3. Two of the estimated coefficients—both of them positive, meaning that an increase in these two variables increases the dependent variable of population growth rate—were significant: whether the precinct was in the Shitamachi section and whether it had higher than average numbers of political gatherings. Model 2 adds voter turnout, and despite fewer observations (since only two of the years in the data set had municipal elections), both of the measures of social capital—voter turnout and number of demonstrations—remain significant, as is the district's location in Shitamachi. The two estimated coefficients for social capital remain positive, meaning that an increase in voter turnout or more demonstrations than average resulted in a measurable population increase.

However, a Hausman test indicated that a fixed effects model might be more appropriate than a random effects model, so model 3 carries out a fixed effects time series cross-sectional analysis. Owing to the structural nature of fixed effects models, those factors in the data that remain unchanging over time—such as the area and the location of the precinct and the percentage of residents killed—drop out of the equation. However, even with the fixed effects model, the social capital variable of political demonstrations remains significant at the $p < 0.01$ level.

To ensure that these findings were not artifacts of the models, I tested a final model (model 4) involving panel corrected standard errors (which Beck and Katz argue more effectively handle the problems of "groupwise heteroskedasticity and contemporaneous correlation of the errors" [2004, 4]), and though the Shitamachi dummy variable is no longer significant, both of the social capital indicators remain positive and significant (at $p < 0.01$). A variance inflation factor (VIF) test produced a mean result of 3.64, which is slightly high—indicating some collinearity—but acceptable (Rabe-Hesketh and Everitt 2007, 69). Even controlling for factors commonly thought critical in the recovery period, social capital remains the most important variable for growth.

Next, to provide a visual representation of the influence of voter turnout and of higher or lower numbers of political demonstrations on precinct-level population recovery, I set all the variables at their means and generated predictions for different levels of these proxies. Simulations together with confidence intervals extract and present information about the variables under investigation and estimate the degree of uncertainty in predictions generated by these analyses. In a simulation, we learn about the distribution of our data by taking many (one thousand or more) random draws from them and estimating the parameters of the actual population in a way that accounts for both sampling error and fundamental uncertainty (Tomz and Wittenberg 1999). Using the statistical program Clarify, I created one thousand simulations of the main and ancillary parameters and then displayed the predicted outcomes bounded by 95 percent confidence intervals (King, Tomz, and Wittenberg 2000). These figures clearly reveal the relation between independent and dependent variables of interest.

The results are displayed in figure 5. Holding everything else constant, a neighborhood where only half of eligible voters participate in municipal elections would see a slightly negative population growth rate. On the other hand, a precinct where more than three-quarters of voters carried out their civic duty would see a population growth rate of close to 4 percent—higher than both national and urban levels.

In Tokyo neighborhoods where residents rallied for a common cause and overcame the typical barriers to collective action that often block voting and demonstrations, citizens built up informal and formal networks and relationships. Through repeated meetings—whether at local bars, the houses of prominent activists, or protests against unwanted projects (Tamanoi 2009)—these residents established expectations of reciprocity and assistance (Small 2009). Although survivors could choose to relocate to new areas or leave Tokyo completely, bonds drew them back to their neighborhoods

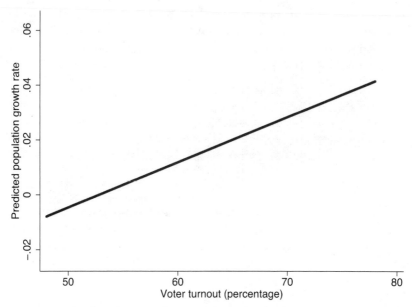

FIGURE 5. Predicted population growth rate per Tokyo precinct based on voter turnout. Figure based on time series cross-sectional panel-corrected standard errors; all dependent variables (area of the precinct [square km], crime damage [in yen] per capita, factory workers per capita, number of commercial cars and trucks per capita, pawnbroker lending per capita, percentage of residents killed in the quake, number of political gatherings, and Shitamachi dummy variable) held at their means except for voter turnout. The gray band indicates the 95 percent confidence interval for these predicted values.

and allowed them to work together to clear debris, erect neighborhood bulletin boards to post information (Hastings 1995), and rebuild homes. Ties between neighbors provided information and other types of informal insurance such as tips on inexpensive places to sleep and eat, suggestions for rebuilding damaged houses, and early insights about job openings. Where these bonds and ties between residents were weak—that is, where trust had not been established—residents could easily contemplate moving elsewhere and seeking new neighbors, practicing exit, not voice (Hirschman 1970). In post-quake Tokyo, precincts with higher levels of social capital had measurably and statistically significant greater population growth than those with lower levels of social capital.

Conclusions

This chapter investigated the ways damage levels, physical, human, or economic capital, and social capital connected to population recovery after a megadisaster in Tokyo in the early twentieth century. Of the factors tested here, social capital—as measured through the propensity to participate in civic affairs such as voting and mobilizing for public events like demonstrations—best explains why communities repopulated quickly after the earthquake or failed to do so. Using bivariate analysis, propensity score matching, and time series cross-sectional models, the chapter underscored the fact that precincts that were better able to mobilize and coordinate their activities showed higher population growth rates after the devastating quake. This analysis found little evidence supporting claims about the standard factors said to alter the pace of recovery—including levels of damage, financial and human capital, area, or population density.

Strong connections and trust among residents help them overcome collective action problems that may prevent other neighborhoods from effectively rebounding. For citizens and decision makers concerned about disasters, social networks are a resource that should not be overlooked. Two points arise from this research on early twentieth-century Tokyo. First, as I mentioned in the book's opening chapter and reiterated more strongly in the theory chapter on social capital, strong social networks can bring negative externalities alongside the benefits of tighter bonds. While most scholars argue that postdisaster riots and violence are said to be somewhat rare (Fischer 1998), after the 1923 quake mainland Japanese residents organized horrific attacks against Koreans across the capital.

The massacre of Koreans began after rumors spread by survivors and police authorities made their way into the popular sphere and were published by newspapers (Yoshimura 2004, 175, 192; Nakajima 1973). On 2 September, the Ministry of Internal Affairs publicly issued a statement that Koreans were involved in riots and warned residents about the danger. The statements themselves led to false rumors accusing Koreans of various crimes—such as poisoning wells, murdering Japanese, and setting fires—in the aftermath of the disaster. After the notification from government officials and then the metropolitan police, neighborhood watch groups formed and started attacking the Korean population (in some cases Chinese were targets of the violence) (Kantō Daishinsai Hachishūnenkinen Gyōji Jikkō Iinkai 2004, 13–19). The Japanese central government issued a warning on 5 September that all vigilante persecution of Koreans should stop (Naimushō Shakaikyoku 1926, 16). Although the exact number of victims is still contested, between two thousand and five thousand Korean residents were slaughtered with at least complicity from police (Yamada 1993).

One explanation for this tragedy rests on the role of social capital—in which bonding social capital solidifies ties between similar individuals but exacerbates differences from others. If bonding social capital was strong in certain neighborhoods but bridging social capital was lacking, the panic of the fires and quakes, combined with existing prejudices and rumors of poisoning, may have inflamed local residents, who sought to attack those "outside" their groups (cf. Varshney 2001). Local mainland Japanese residents mobilized collectively to carry out violence and murder; their networks connected them and facilitated this ethnic violence. In the future, scholars could seek to correlate the locations of such attacks with neighborhood-level measures of social capital to test for measurable connections. Such investigations would further our understanding of the "dark side" of social capital (Putnam 1995).

A second point that comes out of this research is the potential for a crisis to alter local institutions and stores of social capital in the short term. Scholars have pointed out that after disasters such as the 1923 quake, many Japanese residents either formed or joined new collective organizations and neighborhood associations—known as *chōnaikai*—across Japan, particularly in Tokyo (Kimbara 1994a, 6). "In their answers to the survey of 1934, 21 percent of the associations of the old section of the city gave the earthquake as the impetus for their founding. More were founded in the five years between the beginning of 1923 and the end of 1927 than any other five year interval" (Hastings 1995, 79). Between 1922 and 1933 the number of Tokyo neighborhood associations skyrocketed from 452 to 986. It was precisely these groups that displaced both political elites and older organizations and pushed for political changes, becoming new players in citywide politics (Sakurai 2002, 199; Ōoka 2001, 188).

After the earthquake, urban planners in Tokyo wanted to provide more meeting halls—including school gymnasium space—to promote community enterprises such as youth, women's, and veterans' groups (Kobayashi 2006, 24). Architects and social planners envisioned institutions such as local elementary schools and locations such as parks serving as new centers of urban communities in much the way churches organized life in Western towns (Ono 1998, 131). This understanding of the power of community-based organizations to create and enhance reservoirs of social capital meshes well with recent research on the topic (Small 2009). Anchoring organizations—whether religious institutions or community centers—can provide "club goods" to communities after disasters (Chamlee-Wright and Storr 2009a). Furthermore, within the urban communities, many local residents left individual family housing and worked together to build cooperative, joint housing that would withstand fire (Murosaki 1973, 19). Although the disaster destroyed many lives directly and resulted in the loss of many Korean lives, it also led to the reification of social networks through new organizations, which diffused information and connected neighbors to each other.

The next chapter moves forward nearly a century to investigate how social resources helped recovery after the next major Japanese earthquake, in 1995, which struck Kobe, at the core of a densely populated metropolitan center in the Kansai area (in the southern part of the nation).

Kobe Earthquake, 1995

The 1995 Kobe earthquake devastated the densely populated port city of more than 4 million, killing 6,500 people, collapsing buildings, the Hanshin Expressway Route 3, and docks, and leaving more than 300,000 residents homeless.[1] Although the quake affected much of the city and remains among the largest economic disasters in Japanese history (Sawada and Shimizutani 2008, 464), responses to the earthquake and resilience afterward varied tremendously across neighborhoods. Surveys showed that in some wards 99 percent of the original residents returned, while in other neighborhoods fewer than 42 percent did so (Hyōgo Ken 2003, 24). In interviews, many respondents argued that the quality of their connections to their fellow residents was a critical factor in recovery, and these ties (or their absence) were visible soon after the quake struck. In the neighborhood of Mano—known for its long-established community movement (Evans 2002, 458)—for example, local residents spontaneously formed a bucket brigade using the equipment available to them and stopped the encroaching fires set off by the quake from spreading farther. But in the neighborhood of Mikura, next to Mano, residents simply watched as fires consumed their homes and businesses. After the quake and fires were over, neighbors in Mano worked together to set up a series of NPOs and umbrella institutions that would organize their demands on city authorities and coordinate their efforts.

Among other endeavors, residents of Mano lobbied for new housing for the elderly, set up cooperative housing units, created neighborhood promotion organizations, and built a day care center. In Mikura, however, residents managed to create only a single organization to work on reconstruction, failing to coordinate on a number of critical issues. Kobe city officials offered free debris clearing if residents could produce signatures from all affected

FIGURE 6. Kobe's nine wards.

property owners in the area. Unable to coordinate the petition, Mikura residents could not obtain permission from the local landowners, and the debris sat uncollected.

This chapter uses case studies along with a new data set focused on Kobe's nine wards after the city's 1995 megadisaster, the earthquake known in Japanese as the Hanshin Awaji Daishinsai (the Great Hanshin—Awaji Earthquake), to investigate the factors that sped up or slowed down recovery at the neighborhood level after a disaster. Controlling for a number of factors including economic status, dependence on welfare, damage, socioeconomic inequality, and geographic conditions, quantitative data demonstrate that the amount of social capital most strongly determines recovery rates. Paired case comparisons across neighborhoods in Kobe and three time series cross-sectional models confirm these findings. Wards with higher levels of social capital—measured in the time series cross-sectional data as the number of new neighborhood-level NPOs created per capita—proved more successful at rebuilding population levels even when controlling for variables thought critical by past research. These results match up well with large-scale surveys of survivors of the Kobe earthquake; those respondents regularly identified social ties as critical to their own recoveries (Tatsuki and Hayashi 2002, 3).

Figure 6 maps out the city's nine wards that will be the focus throughout the chapter.

The Kobe Earthquake

On 17 January 1995 at 5:46 a.m., a series of shocks measuring 7.3 on the Richter scale struck the densely populated area in and around Kobe, in the southern part of Japan's mainland. The city sits on a small strip between Osaka Bay to the south and east and the Rokkō Mountains to the north and west. The initial tremors caused great devastation, and uncontrollable fires caused additional damage. More than two hundred fires broke out across the Hyogo area, with more than a hundred in Kobe itself, and in the two days of conflagration that followed, more than seven thousand buildings in the city burned to the ground. The quake and inferno claimed 6,400 lives and injured more than 15,000 in a densely populated urban area, which at the time was home to 4 million people. Vibrations and fire completely destroyed over 110,000 buildings in the area and left 320,000 people homeless, causing close to $64 billion in damage (Horwich 2000). Eighty-five percent of the schools, hospitals, and public facilities in the area were damaged (Olshansky, Kobayashi, and Ohnishi 2005). As with most disasters, those killed were mainly women and people older than sixty because of their physical vulnerability and lack of mobility (Yasui 2007, 95; Tajika 2000, 119).

Responding to the Kobe earthquake, professional city fire departments and the Japanese Self-Defense Forces (SDF) mobilized slowly because of blocked roads, collapsed bridges, and a lack of electric power.[2] Many reporters and survivors claimed that members of Japan's mafia—known as *yakuza*—from the local Yamaguchi-gumi syndicate appeared with food, water, and supplies more quickly than the government authorities (Pilling 2005; Begley and McKillop 1995). As has been the case in other crises, neighbors and residents—not police or military officials—were often first responders on the scene (Tsuji 2001, 56; Shaw and Goda 2004, 21; Zhao 2010).[3] Beyond pulling survivors from the rubble and getting neighbors to safety, these "emergent groups" (Stallings and Quarantelli 1985) were the first to encounter the fires. Neighborhood residents responded to the fires in different ways: while some citizens watched in horror as flames consumed their homes and stores, others organized themselves into civilian fire fighting corps and tried to put out the fires (Murosaki 2007). Pushing children in strollers and pulling suitcases on wheels, some survivors walked six miles to find working public trains (Begley and McKillop 1995). A million households lacked water and natural gas for heating or cooking, while another fifty thousand had no electricity for some time after the quake. One elderly sur-vivor said, "I couldn't believe my eyes. It looked like the last days of the war" (quoted in van Biema and Desmond 1995). Although the Japanese govern-ment was initially reluctant to accept foreign assistance, it did so once the scope of the disaster became clear (Nordahl 1995).

After the quake, some 236,000 people evacuated to more than a thousand city–based emergency shelters, including elementary schools, junior high schools, and temporary housing units (Tajika 2000, 126). Soon afterward, roughly 60 percent of the households in the area had moved into public hous-ing (Nakabayashi and Ichiko 2004, 9). Within seven months the emergency shelters were closed, but about 4,500 residents remained in temporary hous-ing units (Ikeda 2004, 33). Most residents in temporary housing were from the heavily damaged wards of Nagata, Hyogo, and Nada (Evans 2001, 162).

Overall, rates of recovery and the success of reconstruction were highly differentiated within the city (Edgington 2010, xv). Structural damage from the fires and quake varied across Kobe based on history and geology (Muro-saki 2007; Evans 2001), so that areas with fewer old wooden houses and more bedrock suffered less damage. However, recovery rates also varied by loca-tion, and these rates were not strongly correlated with damage (Hagiwara and Jinushi 2005; Yasui 2007, 112).[4] One study uncovered housing reconstruction rates of 107 percent (that is, more houses were in place after reconstruction than before the quake owing to land availability) in Higashinada ward com-pared with only 44 percent in Nagata ward (Evans 2001, 150). By 2007, the overall city population had increased beyond pre-quake levels, but certain wards remain at lower levels of occupation while others have grown substan-tially (Yasui 2007, 112). This variation in population growth rates across the nine wards provides a tragic "natural experiment" that allows us to test the factors influencing recovery (cf. Rosenzweig and Wolpin 2000).

Qualitative Data: Cases of Social Capital and Recovery

Case studies of similar neighborhoods in Kobe illuminate the role of social cap-ital in accelerating and facilitating post-disaster recovery. Mano and Mikura make up the first pair of neighborhoods under study; both are in the downtown section of Kobe's Nagata ward and have mixed residential and industrial zones full of factories, workshops, and large numbers of residences (Evans 2001, 177). Both areas face the problems of population decline, an aging population, flimsy old wooden housing, and high building density (Yasui 2007, 15). Although the wards were physically, demographically, and geographically similar, Mano displayed high levels of social capital, while Mikura possessed far lower levels.

Since the late 1960s, Mano's residents have worked cooperatively on issues such as antipollution campaigns and neighborhood development schemes and have a history of advocacy and civic participation (Evans 2002, 452).

In the Mano neighborhood, self-organized citizens' fire brigades[5] made up of neighborhood residents successfully fought the post-quake fires, unlike adjoining neighborhoods—including Chitose and Mikura—facing similar conflagrations. In interviews, the secretary general of the Mano Town-Building Council, Shimizu Mitsuhisa, argued that citizens in Mano spontaneously organized bucket brigades, not waiting to see if fire trucks would arrive (Yasui 2007, 186). Residents coordinated their firefighting efforts, borrowing hoses and water from nearby shoe manufacturers and other companies while others drew water from the Shin Minato River (Yasui 2007, 188). Residents of Mikura, in contrast, lacked the coordination to act and stood by helplessly as flames destroyed their businesses and homes.

Furthermore, the Mano neighborhood undertook a tremendous number of projects after the quake, including the "establishment of Mano Rehabilitation Machizukuri office, construction of Machizukuri center, establishment of 'Manokko (private limited company)' for community development, signature collection campaign for construction of public houses for disaster affected people, lobbying for special houses for elderly, construction of a model house as collective housing, preparing joint housing project proposals, and running a day-care center" (Nakagawa and Shaw 2004, 8). Although critics have argued that even in Mano not all residents participated in community endeavors (Inui 1998, 245), they agree that the neighborhood has demonstrated a tremendous number of broader activities, including sixteen community organizations that frequently hold public events (Inui 1998, 246). Such communal participation dwarfs that of Mano's neighboring wards. For example, Mikura created only a single organization—Machi Communication—to coordinate its recovery (Yasui 2007, 15). Mano stands out as a community whose strong social networks promoted a smoother and faster recovery than in similar neighborhoods with weaker ties.

Other paired comparisons between similar Kobe neighborhoods with high and low levels of social capital have uncovered differences in the course of recovery. Katsuji Tsuji (2001, 231, table 9-3) compared two neighborhoods that he labeled Nagata A and Fukushima B. Both had similar average ages of residents before the quake (approximately fifty-one years), population levels (about 185 residents), income (4.4 million yen on average), employment (approximately 66 percent employed), and household leadership (77 percent headed by men). However, close to three-quarters of the residents of

Fukushima B were born there, while fewer than 10 percent of Nagata A residents were natives. Further, nearly twice as many Nagata A residents rented their homes—roughly 35 percent, compared with 16 percent in Fukushima B. Sociologists have long underscored that in advanced industrial democracies homeowners with longer tenure in neighborhoods are more involved in community and political affairs than renters (Cox 1982; Rohe and Basolo 1997). Fukushima B had more bonding social capital than Nagata A, primarily seen in the long-term residence of its population and its higher rate of homeownership.

Tsuji further characterized Fukushima B as employing a net support scheme based on strong traditional social bonds, while Nagata A relied on a small cadre of leaders. That is, Fukushima B's strong social networks promoted interaction, coordination, and information diffusion. Nagata A relied instead on a top-down structure with a handful of active leaders who set the agenda for community functions. In discussing the post-earthquake outcomes for each neighborhood, Tsuji (2001, 309) argues that "Nagata A experienced a hollowing out, while [Fukushima] B was depopulated." While both neighborhoods lost residents owing to the disaster—either from direct harm or from outmigration—the stronger bonds in Fukushima B allowed it to hold together as a community. After the quake, Nagata A was left with few of its original residents and little community resilience or collective memory. Other evidence from the Kobe earthquake links deeper social capital with stronger recovery.

Collective action and coordination problems proved severe after the earthquake across parts of Kobe; many condominium owners, for example, could not agree on the procedure for rebuilding or repairing their damaged co-owned properties (West 2005). Areas with higher levels of social capital overcame these obstacles, not only to repair their houses but also to design and build new cooperative housing. In the Mano neighborhood, survivors organized soon after the quake to discuss constructing cooperative housing, known as *kyōdō tatekae* (literally "joint rebuilding"), to replace the older individual family homes that were vulnerable both to fire and to quake damage (Yasui 2007, 194). One such project, the Higashi Shiriike Kōtō in the Higashi Shiriike area, involved the "cooperation of the five freehold house-owners and three landowners who owned the land on which were previously eighteen housing units (occupied by five house-owners and thirteen tenants)" (Evans 2001, 223). The tenants worked together to plan their shared housing with the help of volunteer architects and engineers and began construction on eighteen units by August 1996.

Mano's Shiriike Kōtō project was one of many cooperative housing schemes that rose from the ashes of the quake; as of 2003, the city of Kobe reported more than 108 such joint housing projects with more than 4,800 housing units. Homeowners could build and sell or rent additional units in the new shared buildings to offset the costs of the project, and many received assistance from city rebuilding schemes (Olshansky, Johnson, and Topping 2005, chap. 6, 33). Surveys of collective housing members demonstrated that the often lower costs motivated their participation in such projects (Seki-kawa, Sakurai, and Song 2006, 93), and that respondents for whom *kinjo tsukiai*, or relationships with neighbors, were important were more satisfied with their living arrangements than their less sociable counterparts. Building on these cases, connecting social capital to accelerated recovery, the chapter now seeks to uncover broader patterns linking recovery not only with civil society but also with other potential explanatory factors.

Factors Correlated with Recovery

Literature on disasters has identified a number of factors that can acceler-ate or impede recovery. Since the first chapter provided in-depth discussions of these approaches, I will only briefly review their core arguments here. A number of scholars have postulated that the amount of physical damage from the disaster best correlates with recovery speed (Dacy and Kunreuther 1969, 72; Haas, Kates, and Bowden 1977; Yasui 2007, 29), while others (Tat-suki 2008, 24) have challenged this logic. Yet other scholars have sought to connect population density in the affected areas with the pace of rebuilding (Haque 2003; Tobin and Montz 1997, 14; Tandon and Mohanty 2000; Nos-siter and Eaton 2007). Parts of Kobe—especially in the downtown area near the waterfront—had very high population densities, while other wards up toward the mountains were far less densely populated.

Much literature on disasters has focused on the role of socioeconomic resources in rebuilding (Sawada and Shimizutani 2008, 465). Matsuda et al. (2002) focused on the slow recovery in areas of Kobe with higher number of home-based workers who had children in local schools, arguing that the data underscored the quake's larger impact on small business owners, who would lack sufficient capital to rebuild both businesses and homes simultaneously.

Economic inequality—the uneven distribution of wealth in a city or town—has been singled out as a cause of delayed rebuilding. Susan Cutter and Christopher Emrich (2006, 105) have underscored how "inequities in health, well-being, and health care accessibility have now become central issues for many emergency managers." City planners struggle to create recovery policies that can capture the needs of the worst-off neighborhoods alongside those of wealthier ones. Further, research based on individual-level data demonstrated that after a crisis, poorer residents in neighborhoods with greater income inequality suffered from depression more than others (Ahern and Galea 2006). Finally, scholars have sought to link the speed and effectiveness of recovery to levels of trust and social capital—that is, the resources available to individuals through their social networks (Beggs, Haines, and Hurlbert 1996a; Tatsuki and Hayashi 2002; Dynes 2005; Nakagawa and Shaw 2004, 18; Yasui 2007, 43; Lin 2008; Tatsuki 2008, 27).

Quantitative Data

The data for this quantitative analysis come from an original data set I developed to follow the economic and demographic development of the nine wards of Kobe between 1990 and 2008 based on multiple sources. Kobe's division into wards allows us to trace the effects of different factors, including earthquake damage, population density, social capital, and so on, over time. Table 4 provides descriptive statistics for the variables used in this chapter.

The data are arranged in a time series cross-sectional structure because Kobe has nine wards (the units), which are observed annually over eighteen years (periods), with ward-based observations organized by year. The ward thus serves as the unit of analysis within the data set; the average ward within Kobe is about sixty square kilometers. The observations at the ward level match up well with the theoretical explanations of post-disaster recovery laid out above.

TABLE 4. Descriptive statistics for 1990s Kobe data.

Variable	Number of observations	Mean	Standard deviation	Minimum	Maximum
Population growth rate	153	0.002	0.048	−0.258	0.225
Percentage of population affected by the earthquake	162	0.228	0.151	0.048	0.559
Welfare-dependent households per capita	135	0.015	0.012	0.002	0.045
NPOs created per capita	81	0.00004	0.00005	0.00000	0.00025
Population density (people per square km)	162	5,322.6	2870.6	824.4	11,923.5
Socioeconomic inequality	126	0.000	0.947	−0.936	1.784

Sources: *Kōbe Shi Shōmukyoku Tōkeika* (various years), *Kōbe Shi Senkyo Kanri Iinkai* (various years), the Kobe City NPO Database, and calculations by author.

To capture the damage done to each ward, the data set measures the percentage of individuals in the ward directly affected by the quake through deaths and injuries. The average neighborhood in Kobe had approximately one in five residents either wounded or killed by the quake, but in some more than half of the residents were affected, while a few neighborhoods had only one in twenty hurt or killed. The measure of households per capita in the ward on welfare serves as a proxy for economic conditions. On average, the Kobe wards had only two households per hundred people on welfare, while the most poverty stricken had close to five in one hundred and the wealthiest had fewer than two households per thousand people. Population density is measured as people per square kilometer, with an average of 5,300 people per square kilometer and a maximum density of close to 12,000. To measure socioeconomic inequality, I created a Z-score, which measures the gap between the economic conditions in each ward in each year and other wards through the equation $Z_{t,i} = \dfrac{x_{i,t} - \mu_t}{\sigma_t}$. This provides a relative measure of inequality by subtracting the mean level of socioeconomic conditions (across all wards) from the observed level in each ward (for each year) and dividing the result by the standard deviation. In this case I have constructed the measure so that higher values of this score indicate higher levels of poverty compared with other neighborhoods and lagged it by one year to capture any causal effects. This measure is set with its mean at zero and a maximum of 1.7 (the highest concentration of poverty) and a minimum of −0.93 (the lowest).

Measures of social capital need to be sensitive to the cultural and historical environment of the case under investigation (Krishna 2007, 944-945). Scholarship has illuminated the measures of social resources available at the individual, community, and national levels (Van Deth 2008, 161), and here, because I use the ward as the unit of analysis, I focus on the community level. To determine the amount of social capital at that level, the data set measures the number of NPOs and community-based organizations created per capita per ward. The term NPO includes groups classified by the Japanese government as nonprofit public-interest entities (*kōeki hōjin*), along with school, religious, medical, and social welfare organizations. Robert Pekkanen points out that in Japan, the borrowed term NGO typically refers to organizations involved in international work, while NPO applies to domestic groups (2000, 116n12).

After the earthquake, a number of wards within the city of Kobe established new NPOs to organize and coordinate recovery, neighborhood work, and long-term planning. Mayor Kazutoshi Sasayama had imposed a post-quake moratorium on rebuilding as the Kobe town planning department hastily worked out reconstruction schemes (Evans 2001, 4), but many residents felt the city was blocking their participation in land zoning planning and decided to do it by themselves (Yasui 2007, 230).[6] The city plan categorized areas as black (city-initiated and administered rebuilding zones, 2.9 percent of total area), gray (eligible for assistance but not administered by the city, 17.9 percent), and white (citizen-initiated zones, 79.2 percent) (Olshansky, Johnson, and Topping 2005). Citizens formed *machizukuri* (town development) organizations to participate in the planning; these groups were often based in existing civil organizations such as neighborhood associations (*chōnaikai*) (Nakagawa and Shaw 2004, 7). These NPOs focused on helping solely individuals within their jurisdiction to develop their ward and serve as a prime example of institutionalized social capital at the neighborhood level. Small (2009) has demonstrated how the individuals embedded within such community organizations benefit from the formal and informal social resources they provide. These community-based nonprofit organizations match well with earlier discussions of bonding social capital (see chapter 2), since they focused on improving life locally, not for the city as a whole.

Because this data set captures information on the timing of events, the proxy for social capital uses a measure of NPO creation lagged by two years to allow time for this institutionalized social capital to affect the residents and their communities. This lag is based on research demonstrating that it takes time for social resources and networks to diffuse through the community (Krishna 2007). Other studies have similarly set a two-year window in which to measure the effects of changing levels of social capital (Pronyk et al. 2008; Brune and Bossert 2009). The most active neighborhoods created roughly three new NPOs per ten thousand residents, while the least mobilized created none.

As with the previous chapter's study of the 1923 Tokyo earthquake, I again use population growth (or decline) as a proxy for overall recovery (Horwich 2000, 523; for a full discussion of population change as a proxy, see chapter 1). I define population growth through the intuitive measure of

$\Delta_{population} = \dfrac{(Y_{i,t} - Y_{i,t-1})}{Y_{i,t-1}}$, which provides a way of comparing population

change across neighborhoods. Growth rate varied tremendously across wards; in some neighborhoods, it reached −0.26, meaning the area lost one-fourth of its population, while in other wards it was as high as 0.23, meaning the area gained roughly one-fourth over that year. The mean across all observations for population growth rate is quite close to zero (0.002).

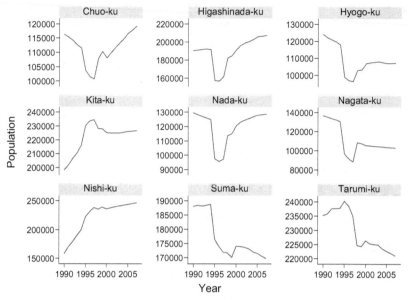

FIGURE 7. Population change per ward over time in Kobe.

Figure 7 displays the raw population levels for the nine wards over time. Note that certain wards, such as Kita and Nishi, had populations that were growing before the earthquake struck in 1995; for these wards the quake was merely a downward blip on the radar in terms of their overall patterns of growth. For others, such as Suma, Hyogo, Nagata, and Tarumi, the earthquake accelerated or catalyzed a loss of population. For Higashinada, Nada, and Chuo, the earthquake stopped a downward trend.

Explaining the variation in these levels of population growth is a critical task for social science. To analyze the factors responsible for accelerating or slowing population growth, I developed three models to test their effects.

Methods and Results

The autoregressive distributed lag (ADL) model incorporates important time and unit information for both the independent and the dependent variables, as displayed below.

$$y_{i,t} = \alpha_1 Y_{i,t-1} + \beta_0 X_{i,t} + \beta_1 x_{i,t-1} + \varepsilon_{i,t}$$

The left side of the equation in this case is the annual population growth rate, while the right-hand side includes lags of the growth rate, potential explanatory variables, and lagged explanatory variables along with error terms.

Known as the workhorse of time series models (Keele and Kelly 2005), this model can adopt values of i (the unit) from 1 to 9 (for the nine wards within Kobe) and values of t (time, measured in years) from 2 to 18 (since the data set contains eighteen years of measurements). The model is known as autoregressive because it contains a lagged Y (the dependent variable, a feature that leads many to call this a "dynamic model"), and as distributed because of the presence of lagged X variables (the independent variables) (Beck and Katz 2009). This model controls for at least some of the potential endogeneity between variable X and outcome Y at time T—known as the instantaneous or contemporaneous effect—through the use of lagged variables as explanatory factors. It allows researchers to make stronger causal claims about the direction of causality between lagged independent and dependent variables because of the chronology of the effect—the system is structured to test the influence of earlier values of X on later values of Y. Since the past values of X predict current values of Y, it cannot be claimed that Y in period T simultaneously or endogenously influenced X in period $T-1$ or $T-2$, since X occurred in an earlier period.[7] Table A4 displays the estimated coefficients for the three models tested on the data set.

Model 1 used the standard fixed effects time series cross-section model, which controls for variables that differ between cases but remain the same over time. As a result, time invariant factors—including the area and the percentage of residents affected by the quake—drop out of the fixed effects models (as indicated in the table). In model 1, the lagged dependent variable (of the previous year's growth rates) proved highly significant, meaning past growth rates within the ward measurably influenced current growth rates. The estimated coefficient for the lagged number of NPOs created per capita is positive and significant, indicating that an increase in this proxy for civil society correlates with an increase in the population growth rate two years later. As I explained above, social capital's effects may not be immediate; rather, the influence of social resources may take a year or two to alter behaviors. Welfare dependence within the ward—which measures socioeconomic conditions—also proved significant, so that as the number of families per capita on welfare increased, the growth rate in that ward decreased.

To ensure that these findings—which support theories connecting stronger social capital to recovery and find little evidence for other explanations—were not an artifact of the fixed effects model, I next used panel-corrected standard error (PCSE) time series models, which Beck and Katz (2004, 4) believe handle the problems of groupwise heteroskedasticity and contemporaneous correlation of the errors. Model 2 uses PCSE, while model 3 uses the Prais-Winsten regression (which adds first-order autocorrelation to the

PCSE model). As in the fixed effects model, the lagged independent variable (of past growth rates) remained positive and significant—showing that the "shadow of the past" for growth rates influences current outcomes. Similarly, in both model 2 and model 3 the proxy for social capital—that is, the lagged number of NPOs created per capita—remained significant at the 0.01 level.

In these models, as in model 1, the estimated coefficient for NPO creation is positive, meaning that the more NPOs created per capita, the higher the population growth rate in the ward later in time. Because these are lagged independent variables, we can more strongly claim that social capital has a causal effect on growth rates—since endogeneity and simultaneity are eliminated through the use of past values. In these two PCSE models, four other variable coefficients proved statistically significant: percentage of the population affected by the quake, population density, socioeconomic inequality, and welfare-dependent households per capita. The coefficients for welfare-dependent households per capita were negative in all three models—meaning wards with higher levels of dependence on local government assistance had negative growth rates. This discovery meshes well with standard arguments about the role financial capital plays in the rebuilding; households seeking government assistance lack a buffer against shocks and are more vulnerable to disasters (Yasui 2007).

Neighborhoods with higher population density recovered more quickly, but the measured coefficient was small and was significant only in the two PCSE models. The measure of socioeconomic inequality showed that areas with greater concentrations of poverty actually had higher growth rates, while the measure for quake damage showed that more heavily damaged areas bounced back more quickly than less damaged ones—but only in models 2 and 3. These nonrobust findings run counter to standard assumptions about damage and inequality.

Since it is difficult to comprehend the magnitude of effect of the independent factors on the dependent variable of population recovery solely from their coefficients listed in table A4, I provide a more intuitive way of interpreting this relation. The proxy for social capital—the number of NPOs per capita—had the largest coefficient of all the variables under investigation and was statistically significant in all three models. Figure 8 uses simulation techniques and confidence intervals to predict the population recovery rate, holding all other factors at their means, for various (lagged) numbers of NPOs created per capita.

Based on this model, a ward in Kobe that mobilized after the earthquake to create three new NPOs per ten thousand residents would show a growth rate of close to 15 percent—a figure that sounds low but is far higher than the

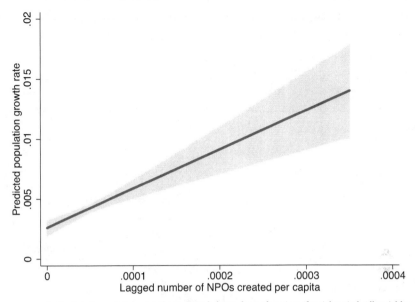

F I G U R E 8. Predicted population growth rate in Kobe's wards as a function of social capital. All variables (percentage of ward population affected by the earthquake, welfare-dependent households per capita, socioeconomic inequality, and population density) were held at their means except for the lagged number of NPOs created per capita. The gray shaded area indicates the 95 percent confidence interval around the predicted value of population growth rate.

average citywide level of growth (hovering just above zero percent per year). Alternatively, a similarly damaged wealthy and welfare-dependent ward that was capable of organizing only one NPO per ten thousand residents would have about a 5 percent growth rate, and a neighborhood unable to create any civil organizations would demonstrate close to zero population growth. While population growth, welfare-dependent households, and to a lesser extent socioeconomic inequality and population density had statistically significant results in some of the models, their effects were far less critical.

Through an analysis of the most common explanations for post-disaster recovery, this chapter reveals that social capital—more than economic conditions, earthquake damage, population density, inequality, or geography—proved essential over the long term. Areas that could organize themselves, not only immediately after the quake to fight fires but also over the rehabilitation period to set up ward associations, recovered better in terms of population than more fragmented neighborhoods. Such communities overcame collective action problems (Olson 1965), demonstrated their voice and not exit (Hirschman 1970), and worked to improve the lives of the citizens within their neighborhood. These wards cleaned up debris, organized antilooting patrols, cooperated and structured aid so that all residents had enough food, and kept up morale and motivation to rebuild through regular social interaction. Neighborhoods in which citizens were less connected to each other and had lower levels of trust suffered and could not regain their population. Survivors regularly discussed the importance of social networks as resources for their recovery after the crisis, and local government agencies focused on it in their follow-up studies (Hyōgo Ken 2003).

Conclusions

Using both paired case study comparisons within Kobe neighborhoods alongside quantitative data from all nine Kobe wards measured over eighteen years, this chapter underscores the important role social capital played in disaster recovery. While past growth rates proved important across all model specifications and welfare dependence had a measurable effect on population growth, no other variables had social capital's robust, measurable influence across all three models. George Horwich (2000, 522) argued that "a fundamental factor is that in most economies physical capital, although the most visible, is not the dominant economic resource—human capital is." Despite this understanding of the power of social infrastructure, decision makers continue to focus resources on standard physical infrastructure—rebuilding roads, bridges, and houses—often ignoring the role of social capital. Shigeo Tatsuki and Haruo Hayashi (2002, 19) argued that "more policy concerns should be paid to assist family systems and to facilitate more active community participation."

Given the importance of social capital in bringing back residents and new migrants, decision makers should take it more seriously as they develop recovery plans. As seen in the previous chapter, the 1923 Tokyo earthquake energized civil society and social networks, motivating previously unorganized neighborhoods to set up their own neighborhood associations after the catastrophe. Here, with the 1995 Kobe earthquake, scholars have uncovered evidence that the disaster at least temporarily disrupted existing social networks: "While 100 percent of the previous condominium owners' voting patterns had been made unanimously, only 12 percent of those following the Kobe earthquake were unanimous" (West 2005, 128). That is, whereas before the earthquake norms of agreement and reciprocity allowed condominium owners to regularly agree on policies, afterward, owing to the challenges of reconstruction and the uncertainties of the future, such cooperation at least temporarily broke down. Further, public policies put in place to help with rebuilding may themselves be responsible for slower recovery by breaking communities apart.

The often random assignment of displaced survivors to temporary housing further disrupted existing social ties after the Kobe earthquake (Tsuji 2001, 59). The priority given to providing housing first to the elderly and infirm "produced a community of elderly and disabled people living alone" (Tanida 1996, 1134). Many of the new housing complexes in and around Kobe were immense—with as many as a thousand living units in buildings similar to *danchi*, or large-scale Soviet-style public housing blocks—so that elderly and disabled residents felt isolated and unable to establish new friendships (Yasui 2007, 110). Scholars and the news media in Japan reported that more than 120 people had died "lonely deaths," *kodoku shi* in Japanese, while living in such isolated conditions (*Mainichi Shinbun*, 17 January 1997, 4; Suga 2007). In one block of apartments that housed more than seven thousand people in temporary shelters, those who died were often elderly victims without kin and others who were socially isolated (Maeda 2007, 42). It was common that new permanent shelters and housing were filled with individuals who had no connections or ties to the original area. Areas like Rokkomochi, for example, were populated primarily by newcomers—only a third of the original community remained geographically together (Horne 2005). In fact, local authorities often deliberately prevented communities from being housed together without explaining this policy. Three hundred quake victims had resettled in a tent city in a park in downtown Kobe, and when they sought permission to construct housing that would shelter them as a group, it was denied (Yoshimune 1999). Only after months of protest did the government agree to begin negotiations about cooperative resettlement. Grouping survivors from the same area together in temporary shelters and in long-term housing can help ensure that existing stocks of social capital are not damaged by the move.

Further, various public policy programs can build up stores of trust and interaction within neighborhoods. After the 1995 earthquake, for example, the city of Kobe itself sought to create stronger solidarity among survivors through programs targeted at increasing trust and participation (Hattori 2003), and such programs could be duplicated elsewhere. Mario Luis Small (2009) demonstrated that individuals who regularly interact with local organizations benefit from their unplanned introduction into broader social networks. Decision makers could seek to increase the density of such organizations—whether day care, *jidōkan* (children's halls), senior care, or communal use halls—across cities.

Scholars have understood that disasters can motivate survivors to participate in civil organizations and governance structures at least for short periods (Tatsuki and Hayashi 2002, 2; Tatsuki 2008, 14; Sorensen 2007, 78). Many
saw the Kobe earthquake as a similar catalyst for growth both in civil society
and in public policies designed to promote its institutionalizing. Thrust together with others after the quake, one survivor told reporters, "Before the
earthquake, I hardly knew my neighbors. This has made me realize how valu-
able communication can be" (quoted in Terry and Hasegawa 1995). Authorities estimated that between 630,000 and a million volunteers streamed into
the area to assist in rebuilding (Tierney and Goltz 1997, 2; Shaw and Goda
2004, 19), and this "renaissance of civil society" spurred national authorities
to streamline the registration of NPOs and NGOs (Pekkanen 2000).[8]

This chapter has sought to demonstrate that, more than being a short-
lived phenomenon involving outsiders, the social networks among residents
of disaster-struck communities serve as a critical component of recovery. Although this recent disaster—unlike the 1923 Tokyo earthquake—has brought
about no obvious negative externalities from strong social ties, the next disaster under study—the 2004 Indian Ocean tsunami—did so all too clearly.

Indian Ocean Tsunami, 2004

The undersea earthquakes that triggered the Indian Ocean tsunami on 26 December 2004 were powerful enough to briefly alter Earth's rotation.[1] The megathrust of Earth's crust created ocean waves as tall as one hundred feet that devastated coastal and inland villages throughout Southeast Asia. Although this large-scale tragedy took the lives of more than 230,000 people in Indonesia, India, Sri Lanka, and Thailand, coastal hamlets in the region bounced back from the disaster at very different rates. In some fishing villages in Tamil Nadu, India, for example, when government of India surveyors arrived on the scene expecting to find chaos and confusion days after the tsunami, they were surprised to find representatives waiting with organized lists of the dead and wounded and specific requests for rebuilding materials, food, and supplies. Once these villages received their aid packages and materials, many of them worked to distribute them equally among members of the *uur panchayat.*

In these well-organized villages and hamlets, uur panchayats served both as an institutionalized form of bonding social capital and a source of linking social capital, connecting residents to each other, providing information and lists to NGOs and government authorities, and coordinating requests and demands for resources from the local population. While this ensured that many members of the village received equitable shares of food, water, boats, and money, it also excluded nonmembers of the dominant groups. Widows, Dalits, Muslims, and other peripheral groups in the villages found themselves even further on the margins of society, unable to benefit directly from the tremendous amount of aid pouring in from both domestic and international sources.[2] However, in villages that lacked the institutionalized social capital and had no such ties to extralocal institutions, the recovery never started.

These hamlets received no visits from NGOs or from government surveyors; they were effectively off the map of the broader recovery process. Without links to NGOs and unable to gain the attention of the government of India, many tsunami-affected villages received little if any aid; at the same time, their recoveries came with a silver lining, since these communities reported no discrimination or exclusions.

This chapter uses three sources of data on the state of Tamil Nadu, India: qualitative case studies of six coastal villages affected by the tsunami, a quantitative analysis of more than sixty villages in the area, and a large-N analysis of approximately 1,600 individuals to investigate the effect of varying levels of social resources on post-tsunami outcomes. Tamil Nadu, the site of my fieldwork and the source of the data for all three sections of this chapter, is on the southeast coast of India and has grown more slowly than most other Indian states over the past decade, but it has displayed higher than average population density and urbanization (for more details see Chandrasekhar 2010). Its overall literacy rates climbed from two-thirds in 1991 to almost three-quarters by 2001, and it has been a leader in digitizing land records and instituting "E-governance" through which government services can be accessed using the Internet (Rural Education and Development Society 2006, 30). Tamil Nadu has roughly four hundred kilometers of beaches, along which sit roughly 230 fishing hamlets, mostly occupied by the Pattinavar fishing caste (Bavinck 2005, 812). Tamil Nadu fishermen, in contrast to workers in other agricultural fields such as farming, come from the same caste, a condition that "encourages the fishermen to emphasize their common bonds and to minimize differences among them" and "provides an ideological and social organizational basis for cooperation and relative equality among fishermen" (Norr 1975, 369, 370).

Based on site visits, interviews with local residents and NGO leaders, and an analysis of these data, I argue that Tamil Nadu villages with high levels of both bonding *and* linking social capital demonstrated better recoveries than those with only bonding connections or none at all. Measures for recovery in this chapter include several proxies; in some cases I measure recovery by access to scarce resources, specifically amounts of aid and assistance. In other cases I capture recovery by the ability of the hamlet or community to rebuild houses and to create new jobs and job training programs.

As past chapters have argued, stronger social capital brings both positive benefits and negative externalities. While villages with tightly connected residents and links to outside organizations experienced enhanced recovery, minorities, outcastes, and nonmembers in those hamlets were often excluded from assistance. It was not merely a lack of social capital that slowed or stalled the recovery of these peripheral groups, although that was certainly part of the story. Rather, hamlets that overcame collective action problems and efficiently extracted resources from donors and government officials also tended to leave some tsunami-affected villagers on the margins of society. Many scholars have emphasized that social capital functions broadly as a "public good" enhancing governance, economic growth, and trust (Coleman 1988; Cohen and Arato 1992; Putnam 1993; Cohen and Rogers 1995) and improving recovery more specifically (Nakagawa and Shaw 2004; Dynes 2005; Adger et al. 2005; Tatsuki 2008). This study of Tamil Nadu underscores a more nuanced view of social capital's role in disaster recovery as described in the first and second chapters, recognizing it as a Janus-faced resource (Szreter 2002) that brings both benefits and costs. Social networks bring about different policy and governance outcomes for groups within the mainstream and for those at the periphery.

The Indian Ocean Tsunami

Two massive underwater earthquakes off the coast of Sumatra on the morning of Sunday, 26 December 2004—measured at 9.0 and 7.3 on the Richter scale—generated tsunami waves that reached as far as Africa (Arya, Mandal, and Muley 2006, 52). The enormous waves surged into coastal villages in Indonesia, Sri Lanka, India, Thailand, and Myanmar (Sheth et al. 2006, S439). Speaking about his experience in Sri Lanka, Dayalan Sanders described "a massive 30 foot wall of sea. . . . it was like a thousand freight trains charging at you, that thunderous roar itself petrified you with fear" (quoted in Bindra 2005, 29). In southeast India, the thirteen coastal districts in the state of Tamil Nadu suffered the worst effects, with approximately 8,000 people killed by the waves (Rural Education and Development Society 2006, 13). In the district of Nagapattinam, 6,000 residents were killed; 817 died in Kanyakumari District and 606 in Cuddalore District (Arya, Mandal, and Muley 2006, 53; United Nations Team for Recovery Support 2005, 3).

As in past disasters, the tsunami affected vulnerable demographic groups most severely, with women and children making up most of the casualties because they were onshore, not out at sea where the tsunami could be ridden out (United Nations Team for Tsunami Recovery Support 2007, 9). Fishing communities sustained the largest loss of lives and property because they were nearest to the water (Alexander 2006, 8). Geographic and cultural context influenced casualties—in Kanyakumari on the southern tip of the continent, for example, the prevalence of Christianity meant that few fishermen were at sea on Sunday and more were onshore when the waves hit. Surveys

FIGURE 9. Map of the districts within the state of Tamil Nadu.

showed that more than 60 percent of families in the area perceived that they had lost a quarter or more of their income, while one in five reported losing between three-quarters and all of it (Fritz Institute 2005a, 4). The roughly two thousand kilometers of coastal area across all of southeast India accounted for 85 percent of the damage (Salagrama 2006b, 5), since more than half of these villages sit within two hundred meters of the shore (Rodriguez et al. 2008, 18). Along with coastal roads, bridges, and ports, more than 150,000 homes were demolished by the force of the waves (United Nations, World Bank, and Asian Development Bank 2006, 8), with $1.3 billion in property and asset losses. The tsunami destroyed or damaged 80,000 fishing boats, killed 32,000 head of livestock, and damaged and salinated close to 40,000 hectares of agricultural land (Office of the Secretary-General's Special Envoy for Tsunami Recovery 2005, 7).

Damage across the southeast coast of India varied by geography—villages and hamlets in alluvial delta regions, such as Akkaraipettai in Tamil

Nadu, experienced maximum wave heights and were often destroyed (Sheth et al. 2006, S440), while areas farther inland or protected by sand dunes often escaped unscathed (see Namboothri et al. 2008 for a full discussion of the importance of coastal sand dunes in the area). Some residents of coastal Indian villages received telephone calls from relatives in cities warning them of the impending wave, but they could not always act on the information in time (Case 7 and Case 12, Tata Institute of Social Sciences 2007). Beyond geographic differences in recovery, certain communities in the Tamil Nadu area affected by the waves have demonstrated more resilience than others with similar levels of damage, as seen through larger proportions of residents back at work, in permanent shelters, and with steady access to needed resources (author site visits, February 2008). Figure 9 details the districts within the state of Tamil Nadu. I now turn to the critical question of what brought about variation in the speed of recovery.

Case Studies

In early 2008 I visited five villages (and two cities)[3] in Tamil Nadu, India, to conduct on-site studies of post-tsunami recovery levels. With the help of a translator, I interviewed twenty-seven people, including survivors, NGO leaders, activists, and disaster scholars, using open-ended questions about their experiences; I used secondary and tertiary materials (translated from Hindi and Tamil when necessary) to study a sixth village. Roughly one-third of my informants were women, and four-fifths were local residents; our discussions averaged thirty to forty-five minutes. Additionally, I was given access to eighty anonymous interviews with local survivors lasting an hour or longer, collected by Indian social service agencies after the tsunami. These transcribed interviews provided additional information about the day-to-day recovery and broadened my understanding of the role of social resources in rehabilitation.

I deliberately selected these six villages because of the variation in both levels of social capital and recovery, using a method known as choice-based sampling (see King, Keohane, and Verba 1994, sec. 4.4.2). Table 5 describes basic characteristics of the six villages under direct study here; communities with a higher percentage of their families in new or repaired housing and with active assistance from NGOs and government officials were categorized as having good recovery outcomes, while those whose residents remained in shelters or that had a smaller percentage in rebuilt or new housing and less assistance from NGOs were categorized as having poor outcomes. Throughout the chapter I refer to them by number, not by name, to preserve their

TABLE 5. Summary of Tamil Nadu village characteristics

Village designation	Hamlet/parish council	Level of damage	Recovery outcome
1	Yes	High	Good
2	No	High	Poor
3	Yes	Moderate	Good
4	Yes	High	Good
5	Yes	Moderate	Good
6	No	High	Poor

anonymity (as is common practice among those who do fieldwork; see Kruks-Wisner 2011).

This first section uses qualitative methodology to make replicable inferences (King, Keohane, and Verba 1994) about the relation between social capital and the levels of post-disaster recovery. I use side-by-side case studies to tease out underlying causal mechanisms (George and Bennett 2004). Process tracing—like its quantitative counterparts—relies on within- and across-case covariational evidence (Gerring 2004) to illuminate the role of relevant factors more effectively. A solid research design requires variation in both independent and dependent variables, and the villages under study had varying levels of both social capital (as indicated by the presence or absence of an uur panchayat) and recovery outcome (determined by quality of housing and NGO- or government-sponsored programs).

Villages with Strong Bonding and Linking Social Capital

In hamlets 1, 3, 4, and 5 parish councils and uur panchayats dominate the social order, as they do in many other fishing villages in coastal Tamil Nadu (Gill 2007, 22). These nonstate organizations embody high levels of bonding social capital in that they connect same-caste residents in one industry to each other—Catholics who work in sea-related industries for parish councils in the south and Pattinavars[4] who are fishers for uur panchayats in the southeast. Many coastal villages in Tamil Nadu are almost completely homogeneous, with Pattinavar fishing families making up 90 percent of the population and the rest of the families coming from Dalits[5] (Bavinck 2008, 79; Sharma 2005, 4). Bonds between members of the fishing communities are strengthened by shared caste and kinship groupings; members of the community who marry outside their caste can be severely punished with ostracism by the community (Gomathy 2006c, 218).[6]

Parish councils and uur panchayats serve both as informal law and norm enforcers and as common pool resource managers (Ostrom 1990; Salagrama 2006a, 76; Bavinck 2008, 81). These councils maintain *gramakattupadu* (discipline in the village) (Gomathy 2006b) through resolving disputes and managing religious events. In the past, councils engaged in hard and soft social control mechanisms (Aldrich 2008b) through social pressure, fines, and ostracism (known as *mariyal*), but at present many of the villages restrict themselves to fining (Gomathy 2006c, 221). More broadly, a council "maintains community structure, rituals, village membership, resource distribution, dispensing of justice and grievance redressal" (Rodriguez et al. 2008, 11; see also Gomathy 2006c, 219). Their distributing shared supplies to members during the rainy season when fishing catches typically run low (Bavinck 2008, 82) is a typical example of their coordinated collective action. These councils, which initially epitomized "bonding" social capital (that is, assisting in-group members), came to serve more as links with outside agencies after the tsunami. Before the tsunami, fishing communities were known to lack awareness of the larger world and connections to it (Salagrama 2006a, 43)—that is, they had little *linking* social capital—but the disaster brought them new roles as bridges to external aid organizations and the government.

The 2004 tsunami transformed these councils into critical gatekeepers for aid distribution, since the government of India relied heavily on them during the relief period.[7] Neither the government of India nor the NGOs involved in recovery could survey or interview every villager about his or her needs, so they relied on lists prepared by fisher panchayat leaders (Rural Education and Development Society 2006, 15) to appraise damage. "In many cases, [hamlet councils] acted as a one-stop shop for the rehabilitation agencies (both Government and NGOs) to channel support into the communities" (International Collective in Support of Fishworkers 2006, 206). Scholars have documented that, long before the storm, the government of Tamil Nadu had little capacity in coastal regions because of its small power and limited ability to enforce the law (Bavinck 2003, 652, 654). Thus villages 1, 3, 4, and 5 held stronger levels of linking social capital than hamlets without these governing bodies, and these links provided survivors with connections to NGOs and the government after the tsunami.

Once the hamlet and parish councils assessed the destruction and provided this information to the government of India and to NGOs, they stored all the incoming aid supplies. Rather than disbursing supplies as they came in, many uur panchayats sought to create an equitable distribution system for their *recognized* members (author interviews 2008; Gomathy 2006). "If the organization could dispense enough relief to all the members, distribution followed. Otherwise they were asked to deposit the materials till more were collected, in order that they could be distributed to all members of the community" (Gomathy 2006c, 232). For example, in one village the council "collect[ed] all boats that are given by the NGOs as well. These boats [were] then sold to those who [could] buy them, with the rest of the money being distributed among other community members" (Tata Institute 2005, 14). In another case, in the village of Pannithittue, fishermen who were offered nearly one hundred new houses refused to move in, arguing "if only a few of us are given the houses, it could create trouble among us" (*Hindu*, 26 December 2006). Individuals or families within the village refusing to conform to these procedures of distribution among members found themselves facing social control mechanisms. "Five fishing families, who had 'refused to surrender to the panchayat the cash and material relief they received from various service organizations,' were excommunicated by the uur panchayat" (Bavinck 2008, 88). Excommunication meant that the families who violated the norms and laws set down by the uur panchayat would be cut off from existing social and economic relationships with the rest of the village.

While the strong social ties embedded in these organizations allowed them to overcome collective action problems and speed up the recovery of their members, those ties also made it difficult—if not impossible—for groups such as Dalits, women, and the elderly to receive aid or participate in the recovery. Because the uur panchayats and parish councils created the lists of families requiring assistance, they could easily exclude—deliberately or by oversight—nonmember families considered unworthy of aid. "[The panchayat] identified all beneficiaries but in some cases they excluded those in conflict with the panchayat along with outcastes" (author interview, 21 February 2008). Women—especially women who headed households—and Dalits had never been formal members of uur panchayats before the disaster (Gomathy 2006c, 224; see also Sharma 2005, 4; Martin 2005, 44), and the recovery procedures highlighted cultural barriers for them and other subgroups, including tribal communities (*adivasi*), single or widowed women, and the elderly (United Nations, World Bank, and Asian Development Bank 2006, 16; Menon 2007, 6). Across Tamil Nadu, Dalit villagers were not allowed to participate in elections for the councils, and Dalit political parties face "strong opposition from upper caste representatives and caste groups" (Menon 2007, 8). Interviews with women in Pattinavar villages showed that they rarely if ever approach the uur panchayat with problems (author interviews, 2008; Kruks-Wisner 2011, 19–20). In one case, when a local family was excluded from receiving new housing and approached the local caste council to seek redress, they were told, "That man said we were not [fishing caste] so we don't qualify" (quoted in Chandrasekhar 2010, 81).

In a survey of sixty villages affected by the tsunami, Dalit, outcaste, and nonmember victims in 16 percent of the villages—a group of roughly 7,800 people—were deemed eligible for relief (because of losses suffered) but did not receive it in part or at all because of discrimination by gatekeepers (data from Louis 2005, 2, 6–7). Other reports claim that in more than 80 percent of villages, Dalits and other groups encountered overt discrimination in compensation procedures (Gill 2007, 30). In some villages, Dalit families were forced out of communal temporary shelters, and their children were made to eat in different places than the other students (Gill 2007, 12). In one case an elderly Dalit woman lost her husband to the tsunami but received nothing owing to the gatekeeping measures of the local panchayat. When two Dalit families in her village tried to stand in line to receive disaster assistance, they were beaten and driven away (Case 43, Tata Institute 2007).

In another village, an NGO sought to give a young widow a new house after the tsunami, but she was told by council leaders that "if the panchayat decided that single women will not be given a house then she has to hand it over to the panchayat." Further pursuing her claim to her own house, she was told that "single women don't need large houses like that" (Case 2, Tata Institute 2007). In a different case where the tsunami had killed both parents in a household and a grandmother took over care of the orphaned children, no attempt was made to collect information on their circumstances so as to distribute aid, because of the gender and age of the primary caregiver (Help Age International 2005, 7). Widows and women in marginal economic positions, such as dried fish vendors, were also denied compensation (Gomathy 2006c, 235) in what some called a "double deprivation" because they belonged to "a socially deprived group" with "lesser access to public services . . . and entitlements" (Sharma 2005, 6). Even when aid had been provided to the community as a whole, these measures made little impact on Dalit families (Dorairaj 2005). Migrants too faced difficulties in being listed for assistance or receiving aid through the uur panchayats. Because the council saw them as nonmembers, "only 281 [migrant] families out of 420 [had] been enumerated for post-tsunami relief" (Gomathy 2006c, 233).

Parish priests and councils, like their uur panchayat counterparts, worked as intermediaries between villagers and NGOs, so that "information from the parish priest and panchayat, not direct information," was taken by relief organizations (Case 7, Tata Institute 2007). That is, in many cases in Kanyakumari, "NGOs provided all relief materials through the parish priest"

(Case 12, Tata Institute 2007). Just as uur panchayats acted as links to government authorities after the crisis, Indian officials contacted religious groups in southern parts of Tamil Nadu to work as go-betweens. In areas like Kanyakumari, residents complained that only families active in the Catholic Church "benefited from the economic, social and educational opportunities made available" (Rural Education and Development Society 2006, 29). As one informant told me, "In the South, if you are not in the church, you are not on the disaster rolls" (author interview, 17 February 2008). In another village, families that did not engage in church-sanctioned education found themselves excluded from the aid process (Case 13, Tata Institute 2007). When local families chose not to send their children to the village's church-run schools, those sixteen families "facing the boycott were deprived of the NGO largesse, routed through the church" (Newindpress.com, 1 May 2006). A number of other reports mention the deep involvement of the Catholic Church in the recovery and resettlement phases (Kannan 2005). The findings that the distribution of aid and sharing of resources were "captured" by institutions such as uur panchayats in Tamil Nadu confirms findings in other cultures such as Fiji where disaster aid was captured by certain clans (Takasaki 2011).

Villages with Low Levels of Bonding and Linking Social Capital

Villages 2 and 6 lacked uur panchayats or parish councils and had poorer recovery outcomes in terms of housing and aid receipt; on the positive side, they also had almost no recorded cases of exclusion or discrimination (author interviews, February 2008). In such communities, "existence depends on the ingenuity of women, mutual support within extended families, and minimal income derived from intermittent, informal sector jobs" (Bunch et al. 2005, 3). Residents who lack a governing uur panchayat must rely solely on existing bonding social capital after a crisis, since they lack linking capital that could connect them to NGOs or government representatives. As many scholars of social networks have pointed out, for underdeveloped regions and for individuals of low socioeconomic status, bonding social capital allows them to get by, but without linking connections to extralocal organizations they have difficulty getting ahead (De Souza Briggs 1998, 178; Woolcock and Narayan 2000, 227; Dahal and Adhikari 2008; Elliott, Haney, and Abiodun 2010, 628).

These isolated villages did not connect to the government of India or to local or international NGOs in the course of post-tsunami recovery. Village 6 lacked an uur panchayat and was unable to collectively mobilize and extract resources from the outside agencies. Lacking trust in each other, communal leadership, and contacts with the broader relief world, the villagers were left out as rehabilitation began in other villages nearby. Unlike other communities that could engage in collective action, "no communal strategies were employed" in "propagating an image of a wrecked and affected tsunami village," and "no efforts were made to contact any outside aid organizations and ask for help" (Mercks 2007, 39–40). Instead, villagers relied on family members for assistance and literally were not on the maps of relief providers; a local NGO eventually came on the scene and tried to help them long after the recovery had started for other hamlets. It is important to notice that nongovernmental actors, not the Indian government, finally provided assistance to village 6.[8]

Village 2—which, like its counterparts governed by caste council, suffered heavy damage from the tsunami—also lacked an organizing caste or parish council before the disaster. Attempts to interface with outsiders both domestic and international floundered, and survivors could rely only on kinship ties and bonding social capital to find assistance. Its process of recovery, then, did not favor one caste group, gender, or demographic over others, but it lacked the resources flowing into strongly connected communities. Some of the residents recognized that their recovery had been compromised by a lack of connections and social capital. As one survivor in the village told me, "We are [now] planning to make a panchayat. . . . I believe that people with panchayats received more benefits because they were better organized" (author interview, 19 February 2008). This recognition of the power of coordination mirrored what other scholars saw in their fieldwork; one observed that "the dalit panchāyat had not been truly functional until after the disaster when the community made a concentrated effort to organize and advocate for their interests" (Chandrasekhar 2010, 100).

Finally, one scholar described poorer post-tsunami outcomes for heterogeneous fishing communities in Tamil Nadu—hamlets that lacked *both* bonding and linking social capital. The lack of coordinating mechanisms such as parish or hamlet councils "precluded their coming together for collective and effective articulation of their views" (Salagrama 2006a, 60). For residents and survivors of these villages, although everyone has received the same treatment and discrimination has evidently been absent, recovery has been slower and impeded by a lack of assistance from either NGOs or government officials.

Discussion

As past studies have argued, higher levels of social capital in tsunami-affected villages in Tamil Nadu provided resources for a faster and more efficient recovery (Nakagawa and Shaw 2004; Dynes 2005; Adger et al. 2005; Tatsuki 2008). However, these studies have overlooked a critical point: although institutionalized bodies with strong bonding and linking social capital—such as uur panchayats—sped up the recovery for their members, they simultaneously slowed it down for outsiders and those on the margins of society. Strong social capital brought a number of benefits, including more robust mental health and greater access to logistical and financial resources for survivors. The strong local institutions of caste and parish councils served as focal points and mediators with the aid community during the relief efforts, ensuring that in-group members received aid. Social capital reduced the need for counseling and external intervention after the disaster (Gupta and Sharma 2006, 74), and social support systems—such as extended and joint families—contributed to the community's resilience (Mehta 2007). Further, the weak ties (Granovetter 1973) extending outside affected communities provided up to one-third of the financial assistance delivered to tsunami-affected households (Nidhiprabha 2007, 26).

Scholars must now begin to recognize that these benefits come with exclusion of outsiders, such as women, widows, Dalits, Muslims, the elderly, non-Christians (in Catholic areas), and migrants. Age-old patterns of discrimination against minorities and outcastes pushed many to the periphery and out of the aid process throughout Tamil Nadu. The results of this section resonate strongly with findings from other experts that women and caste minorities sought assistance from formal government channels while men from the dominant caste relied on traditional caste associations (Kruks-Wisner 2011). Marginalized members of these communities had to go through different channels to make their voices heard.

Quantitative Analysis: Sixty-two Villages in Tamil Nadu

Having underscored the role social resources played in recovery in a handful of villages, I now examine recovery patterns in a larger sample of villages. Here I investigate whether characteristics of the villages—such as their caste makeup, location, or reservoirs of social capital—influenced their access to resources after the disaster. Research has demonstrated that in standard circumstances the provision of foreign aid to developing countries is biased: that is, nation-states rarely provide loans, grants, and technical assistance in solely apolitical ways. Instead, the size of the recipient (in terms of population), its connections to the giver, and other political factors matter (Dowling and Hiemenz 1985; Arvin, Pirvetti, and Lew 2002). Given these findings in the international arena, many have argued that aid, whether distributed domestically by NGOs or by the national government, reaches certain groups and victims while bypassing others (Martin 2005; Gill 2007). On the other hand, donors, NGOs, and state governments insist that distribution is based solely on need (Brookings-Bern Project on Internal Displacement 2008). The 2004 Indian Ocean tsunami provides a tragic test case for investigating the patterns of aid provision to affected villages and communities (cf. Rosenzweig and Wolpin 2000). Using a new data set based on sixty-two similarly damaged inland fishing villages (also known as "non-ocean fishing communities") across coastal southeast India, this section underscores the role that caste, regional governance, family status, and location play in the receipt of aid.

For the first two days after the tsunami, villagers worked together to pull survivors and bodies from the wreckage, seek higher ground, and treat the wounded. The government of India soon intervened, with the help of domestic and international NGOs, to provide relief supplies, medical assistance, and temporary housing to the survivors. Families initially received food, equipment, and clothing to help them immediately after the tsunami (aid known as the "relief package"), followed by money for those who had lost loved ones, homes, or jobs, and, over time, payments to assist them in rebuilding. In this chaotic environment, government officials sought to help as many victims as they could.

Observers argued that the reaction to the Indian Ocean tsunami from the international relief community was "the most publicized and best-funded response of all times" (Alexander 2006, 5). A number of Western nations had immediately pledged financial and medical assistance, and "the US soon increased its contribution to $950 million, Germany pledged 727 million, Australia 830 million, France 443 million, Japan 300 million, Britain 120 million, China 83 million" (Bindra 2005, 181). Naomi Klein (2007) has dubbed the way large corporations and US contractors profit from crisis "disaster capitalism," but the organizations building houses, repairing roads and bridges, and assisting villagers in the recovery were on the whole not US–based corporations (for details on the reconstruction process see United Nations Team for Tsunami Recovery Support 2007). However, this tremendous outpouring of aid brought a number of often unexpected externalities. Local NGOs referred to the aid that flowed in as a "second tsunami" (Nelson 2007) because of the damage it did to social and traditional economic structures in coastal India. Others have called these post-crisis policy changes the "disaster after the disaster" (Schuller 2008) and pointed out that they may have created as many problems as they solved (Tobin and Montz 1997, 226).

The government of India, NGOs, and uur panchayats sought to coordinate their efforts to distribute the massive amount of aid to tens of thousands of victims. Observers praised the government of India for handling the disaster "admirably" as it "went about the rehabilitation programmes in a transparent manner by putting all relevant information on the Internet and updat[ing] frequently" (Salagrama 2006a, 55). Other assessments of the aid and relief distribution were more mixed: "Though the relief coordination with NGOs and [government] local system worked well at the initial stage, aid did not reach to the most vulnerable communities like Dalits, tribals, differently-abled people, senior citizen[s], widows and women in general" (Chandran, n.d.). In its post-disaster overview of the recovery, the United Nations Team for Tsunami Recovery Support admitted to problems of "unequal distribution" (2007, 14). Some saw any problems in distribution as localized, not systematic: "There were instances (in Kanyakumari) where members of particular groups were reportedly discriminated against in rehabilitation programmes" (Salagrama 2006a, 62).

Local and international observers, however, soon argued that they had evidence of what they labeled "systematic discrimination" in the provision of supposedly guaranteed aid to survivors and displaced people—not everyone who was eligible to receive supplies and cash assistance got received it, especially among peripheral groups. The NGO Social Needs Education and Human Awareness (SNEHA) documented stories of many survivors of the tsunami who lost family members but did not receive compensation from the government (2006, 20). Human Rights Watch (2007) detailed systematic discrimination against the Scheduled Castes in two recoveries in India, including the 2001 Gujarat earthquake and the 2004 Indian Ocean tsunami. Similarly, Louis (2005) listed the names of nearly eight thousand individuals—many of them Dalits—eligible for compensation and assistance from the government who did not receive it. Many critics have argued that aid was overprovided to coastal fishing communities in the area, while inland, non–ocean fishing villages were left out.

The government of India set up multiple aid policies after the tsunami. In interviews with social workers from the Mumbai-based Tata Institute of Social Science, a number of victims stated that they had not received compensation from the government despite being eligible. For example, one resident reported, "I am from a Dalit community. So far I didn't get any tsunami relief materials. Ours is also a tsunami-affected area. Now, due to the entry of the saltwater our agricultural fields are destroyed and we lost our livelihood. . . . But still I didn't get any benefit." National and local government officials worked with local institutions to set up, on higher ground, temporary

TABLE 6. Descriptive statistics of sixty-two Tamil Nadu villages

Variable	N	Mean	Standard deviation	Minimum	Maximum
Days spent in camps for internally displaced people	61	18.6	29.1	0	210.0
Percentage of eligible families receiving relief supplies	62	1.0	0.2	0	1.7
Percentage of eligible families receiving 4,000 rupees compensation	43	0.8	0.3	0	1
Nagapattinam District (dummy)	62	0.5	0.5	0	1
Cuddalore District (dummy)	62	0.2	0.4	0	1
Thiruvallur District (dummy)	62	0.1	0.3	0	1
Scheduled Tribe percentage	62	0.1	0.3	0	1
Scheduled Caste percentage	62	0.6	0.5	0	1
Most Backward Caste percentage	62	0.2	0.4	0	1
Homes owned per family	62	1.0	0.2	0.7	2.0
Homes owned per capita	62	0.3	0.0	0.1	0.4
Percentage of families making between 0 and 500 rupees per week	62	0.7	0.4	0	1
Contact only with the government of India	62	0.1	0.3	0	1
Contact only with NGOs, private organizations, political parties, or the villagers themselves	62	0.6	0.5	0	1
Contact with the government and at least one other translocal institution	62	0.3	0.5	0.0	1

camps for internally displaced people (IDP) where families and individuals could stay until they could return to their often-damaged homes. Some, like Lourdamma, a widow from the village of Keelamanakudi, were in a relief camp for a week, while others, such as Mr. Nainappan, from Kallar, spent only a day or so away from their villages. The conditions within many of the temporary housing camps were poor, as various Indian government officials admitted at the time (*Hindu,* 23 September 2006). As one observer underscored, "The problem of overheating, in 42 degree Celsius temperatures, in the temporary shelters—often derisively called cowsheds, shoeboxes, or ovens—is well known" (Gangadharan 2006).

This section tests which factors affected three post-tsunami policies providing relief and assistance at the village level by the government of India with the assistance of NGOs: the number of days spent in the relief camps; the percentage of eligible families receiving the initial bundle of relief supplies; and the percentage of eligible families receiving 4,000 rupees in assistance. These three policy outcomes vary widely, as can be seen in the descriptive statistics provided in table 6.

Here, I seek to understand why survivors in some of the sixty-two villages stayed in IDP camps for days while others stayed for weeks, and why some villages had more than their registered number of families receiving assistance while in others only three-quarters of eligible families received anything.

Theories Explaining Aid Access

Scholars of catastrophe have suggested a number of factors that may influence how aid is distributed and received by survivors; although the six factors detailed below may not be exhaustive, they cover the core concerns raised by past research, by aid practitioners in the field, and by the survivors I spoke to.

Many government agencies and decision makers see providing disaster aid as—at least ideally,[9] if not in practice—an *apolitical* process based on need, not on factors such as minority status, location, and wealth. For domestic disaster aid in the United States, FEMA states that "any person eligible to receive disaster aid or other services from FEMA is entitled to those benefits without discrimination," based on Title VI of the United States Civil Rights Act of 1964. North American legislation on international assistance—primarily codified in the Foreign Assistance Act (enacted in 1961 and amended since)—similarly relies on Title VI of the Civil Rights Act. Article 2 of the Principles of Conduct for the International Red Cross states: "Aid is given regardless of the race, creed or nationality of the recipients and without adverse distinction of any kind. Aid priorities are calculated on the basis of need alone" (quoted in Bakewell 2001, 6). One manual for disaster relief stated, "The principles of equality and non-discrimination . . . should underpin all disaster relief, recovery and reconstruction efforts" (Brookings-Bern Project on Internal Displacement 2008, 10). After the disaster, every family whose house and/or belongings were destroyed by the tsunami should have received a single initial aid package, while affected families should also have received distributions of 4,000 rupees.

Although apolitical, equitable distribution may be the goal, empirical evidence contradicts such optimism. Instead, scholars have argued that the resources available to community members before the disaster or crisis strongly determine the community's ability to extract assistance afterward. Hence the *wealth* of the village may determine how many of its eligible inhabitants actually received aid, since it serves as a proxy for legitimacy and education. By their financial resources, language abilities, and recognized authority, survivors with more wealth may be well positioned to contact NGOs, aid agencies, and government officials through informal or formal channels; hence they can ensure aid receipt. Alternatively, households with more wealth may be more highly educated and better able than poorer and less educated residents to complete the often complex procedures of aid distribution.

Related to wealth is the structure of the families in the affected area. Traditionally, rural Indian extended families lived together under the same roof in joint structures. In the past decades, cultural practices have created a social environment in which smaller nuclear families are the norm. Where multiple generations of families share homes, fewer homes are owned per family, yet aid policies may be built on the assumption that single families in one home are the standard. Hence aid may be less likely to be delivered to multiple families living in the same household.

Rather than aid distribution being a technocratic process or one based on the socioeconomic or family conditions of the village, the ability of the villagers to connect with extralocal organizations—regardless of wealth—may instead be crucial (Szreter and Woolcock 2004, 655). Hence the amount of linking social capital the residents hold may determine access to government and NGO resources. Anna Wetterberg (2004) demonstrated that, in Indonesia, households tied in to external organizations were best able to access resources after the devastating shock of the Asian financial crisis. Linking social capital, which transcends geographical distance and social hierarchy, can help even resource-poor areas draw attention to their plight (Szreter 2002). In Thailand, villages with linking social capital created connections and alliances with elites to influence public policy (Birner and Wittmer 2003). Similarly, Indian hamlets unable to attract visitors, NGOs, and government officials to view damage to their villages were not provided with assistance after the tsunami (Praxis Institute for Participatory Practices 2006).

Another critical factor in the distribution of aid may be location. The affected area itself may be envisioned as being more (or less) disadvantaged based on damage from the catastrophe; it may have stronger native governance institutions; or it may be easier (or more difficult) to reach by standard roads and transport networks. Damaged or destroyed villages in certain regions may not be seen as "needy" after a disaster because of a belief that the area as a whole survived without incident: some areas "received less attention as the focus had been mainly on the worst affected districts like Cuddalore and Nagapattinam" (Salagrama 2006a, 22). Other communities may be far removed from standard transportation systems, so that "in other communities, particularly remote ones, the distribution of aid seemed to be quite slow and limited" (Rodriguez et al. 2006, 170). Logistical costs of reaching out-of-the-way areas without paved or even dirt roads may keep administrators from sending aid to such locations. Local activists argued that Nagapattinam had stronger governance institutions before the tsunami, which allowed a flourishing of NGOs afterward, such as the Tamil Nadu Tsunami Resource Centre in Chennai and the Nagapattinam Coordination and Resource Centre (author interviews, February 2008).

Finally, ethnic or racial discrimination may play a role in the distribution of aid after a disaster. In India, the caste system, with Scheduled Tribes and Scheduled Castes (abbreviated in Indian records as ST and SC) as the lowest on the ladder and with Backward Castes and Most Backward Castes (BC and MBC) in the middle, may influence how officials and local officers provide aid (Rural Education and Development Society 2006, 16). Some charged that "across the backwaters, NGOs are moving in to assist fishing communities but they do not cross over to this tribal hamlet or the nearby Dalit community" (Martin 2005, 44). Other observers of the post-tsunami recovery argued that caste discrimination was an "unquestionable fact. The testimonies of Dalit victims of the tsunami all along the Indian coast of Tamil Nadu show remarkable consistency, pointing to a systematic and predictable type of discrimination" (Gill 2007, 7). Given the variety of factors that may affect how aid is distributed to survivors, I next use data from a sample of villages hit by the tsunami to illuminate patterns in access to assistance.

Data

This section uses a quantitative data set, created by M. Louis and his researchers, made up of sixty-two noncoastal fishing hamlets and villages most strongly affected by the tsunami; the unit of analysis is the hamlet or village (Louis 2005).[10] Louis selected these localities because they should have received aid from the government for the damage caused by the tsunami. By deliberately selecting observations across a range of values of the dependent variable the team utilized a choice-based sampling method (King, Keohane, and Verba 1994, 141) rather than a larger, completely random sample. Observers categorized these villages as marginalized and vulnerable. Their residents worked in a variety of occupations including backwater fishing, shell collecting, pearl fishing, algae harvesting, lime powder production, shell ornament manufacturing, and seasonal agriculture (Louis 2005, 9). Actual levels of aid received varied across villages; the research team did not know levels of assistance when they chose villages for the study. Louis and his sampling team spent eighty person-days in the villages in July 2005 gathering data by walking transects, mapping social characteristics, resources, and livelihoods, and distributing questionnaires (3–7).

The existing variables within the data set match up well with the theories about distribution patterns detailed previously. Wealth is captured through the number of homes owned per capita and the percentage of families making between 0 and 500 rupees per week. Family structures are measured through the average number of homes owned per family in the village (with nuclear families having higher scores and extended families having lower scores). Levels of linking social capital are captured through the village's connections to the outside world—specifically whether the village had contact solely with government officials, solely with nongovernment sources (such as NGOs, the villagers themselves, private donors, etc.), or with a mix of the two. Location information for each village was captured by dummy variables for Nagapattinam District, Cuddalore District, or Thiruvallur District. Finally, caste was measured through percentage of the village in the Scheduled Tribe, Scheduled Caste, and Most Backward Caste categories.

Methodology

All the regression models here seek to untangle the effects of individual variables from potentially confounding factors. The three dependent variables under investigation—the number of days spent in the relief camps, the percentage of eligible families receiving the initial bundle of relief supplies, and the percentage of eligible families receiving 4,000 rupees in assistance— require nonstandard models because each variable is dispersed or censored differently.

When dealing with a count variable (that is, a positive dependent variable bounded at zero), standard ordinary least squares (OLS) models are inappropriate. Instead, the general class of event-count models, including the Poisson model and negative binominal models, best fit the data. Given the overdispersal of the dependent variable—the number of days spent in camps—the negative binominal model fits the data more closely than the Poisson model. Similarly, standard OLS models are inappropriate when dealing with a bounded or censored dependent variable such as percentages. Wooldridge (2006, 596) points out that if scholars used an OLS model, "we would possibly obtain negative fitted values, which leads to negative predictions for y" and would additionally provide inconsistent estimates of beta coefficients. Rosett and Nelson (1975) developed the mathematics behind a model for percentages, known as a censored regression model or a "two-limit tobit." J. Scott Long (1997, 189, 212) shows how the "two-limit tobit model uses all of the information, including information about the censoring, and provides consistent estimates of the parameters" that can be applied when "the outcome is a probability or a percentage." Therefore the two main approaches used for analyzing the data set are two-limit tobit and negative binominal models.

Next, rather than relying on long lists of hard-to-interpret coefficients (although coefficient tables are provided in appendix 1), this section continues to use simulations and confidence intervals to clearly illustrate its quantities of interest. Simulations together with confidence intervals extract and present information about the variables under investigation and estimate the degree of uncertainty in predictions generated by these analyses (Tomz and Wittenberg 1999; King, Tomz, and Wittenberg 2000).

Results

NUMBER OF DAYS IN RELIEF CAMPS

After the tsunami, survivors fled their homes to seek shelter on higher ground. Residents of some villages spent only a short time in these IDP camps, but others stayed for weeks or even months. All the villagers in this study suffered significant damage to their homes. An important question is why residents of villages with similar damage would not return home at the same time. Based solely on the negative binomial regression results, proxies for location and Scheduled Caste proved to be both significant and important in predicting the amount of time spent in IDP camps, but follow-up with simulations proved that only caste remained significant. Table A5 provides the estimated coefficients, standard errors, and significance of the full list of proxies. Figures 10 and 11 display the relation between caste, location, and interval in the relief camps.

Figure 10 illustrates that the greater the percentage of Scheduled Caste individuals within the village, the longer the villagers stayed in relief camps, holding all other variables—including location, wealth, family structure, damage, and so forth—at their means. Residents of a village with fewer than 20 percent Scheduled Caste members would be expected to stay approximately ten days in the camp, while residents of a similar village with 80 percent or more Scheduled Caste members would stay closer to three weeks. The gray outline around the predicted variable line is wider where predicted outcomes are less certain and narrower where there is more infor-

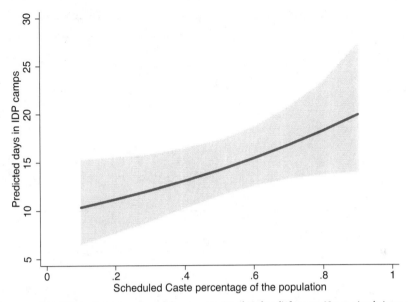

FIGURE 10. Relation between caste and days spent in Tamil Nadu relief camps. $N = 61$, simulations = 1,000. All other variables held at their means except for Scheduled Caste percentage of the population, which varied. The gray outline indicates the 95 percent confidence interval around the predicted value.

mation (observations). The confidence intervals confirm the overall trend that villages with more Scheduled Caste members remained in the temporary camps longer.

Figure 11 shows that survivors from villages in the districts of Nagapattinam, Cuddalore, and Thiruvallur are predicted to spend eight, four, and three days, respectively, in IDP camps. However, the 95 percent confidence intervals surrounding these predictions overlap. This indicates that, based on this sample of cases, we cannot dismiss the null hypothesis that—holding all other variables at their means—the influence of being in any of these three villages was the same. Survivors in these three areas stayed longer in the camps, all else equal, than residents of other areas, but the effects of being from any one of these villages compared with the others are not statistically significant.

This finding is important because many observers intuitively believed that Nagapattinam residents would spend more time in the camps because of perceptions of severe damage to this region (Louis 2005, 17). That is, there were far more deaths in the Nagapattinam area than in Thiruvallur or Cuddalore. However, reported tsunami damage levels across these sixty-two villages were very similar, so we cannot rely on this factor alone. Further, while

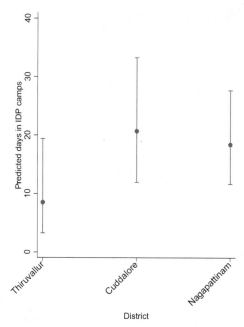

FIGURE 11. Effects of location on days spent in camps. $N = 61$, simulations = 1,000. All other variables held at their means. Vertical lines represent the 95 percent confidence interval around the predicted value, which is represented by the dot. Where lines overlap, we are unable to statistically distinguish between the variables.

conditions in some temporary shelters—such as those in Thiruvallur—may have been poor (Fritz Institute 2005a, 4; Martin 2005) owing to inappropriate construction materials, and while some argued that residents of certain fishing villages deliberately spent more time outside their homes in order to draw more attention (Bavinck 2008), these data do not support these factors as systematically altering the length of IDP camp stays. Location and other variables thought important did not measurably alter the length of stay, while caste did.

Results

PERCENTAGE OF ELIGIBLE FAMILIES RECEIVING RELIEF SUPPLIES

I next explore the percentage of eligible families who received the initial relief packet from the government.[11] As I mentioned previously, if the apolitical approach to distribution were actually carried out, the percentage of eligible families receiving aid should be 100 percent—and it was not. Table

A6 lists the estimated coefficients for the variables that influenced what portion of eligible families received the relief packet, and figures 12 and 13 display simulations generated from these data. Based on these estimated coefficients, villages in Nagapattinam were more likely than their counterparts in other districts to receive this aid—perhaps because of the superior organization of the local governance structures and the umbrella organizations that mobilized the NGO response in this area.

Figure 12 demonstrates that, holding all other variables at their means, villages where more families each owned one or more dwellings were the most likely to receive aid. In villages where fewer than half of the families owned a house, the predicted percentage of families receiving the initial relief supplies is close to 60.

However, in villages where all households owned at least one house, the predicted percentage of families receiving relief supplies was 100 percent or more. That is, villages with more nuclear family structures (with fewer generations living in one house) are forecast to pull in more relief packets than extended families (with fewer houses per family; that is, more families living under one roof).

Figure 13 holds all other variables at their means except for the group(s) contacting the affected villages. Villages and hamlets that were contacted

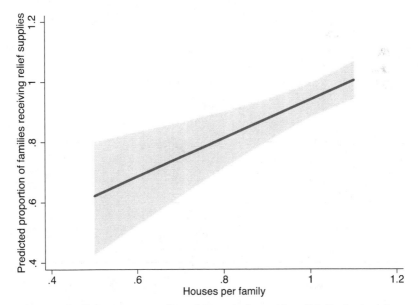

FIGURE 12. Family structure as a predictor of propensity for receiving relief. $N = 62$, simulations = 1,000. All other variables held at their means while houses per family varied. The gray outline indicates the 95 percent confidence interval around the predicted value.

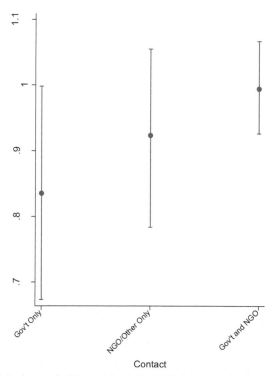

FIGURE 13. Relation between bridging social capital and aid relief. $N = 62$, simulations = 1,000. Vertical lines represent the 95 percent confidence interval around the predicted value, which is represented by the dot. Where lines overlap, we are unable to statistically distinguish between the variables.

only by officials from the government of India and local governments are labeled "Government Only." Those that had contact only with NGOs such as World Vision (India), CARE (India), Catholic Relief Services (India), Project Concern International, ECHO, Oxfam, Dhan Foundation, League for Education and Development, Tamil Nadu Voluntary Health Association, and Jesuits in Social Action (United Nations Team for Recovery Support 2005, 5), private organizations, or other villagers are labeled as "NGO/Other Only."[12] Finally, those organizations that were approached after the tsunami both by the government of India and by one or more NGOs are labeled "Government and NGO." The dot indicates the predicted values, with the ends of the lines marking the 95 percent confidence intervals for the prediction.

Although the predicted portion of families receiving aid is highest in the figure when the village had contact with both government and non-government sources, and the coefficient for this measure of linking social capital is significant at the 0.05 level, the simulations demonstrate that we cannot draw any strong inferences about this outcome. That is, because the confidence intervals overlap across the types of translocal connections, we cannot reject the hypothesis that different amounts of linking social capital had no effect on the proportion of eligible families receiving supplies. This outcome may be a function of the relatively small sample size here (sixty-two villages). Based on these data alone, family structure—and not linking social capital or other factors—proved most important in this policy area. Nevertheless, the coefficient (but not the simulations) for linking social capital indicates a strong relation between the types of contacts villages had and their ability to receive relief supplies and confirms the pattern found throughout other disasters studied in this book and by other scholars.

Results

PROPORTION OF ELIGIBLE FAMILIES RECEIVING 4,000 RUPEES IN ASSISTANCE

The final aid policy I explore is the portion of eligible families receiving 4,000 rupees in assistance. Table A7 provides the estimated coefficients for factors thought to influence what fraction of the families deemed deserving of the 4,000 rupees actually received it. First, based on the estimated coefficients, villages and hamlets in Kanyakumari and Nagapattinam were more likely to receive the 4,000 rupees than their counterparts elsewhere.

Figures 14 and 15 use these data to illustrate the connections between the two most important quantities of interest: caste and wealth. Figure 14 holds all other variables at their means and demonstrates that wealth—measured here as homes owned per capita—was an important influence on the probability of eligible families' receiving 4,000 rupees in assistance. In villages where individuals owned only one-tenth of a house—meaning only one home was owned for every ten people—the predicted probability of receiving this aid package was approximately 50 percent. But for villages where individuals had 0.5 houses per person—meaning one home was owned for every two people—more than 100 percent of the registered, eligible families would receive this packet.

Finally, figure 15 holds all other variables at their means while allowing the percentage of the village made up of Scheduled Caste members to vary. Here the results indicate that hamlets and villages made up primarily of Scheduled Caste members were less likely to receive the 4,000 rupees than similar villages with fewer Scheduled Caste members. In a village where fewer than

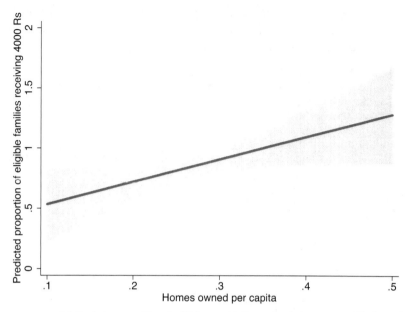

FIGURE 14. Relation between wealth and post-disaster aid. $N = 43$, simulations = 1,000. All other variables held at their means while homes owned per capita varied. The gray outline indicates the 95 percent confidence interval around the predicted value.

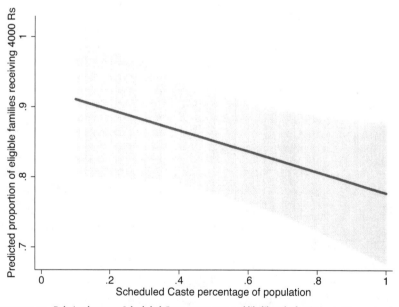

FIGURE 15. Relation between Scheduled Caste percentage and likelihood of assistance. $N = 43$, simulations = 1,000. All other variables held at their means while Scheduled Caste percentage was allowed to vary. The gray outline indicates the 95 percent confidence interval around the predicted value.

20 percent of the population are Scheduled Caste members, the predicted probabiity of eligible families' receiving the money is over 90 percent. But in similar villages where all the members are Dalits, the chances drop below 80 percent. Caste discrimination may be taking place at the regional or administrative level as decision makers either deliberately or accidentally overlook villages populated primarily by Scheduled Caste families.

Discussion

Using three types of post-tsunami aid as dependent variables, this section has explored a number of factors said to account for patterns of distribution. While many have speculated that these marginalized inland villages received less aid overall than more visible and better-organized coastal fishing villages, this chapter has shown a systematic exclusion based on caste. The Scheduled Caste percentage of the village proved a robust predictor of worse outcomes for individuals and families seeking to recover after the disaster. Members of villages with more Scheduled Caste families were likely to spend longer in relief camps and, more important, fewer individuals from these villages would be eligible for cash assistance, despite claims of objectivity and transparency. Further, preexisting wealth was another excellent predictor of more assistance after the disaster. Families and individuals owning their homes were more likely to be able to attract and extract aid than those who rented. This may be because of resource availability and familiarity with the bureaucracy or because administrators of aid were more responsive to certain demographic groups. Villages with more poorer families who rented or leased their homes were less likely to get the promised assistance from the government. Finally, family structure—whether nuclear or extended—altered receipt patterns. Villages and hamlets with more extended families in traditional social structure were less likely to receive help than localities where nuclear families dominate.

Qualitative studies of post-tsunami recovery in India underscored how members of Scheduled Caste hamlets often lacked the bridging social capital that could organize their relief activities and put them in contact with out-network resources (Mercks 2007, 39). Using quantitative evidence, this chapter has confirmed arguments about the role of caste in distribution. While some (Mathbor 2007) have emphasized the "public good" role that social capital can play in mitigating the effects of disaster, this view may overlook the role of institutional discrimination in the provision of aid. I next search a much larger data set at the individual level, not the village level, to seek patterns in post-disaster recovery.

Quantitative Analysis: 1,600 Residents

The first two analyses in this chapter have focused on the village as the unit of analysis and have sought to test claims about the positive (and negative effects) of social capital. However, relying solely on this level of analysis, we cannot make arguments about the actual conditions of individuals without running afoul of the ecological inference problem (see King 1997 for details).[13] To overcome this problem, I used a survey of nearly 1,600 respondents, which captures many of the factors thought important in past research, including demographic characteristics, socioeconomic conditions, and damage done by the tsunami. Most important, the data set incorporates measures for both bonding and linking social capital. I find that individuals who were connected more fully to fellow residents in their communities before the tsunami and those who had more connections to organizations outside their villages were more likely to receive larger amounts of relief aid than similar individuals with weaker social networks. These results confirm past claims that social networks connect even low-income, less educated residents to both information and resources that aid their everyday lives (Small 2009).

Despite attempts to provide equitable assistance to everyone who needed it, not all victims and survivors of the tsunami who were supposed to receive aid did so. In interviews with social workers from the Tata Institute of Social Science, a number of victims stated that they had not received compensation from the government despite being eligible for it. Researchers found evidence of denial of aid to individuals across the affected area because of caste (Louis 2005) and gender (Martin 2005). Based on the data used here, some victims of the tsunami in the state of Tamil Nadu, India, reported that they had received as little as 500 rupees in assistance, while others reported assistance worth close to 400,000 rupees. Survivors repeatedly have described how important aid was in rebuilding their shattered lives (author interviews, February 2008; Kapur 2009); the more aid residents could access, the more quickly they could restore stores, homes, and lives. This section seeks to answer what caused the tremendous variation in the amount of aid received by survivors and their families.

Theories Explaining Disaster Recovery through Access to Aid

A number of factors may affect survivors' access to disaster aid, including demographic, socioeconomic, and damage conditions along with levels of social capital. Having discussed these factors at length in the first chapter, I will only briefly review them here. First, a number of theories connect

levels of education, gender, caste, and age—demographic characteristics—
with disaster outcomes. Women and the elderly often face institutionalized
discrimination, as do minorities or lower castes, especially in hierarchical
societies (Cutter and Emrich 2006; Cutter and Finch 2008); hence they may
receive less assistance. Alternatively, individuals with more education may
be better able to interpret the often confusing signals from government pronouncements and regulations and more efficiently navigate the complex distribution system to acquire aid.

Beyond demographic characteristics, scholars have argued that the financial resources available to community members before the disaster strongly
determine the community's ability to extract assistance. Survivors with higher
socioeconomic status may be better positioned because of their financial resources and their recognized authority to contact NGOs, aid agencies, and
government officials through informal or formal channels; hence they can
ensure that they receive aid (United States Small Business Administration
2006; Yasui 2007, 95; Sawada and Shimizutani 2008, 465). Alternatively, a
number of scholars postulated that the amount of physical damage from the
disaster may correlate with the amount of aid received, so that more heavily
damaged areas would be expected to collect more assistance (Dacy and Kunreuther 1969, 72; Haas, Kates, and Bowden 1977; Yasui 2007, 29).

Moving beyond these traditional explanations for recovery, scholars have
sought to link the speed and effectiveness of recovery to social capital—
broadly speaking, the resources available to individuals through their social
networks. DaCosta and Turner (2007, 195) pointed out that for developing
or underdeveloped communities, linking social networks are particularly important for economic development, since they provide resources and information to cities and towns that otherwise are off the grid or under the radar.
In rural southeastern India, for example, where many villagers do not come
into direct contact with government representatives or NGOs, linking social
capital would provide a pipeline to external resources and information. The
data set used for this section includes indicators of bonding social capital—
measured as the interactions between the respondents and their neighbors
and colleagues before the disaster—and of linking social capital, measured as
the connections between the local, village-based respondents and outside aid
agencies or the government of India.

Data and Methodology

This section uses a new data set created by Sawada, Sarath, and Shoji (2006),
known as the University of Tokyo–Tamil Nadu Agricultural University

(UT-TNAU) Household Survey on the Tsunami-Affected Villages, along with follow-up interviews I carried out in 2008. From January through April 2006, the UT-TNAU research team canvassed nearly 1,600 individuals about factors related to demographics, socioeconomic status, tsunami damage, caste, social capital, and recovery outcome. Table 7 provides descriptive statistics about the data set.

TABLE 7. Descriptive statistics of 1,600 Indian Ocean tsunami survivors

Variable	N	Mean	Standard deviation	Minimum	Maximum
Demographic information and education					
Age (at tsunami)	1595	29.20	17.89	0.00	100.00
Education (by grade)	1594	5.90	4.14	0.00	15.00
Sex (male = 1)	1589	1.44	0.50	1.00	2.00
Position in family (head, wife, child, parent, grandchild, grandparent, nephew, parent-in-law)	1579	2.37	1.10	1.00	8.00
Marital status (1 = married, 2 = not married, 3 = divorced, 4 = widow)	1585	1.50	0.57	1.00	4.00
Socioeconomic status and employment					
Family business/self-employed (dummy)	1595	0.29	0.45	0.00	1.00
Hired worker (dummy)	1595	0.06	0.24	0.00	1.00
Housewife/unpaid family worker (dummy)	1595	0.25	0.43	0.00	1.00
Student (dummy)	1595	0.28	0.45	0.00	1.00
Fisher (dummy)	1595	0.10	0.31	0.00	1.00
Farmer (dummy)	1595	0.21	0.40	0.00	1.00
Tsunami damage					
Family lost house in tsunami (dummy)	1595	0.06	0.23	0.00	1.00
Family lost member in tsunami (dummy)	1595	0.08	0.26	0.00	1.00
Family's house, assets, or utensils damaged by tsunami (dummy)	1595	0.87	0.33	0.00	1.00
Caste					
Family Scheduled Caste	1595	0.02	0.15	0.00	1.00
Family Scheduled Tribe	1595	0.00	0.00	0.00	0.00
Family Backward Caste	1595	0.36	0.48	0.00	1.00
Family Most Backward Caste	1595	0.62	0.49	0.00	1.00

TABLE 7. (*continued*)

Variable	N	Mean	Standard deviation	Minimum	Maximum
Linking social capital					
Family relief aid from government only	1595	0.11	0.31	0.00	1.00
Family relief aid from NGO sources only	1595	0.03	0.18	0.00	1.00
Family relief from government and NGO	1595	0.78	0.42	0.00	1.00
Family contact with government only (Dec.–Jan.)	1595	0.88	0.33	0.00	1.00
Family contact with government only (Jan.–Feb.)	1595	0.91	0.29	0.00	1.00
Bonding social capital					
Number of funerals family attended (Oct.–Dec. '04)	1595	4.52	4.58	0.00	35.00
Amount of money family gave at weddings (Oct.–Dec. '04)	1595	175.3	183.09	0.00	1500.00
Dependent variable					
Family relief amount (rupees)	1586	12422	46849.18	500.00	400000

The procedure for selecting interviewees involved a mix of choice-based sampling (King, Keohane, and Verba 1994, sec. 4.4.2) and random sampling. Researchers initially listed all tsunami-affected villages in the district of Nagapattinam in Tamil Nadu, ranking those seventy villages in terms of damage from the tsunami. Then the eight most damaged villages were selected as locations for nonstratified random sampling of individuals; trained local interviewers carried out roughly two hundred face-to-face surveys in each village. I carried out additional follow-up interviews in five villages in 2008 as described earlier in the chapter.

The variables in the data set line up well with the theories of disaster recovery described above, along with necessary controls for potential confounding conditions. Demographic information is captured through variables that measure age, education, sex, position in the family, and marital status. Socioeconomic status and employment are encapsulated by a series of dummy variables describing the individual's position as a member of a family business or self-employed worker, hired worker, housewife or unpaid family worker, student, fisher, or farmer. The amount of damage caused by the tsunami is recorded by dummy variables indicating whether the individual's family lost a house or any members in the tsunami or whether the family's home, assets, or utensils were damaged. Caste is captured through variables for Scheduled Caste, Scheduled Tribe, Backward Caste, and Most Backward Caste.

As I mentioned previously, measures for social capital must seek proxies appropriate for the context (Krishna 2007, 944–45). Serra (2001) argued that standard Western measures of social capital, such as those Putnam used in his 1993 study of northern and southern Italy—including literacy, voter turnout, and membership in associations—do not map well onto the empirical realities of Indian states. Anirudh Krishna (2003, 9) similarly argued that measures that capture the "density of formal organizations" would be "particularly inappropriate for Rajasthan villages." Instead, Serra (2001, 699) posited that in India, "kinship ties . . . which provide vital support to individuals" best reflect social resources.

This data set captures linking social capital through variables indicating the degree of connectedness to associations outside the village. The data set measures whether the individual's family received aid only from the government of India, only from nongovernment sources, or from a combination of government and nongovernment sources. Based on interviews with survivors (February 2008), many argued that they sought to contact as many outside agencies as possible to maximize aid, but their ability to capture the attention of outside decision makers varied (Mercks 2007). Some believed their caste prevented policy makers from further engaging them in the recovery process, while others saw wealth and prior contact with authorities as critical. Based on these interviews, this data set records whether the individual's family had contact solely with the government in the periods immediately before and after the tsunami (December 2004 through January 2005) and soon afterward (January through February 2005).

Past scholarship on measures of bonding social capital for India and Southeast Asia has focused on local, informal communal practices that reinforce reciprocity, gift giving, and community ties, especially the important festivals of weddings and funerals (Worthington, Ram, and Jones 2006, 212; Adger 2003, 399). The World Bank's Social Capital Questionnaire (question 5.15), for example, asks respondents how often they have participated in family, village, or neighborhood festivals and specifies weddings and funerals as prime examples (Grootaert et al. 2003, 57). Quantitative studies of social capital in India regularly look to weddings and funerals as ways of measuring these noncommercial networks (Blomkvist 2003). Newer research has shown the ways rituals, such as annual festivals in Japan, build levels of trust and social capital and create resilience (Bhandari et al. 2010). This data set builds on this research to record the number of funerals the individual's family attended before the tsunami (from October to December 2004), along with the amount of money given at weddings during that same period, as proxies for linking social capital. Survivors who extended their own resources to participate in weddings and funerals built up connections to each other and created expectations of reciprocity and obligation within a broad network. Using pre-tsunami data avoids potential methodological pitfalls due to endogeneity—that is, these measures of social capital cannot be "caused" by the tsunami, since they occurred before it. Finally, this data set captures the amount of money (in rupees) the individual's family received in relief aid, which I use as the dependent variable.

Since the focus in this chapter is on the amount of relief aid—a variable left-bounded at zero (since families cannot in practice receive negative amounts of aid)—I use regression analysis (OLS), checking the results using a left-limited tobit (a maximum likelihood model for which we can set bounds, such as zero, for the dependent variable). Next, rather than relying on long lists of hard-to-interpret coefficients (although coefficient tables are provided), this section again uses simulations and confidence intervals to illustrate its quantities of interest (Tomz and Wittenberg 1999; King, Tomz, and Wittenberg 2000).

Results

The estimated coefficients from the maximum likelihood regression are reported in table A8. As expected, age, education, and marital status were significant (as indicated by their p values) and had a measurable impact on the amount of aid received (as indicated by their estimated coefficients). Thus older, more educated, and married individuals received more aid after the tsunami, in line with predictions. Similarly, those individuals who lost family members or a house to the tsunami received more aid, an outcome that reflects the policy goal of the government and NGO assistance programs. Individuals who lost homes and family members in the tsunami were supposed to receive additional aid to cover these critical losses. Gender and occupation were not measurably important in determining aid amounts—that is, the coefficients for these factors were not statistically significant.

Perhaps the most surprising results from this study were the findings that both types of social capital—binding, which connected villagers to each other, and linking, which connected villages to outsiders—highly determined levels of aid. These figures use the data set along with the maximum likelihood models tested to predict the amount of aid under different conditions.

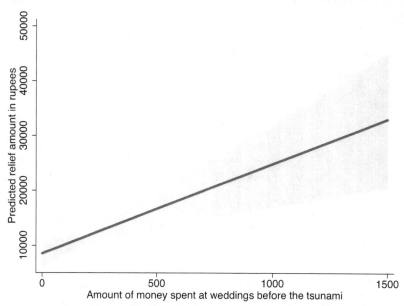

FIGURE 16. Relation between bonding social capital and tsunami relief. N = 1,590, simulations = 1,000. Simulations hold all other variables (age, education, sex, position in family, marital status, family business/self-employed, hired worker, housewife/unpaid family worker, student, fisher, farmer, family lost house in tsunami, family lost member in tsunami, family's house or assets damaged by tsunami, family Scheduled Caste, family Scheduled Tribe, family Backward Caste, family Most Backward Caste, relief aid from government only, relief aid from NGO sources only, family relief from government and NGO, contact with government only [December to January], number of funerals attended by family [October to December 2004]) at their means, with amount of money spent at weddings (October to December 2004) allowed to vary.

Figure 16 holds all the other variables at their means and calculates the predicted amount of aid individuals received depending on their connections to others, as measured through their pre-tsunami wedding donations. Holding all other variables equal, individuals who spent 1,500 rupees or more on weddings during the three months before the tsunami are predicted to receive roughly three times as much as their counterparts who spent nothing on gifts (30,000 rupees versus 10,000 rupees). Higher levels of spending on fellow residents indicated more regular attendance and gift giving at social rituals and ceremonies that create and reinforce social ties. Past research has underscored the ways rituals—whether in urban or rural settings—enhance social capital and create disaster-resilient communities (Bhandariet al. 2010). Anthropologists include weddings and funerals in the broader category of "life cycle events" that play large roles in the social interactions of rural residents. Residents—even in developed nations—who do not attend such life cycle events are seen as being disengaged from existing social networks (Hayes, Gray, and Edwards 2008). Given that "especially in rural areas in India many people will rely on informal, noncommercial relationships to deal with some important occasions or decisions in life" (Blomkvist 2003, 13), weddings and funerals provide opportunities for developing and strengthening community ties. Villagers in these Nagapattinam localities who gave more and participated in more of these events used their financial resources to develop a network of connections within and throughout their locality; such ties enabled them to "stand out" from fellow survivors after the tsunami. When distributors of aid sought to disburse funds, these better-connected survivors rose to the top of the list.

Figure 17 similarly predicts the amount of aid individuals received depending on their attendance at funerals before the disaster. The model forecasts that, all else being equal, individuals who attended funerals with great

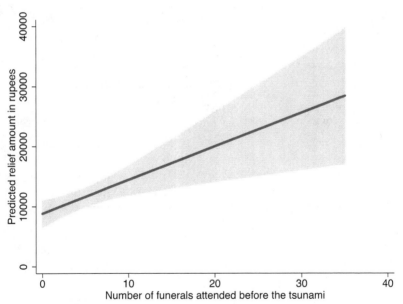

FIGURE 17. Relation between bonding social capital and disaster relief. $N = 1,590$, simulations = 1,000. Simulations hold all other variables (age, education, sex, position in family, marital status, family business/self-employed, hired worker, housewife/unpaid family worker, student, fisher, farmer, family lost house in tsunami, family lost member in tsunami, family's house or assets damaged by tsunami, family Scheduled Caste, family Scheduled Tribe, family Backward Caste, family Most Backward Caste, relief aid from government only, relief aid from NGO sources only, family relief from government and NGO, contact with government only [December to January], family contact with government only [January to February 2004], amount of spending at weddings [October to December 2004]) at their means, with number of funerals attended in October to December 2004 allowed to vary.

regularity—ten or more a month before the disaster—will receive three times as much aid as counterparts who attended none. Although funerals are grim occasions, they are also chances to network and to demonstrate involvement in communal activities. In Japan, for example, local and national politicians regularly keep track of local funerals so that they can participate, comforting the mourners and displaying their local connections (Aldrich and Kage 2003). In Kenya, social scientists have seen collaborative ceremonies and donations at funerals as evidence of civil society development (Ouma and Abdulai 2009). Residents of these Indian villages who connected to a wider range of village members through rituals marking death held additional leverage and higher status when they sought to receive disaster relief. Although government officials and NGOs hoped aid would be given primarily based on need—that is, damage from the tsunami—the survivors' connections strongly influenced their ability to collect assistance.

The ability to connect to agencies beyond the government of India was also crucial for victims who sought larger amounts of aid. First, individuals receiving aid from NGOs are predicted to have received roughly twice as much aid as their counterparts who received aid only from the government of India. Further, contact outside the village was important in itself. For families and individuals who had contact with multiple external agencies, including the government of India and NGOs, the predicted amount of aid received would be 31,817 rupees (holding all other variables constant, with a 95 percent confidence interval around that prediction running from 26,074 to 37,561 rupees). However, for victims who had only the government to rely on, the predicted aid would be only 9,303 rupees (with a 95 percent confidence interval running from 7,615 to 10,990 rupees). Through their linking social capital, survivors who had ties to the government and to NGOs could leverage their connections to ensure that they received more aid. Local residents who lacked these connections had to rely on the aid distribution system to receive assistance; they had no contact persons within the civil service or community service organizations whom they could contact should they feel underserved.

Conclusions

Using three sources of data—qualitative case studies of six villages, quantitative studies of more than sixty villages, and a large-N data set of approximately 1,600 tsunami survivors—this chapter has demonstrated the critical nature of social resources after a crisis. While many theories on recovery are based on standard assumptions about damage, demographics, and other variables, the chapter has underscored that, controlling for these factors, social capital proves crucial in accessing aid and building back after a disaster. I provided evidence that social capital simultaneously brought solutions for collective problems along with negative externalities, especially for out-group residents and nonmembers of local organizations (Berman 1997; Callahan 2005; Aldrich and Crook 2008). Building on past research, this chapter has also sought to correct a naive conception of social infrastructure in which social capital enhances resilience without bringing harm (cf. Adger et al. 2005). Observers envisioned the high cohesion within Southeast Asian fishing communities as a symbol of a "strong sense of camaraderie and community membership among the individuals residing in the same area" that leads to altruistic behavior (Rodriguez et al. 2006, 173). However, Anne Wetterberg (2004, 27) pointed out that "social capital must be thought of as a potential source of benefits, rather than the benefits themselves," and this chapter would further amend our understanding so that social capital needs to be seen as source both of benefits for some and of costs for others.

Despite the dawning recognition of the importance of social capital in mitigating the effect of disasters (Hutton 2001; Mathbor 2007), standard disaster aid procedures continue to focus primarily on restoring the damaged physical infrastructure. For example, when discussing the grants and loans provided to Indian coastal communities, the United Nations, World Bank, and Asian Development Bank (2006, 26) argued that "during disaster situations, roads and bridges serve as links not only for launching rescue and transporting [supplies] for relief and rehabilitation, but also as escape routes. Therefore, the criticality of roads and bridges is indisputable." As an afterthought, these organizations acknowledged that community-level social workers should encourage victims to participate in community events (2006, 34) to help them rebuild their social networks.

One obvious recommendation to policy makers setting up evacuation plans is to maintain existing social networks after a crisis or disaster; this can be carried out through policies that maintain the integrity of communities and neighborhoods even immediately after a crisis and in temporary housing. Disaster planners should evacuate people in socially intact groups, or at least reassemble evacuees in intact communities. In interviews, survivors of the tsunami described how they were randomly assigned to temporary shelters and how "people were placed with people of different communities" (Case 7, Tata Institute 2007). As one displaced person told me, "My old neighbors are not nearby; they are in the locality but far from my house. It was a lottery to choose locations for houses" (author interview, 20 February 2008). Local residents recognized the benefits of maintaining and strengthening networks after the tsunami. In one study an older woman reported that "many people in this camp are from the same street and village in which I live and we all help each other" (HelpAge International 2005, 12). Some organized themselves in their evacuation, so that "post tsunami, all the members of one village decided to stay together in the temporary sheds in a gesture of unity, especially to support people who have lost their dear ones" (Gomathy 2006a, 218). These tsunami survivors intuitively recognized that "women who are able to access familiar religious sites, markets, hospitals, relatives, friends and other resources will be far less vulnerable to abuse, exploitation and psychological distress" (Banerjee and Chaudhury 2005).

A second goal for disaster planners should be to consider how to expand both bonding and linking social capital so as to include excluded groups and at the same time develop outreach skills for these peripheral residents. Initial signs indicate that this may be happening. The Mumbai-based Tata Institute of Social Sciences has developed a leadership seminar to increase the capacity of indigenous groups and tribal peoples in India to mobilize effectively and connect with outside communities. Through such programs, otherwise insular groups may develop new linking social capital that puts them in touch with new resources and organizations. Local NGOs, such as the National Council of YMCAs of India, have begun training women to expand livelihood options including mat weaving and diamond polishing (site visit, 19 February 2008). So, too, the Self Employed Women's Association in India has sought to increase job security for women and decrease their vulnerability to disaster (Vaux and Lund 2003). These new skill sets, and new government regulations requiring the names of both husband and wife on land titles, will provide women with additional leverage to push for broader participation in both political and economic spheres.

Future post-disaster distributions would do well to heed the advice of program coordinators who have suggested that relief programs begin with comprehensive profiles of affected areas. "Without this profile, the programme risks falling short of the beneficiaries' entitlements and becoming (involuntarily) discriminatory" (Brookings-Bern Project on Internal Displacement 2008, 11). By relying heavily on uur panchayats, both the government of India and NGOs were dependent on these tribal councils to list needy recipients and deliver aid. Dalits, women, Muslims, widows, and other often marginalized groups slipped through the cracks and were often helped only after weeks or even months of waiting. Through their gatekeeping roles, uur panchayats throughout coastal southeast India may have denied assistance to a number of eligible families and villages, further widening the gap between the haves and the have-nots. The next chapter focuses on a case that again brings up the benefits and costs to strong social capital: siting temporary housing after Hurricane Katrina.

Hurricane Katrina, 2005

A walk through two neighborhoods in New Orleans, Louisiana, in the spring of 2011 revealed two very different landscapes.[1] Even more than five years after the collapse of the levees, much of the Lower Ninth Ward remains like a ghost town that could double as a movie set for post-apocalyptic wastelands, overrun by weeds and empty of residents.[2] Many houses sit ruined and unoccupied, with high-water marks visible along walls and roofs: a newspaper described "gutted homes with smashed windows list[ing] to one side" (Wilson 2011). Overall, the area has recovered only one-fourth of its pre-Katrina population—although half a decade has passed since the tragedy (*New York Times*, 27 August 2010). Stroll through other areas, though, like the primarily Vietnamese and Vietnamese American community in Village de L'Est in the northeast corner of the city, and you would never know the levees had broken (Weil 2010). While Village de L'Est also suffered tremendous damage after the hurricane and has struggled with similar levels of poverty, it experienced a 90 percent population recovery and business reopening within two years of the disaster (LaRose 2006; Faciane 2007). Recovery has seemingly stalled for parts of Big Easy, yet in other areas resilience was dramatic and rapid. How can these flood-damaged neighborhoods in the same city look so different?

In areas like Village de L'Est, local activists worked to maintain strong bonding social capital among residents both during the evacuation and afterward (see Krishna 2002 for a full discussion of agents and social capital). Father Vien Nguyen of Mary Queen of Vietnam Church and other community leaders drove to temporary evacuation shelters in Texas, Arkansas, and Louisiana to meet with church members, neighbors, and community members who had left the city with the arrival of Hurricane Katrina. Father Vien took photographs "of every member of the community he met to confirm their safety to friends and family in distant cities" (Chamlee-Wright 2010, 62). While many communities found their residents often alone and isolated in temporary locations in Houston, Dallas, or other far-flung cities, members of this community did everything they could to maintain their connections during the evacuation.

Father Vien set up Vietnamese-language radio broadcasts in cities with Vietnamese evacuees to announce community plans for rebuilding. When New Orleans allowed residents to return in October 2005, Village de L'Est residents did so en masse, with the parish church organizing to supply necessities including bleach, bottled water, food, and building supplies. When five hundred signatures were needed to prompt Entergy—the local utility—to restore electrical power to the neighborhood, more than a thousand residents signed by the end of the day (author interview, 12 May 2010). Village de L'Est displayed its ability to overcome barriers to collective action—whether gathering signatures on a petition or bringing residents back simultaneously and avoiding the waiting game. Residents there drew on deep reservoirs of social capital when calling on each other for informal insurance; the neighborhood remains an emblem of resilience in a still struggling New Orleans (Leong et al. 2007; Weil 2010). Other communities similarly lacking in socioeconomic resources also lack the social ties that would enable a more efficient and coordinated recovery—and this has dampened their resilience.

Chapter 2 underscored the different types of social capital—bonding, bridging, and linking—and the mix of these types of social networks matters tremendously. Recent research on the post-Katrina recovery has discovered that certain neighborhoods had different social network capacities and that areas with deeper reservoirs of multiple types of social resources displayed more resilience. More precisely, although neighborhoods such as the Lower Ninth Ward had strong levels of bonding social capital,[3] they lacked the linking connections that could provide assistance when local institutions could not. Neighborhoods in the city with high levels of damage and both bonding and linking social capital have proved more resilient than communities whose residents connected primarily to each other and not to extralocal figures or institutions (Elliott, Haney, and Sams-Abiodun 2010). A past president of the Lower Ninth Ward Neighborhood Association noted, "My area has not traditionally been open to connecting with other groups due to the fact that we felt we did not need to work with others" (author interview, 11 May 2010). Another resident of the area spoke of a "disconnect" between

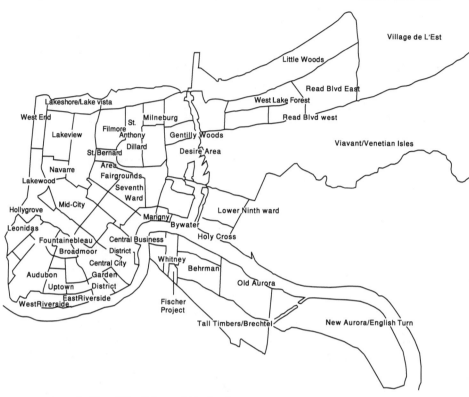

FIGURE 18. Map of New Orleans neighborhoods.

citizens and decision makers and argued that while local leaders could unify members of their own community, few of them had connections outside the area; she theorized that this hurt their ability to have their voices heard (author interview, 10 May 2010). These comments underscore the critical nature of bonding, linking, *and* bridging connections after the disaster.

This chapter uses data on the post–Hurricane Katrina recovery of New Orleans to demonstrate how social capital played a role in improving the quality of life for individual neighborhoods while at the same time slowing the overall recovery. A quantitative analysis of the siting of FEMA trailers in the year after the hurricane provides evidence that organized and mobilized neighborhoods pushed away projects they did not want. Controlling for a number of factors thought to influence how sites were selected for post-disaster temporary housing, the factor of social resources remains critical. Decision makers avoided placing trailers in areas with more prominent civic norms and hence may have slowed the overall provision of temporary housing. Figure 18 is a map of the neighborhoods of New Orleans.

Hurricane Katrina

In late August 2005, a hurricane that formed over the Atlantic Ocean devastated the Bahamas before moving toward the Gulf Coast of the United States. The storm weakened before making landfall, and though it did severe damage to many coastal towns in Mississippi, Florida, and Texas, initial reports from the urbanized area of New Orleans described relatively minor wind and water damage. In one of the largest evacuations in North America since the Dust Bowl, more than a million people left New Orleans for higher ground (Appleseed 2006, 1). Fourteen inches of rain overpowered the city's pumps; on the morning of Monday, 29 August, the levees built by the Army Corps of Engineers, which served to keep the below sea level bowl of New Orleans dry, failed in dozens of spots. Major breaches occurred in the Industrial, Seventeenth Street, and London Avenue canals. These structural failures released water that flooded close to 80 percent of the city as it equalized with sea level. More than 1,500 residents died from the storm—approximately two-thirds from drowning or injury from the water, the others from exposure, lack of food and water, or preexisting medical conditions. Studies showed that residents living closest to the levee breaches were most likely to have drowned. As with past disasters, most Katrina victims were elderly and infirm—those who were unable to evacuate or who suffered trauma from the flooding itself. Katrina's damage to lives and property (1,500 killed, 2 million displaced and evacuated, more than 300,000 homes destroyed, $130 billion in damage) outpaced previous storms such as 1969s Hurricane Camille (category 5) and 1992s Hurricane Andrew (also category 5) (United States Government Accountability Office 2007).

Although the damage and destruction from the hurricane were tremendous, the notion that New Orleans might find itself underwater was not a new one. Certainly the city had experience with broken levees; on 9 September 1965, Hurricane Betsy caused tremendous flooding throughout the city, including the Lower Ninth Ward (Rogers and Rogers 1965). Journalists and disaster specialists alike had regularly speculated that New Orleans might find itself flooded again, given its location below sea level (McQuaid and Schleifstein 2002). Many predicted that with the advent of a major tropical storm or hurricane, a million people would evacuate, but 200,000 would be left behind, and the levees would be overtopped by a storm surge that would produce "the worst natural disaster in the history of the United States" (Bourne 2004). Some organizations prepared for the event, such as the New Orleans Zoo, which quickly implemented its disaster plans and so saved many of its animals. Similarly, observers credit the United States Coast Guard with performing admirably despite having fewer resources and receiving less press coverage than the other armed services. Critics regularly singled out national political leaders, FEMA, and the local New Orleans police department for their poor performance.

Soon after the disaster, with more than a million evacuees dispersed across the country, New Orleans politicians, city officials, and FEMA officials repeatedly stressed housing as their number one priority. The levee breaches damaged some 434,000 homes in the New Orleans area and destroyed nearly 140,000 of them. While everyone in New Orleans publicly agreed that housing remained the most critical obstacle to rapid recovery after Hurricane Katrina, local controversy stalled the siting of temporary housing. Most citizens recognized the need for facilities like trailer parks and modular homes, but many insisted they be placed elsewhere. Which communities would be selected to host these trailers and their occupants was a critical but unanswered question.

This chapter, set against a backdrop of local opposition, investigates which communities and areas in and around New Orleans were selected as hosts for FEMA travel trailers and mobile homes. Controlling for a large number of factors, the strength of local-level social capital best predicts which zip codes would be chosen as hosts for more trailers and trailer parks. Those localities with more politically active and involved citizens who voted in past elections—a proxy I interpret as defining an area with stronger social ties and civic norms—received the fewest trailers. Conversely, authorities selected those zip codes that demonstrated weaker political activism to get more trailers. Those areas where citizens mobilized collectively were zones where authorities encountered or expected to face the strongest resistance to often controversial projects. By not placing trailers in areas they judged to be stronger in social capital and searching for alternative locations for temporary trailers because of actual or potential local resistance, they diverted administrative, financial, and personnel resources from other purposes. Hence pockets and blocks of stronger social capital improved local quality of life but may have slowed the overall recovery.

Trailers as "Public Bads"

Scholars and policy makers alike claim that temporary shelters, housing, and housing infrastructure are among the critical needs after disasters (Anderson and Woodrow 1998, 10; Richardson 2006). "Without housing, the individuals necessary to populate the economy, fill the jobs, and restart and open businesses as well as consume the services and purchase the goods will be absent"

(Peacock, Dash, and Zhang 2006, 259). However, in post-Katrina New Orleans, many local residents viewed trailer parks as an additional blight rather than the solution to the housing problem. At Lakewood Estates in the Algiers section of New Orleans, local residents used chains of people and vehicles to block construction and surveying equipment brought by federal workers who intended to begin siting a new temporary housing development.

One resident told reporters, "I don't want my neighborhood ruined because theirs is," epitomizing the problem of siting temporary housing after the storm. Councilwoman Cynthia Hedge Morrell summed up the thinking of many locals when she stated, "You can't rebuild a community if you are taking sacred parts of that community and destroying it" (quoted in Varney and Carr 2005). New Orleans councilman Jay Batt put up campaign posters with an image of a temporary FEMA trailer within a red circle with a line through it next to the heading, "He protected the integrity of neighborhoods in district A by not allowing trailers to be placed in parks and playgrounds where our children play."

Half of sixty-four parishes across the state of Louisiana immediately banned new group trailer sites after the storm. Scholars have estimated that approximately one in four FEMA trailer parks initially proposed for previously undeveloped sites by either FEMA or the city of New Orleans were rejected by the potential host communities (Davis and Bali 2008). Mayor Ray Nagin criticized the influx of "not in my neighborhood" thinking and pleaded with residents to "come together as neighbors, as friends" (quoted in Nelson and Varney 2005). Against this backdrop of NIMBY (not in my backyard) opposition, Mayor Nagin and the Housing Department within his administration worked with FEMA to create, revise, re-revise, and eventually release a list of approved sites for temporary trailers and housing.[4]

Trailer parks, often on the "wrong side of the tracks," are heavily stigmatized (Takahashi 1998). They are viewed as magnets for increased foot and vehicle traffic, loitering, drug use, and crime and as lowering property values (MacTavish 2006). Further, despite reassurances that temporary trailers are in fact temporary, many communities, such as those in Florida that accepted trailer parks after Hurricane Andrew, continued to host them several years after disasters (Peacock, Morrow, and Gladwin 2000). Some critics interpreted local reactions to trailer parks as evidence of the continuing racial and class divisions that have plagued New Orleans for decades (Nelson and Varney 2005). Beyond issues of race and crime, a number of studies showed that the FEMA trailers posed health hazards to occupants and nearby residents from formaldehyde and other toxic chemicals (Blumenthal 2007). Some scholars have argued that mobile homes are "seen as less desirable from a community planning perspective, but acceptable since local residents can remain in or near the community" (Nigg, Barnshaw, and Torres 2006, 120).

I categorize temporary trailers and trailer parks as examples of "public bads," projects that impose focused costs on local communities but provide diffuse benefits to cities and regions as a whole (Aldrich 2008a, 2008b). The term public bad is used to contrast them with public goods, such as lighthouses and national defense, which provide diffused benefits and diffused costs (Frey, Oberholzer-Gee, and Eichenberger 1996, 1298n1; cf. Reuter and Truman 2004). Trailers provide necessary housing for workers and families who will improve the economic conditions of the city and region, but they focus potential externalities, whether actual or expected, on local host communities. States and developers around the world regularly struggle to site controversial projects, including nuclear power plants, incinerators, and airports. Temporary housing after a disaster seems to be no exception.

Explanations for Siting Decisions

Different observers see dissimilar landscapes when envisioning how authorities decide where to locate controversial facilities. Previous research has sought to identify the factors that influence whether local residents end up with unwanted projects in their vicinity. Some authors have focused on technocratic criteria, such as the space available in the target area and the density of the local population. Others have underscored the potential for environmental racism, where authorities deliberately site unwanted projects in the backyards of ethnic and racial minorities. Socioeconomic conditions, such as poverty, unemployment, and homeownership may be linked to the potential for receiving such projects. After a megacatastrophe like Hurricane Katrina, the amount of damage in an area may best predict siting outcomes. Finally, some scholars, such as Hamilton (1993), Clingermayer (1994), and Aldrich (2008b), argue that authorities take into account the potential for collective action in local communities. As chapter 2 explained, neighborhoods with denser social networks can better overcome barriers to collective action and mobilize as a group to stop unwanted projects.

Scholarship has proposed five approaches to how locations are chosen for divisive facilities: technocratic criteria, discrimination against minorities, socioeconomic characteristics, amount of damage, and civil society. Technocratic criteria, such as the amount of land in an area or zip code block, or the density of population nearby, may push developers to select or exclude communities as hosts for trailer parks. Areas that have little land or are densely populated, such as metropolitan areas, may be worse candidate sites than more rural, sparsely populated ones. To test this theory I include measures of the area (in square miles) of the zip code block and measures of population density (people per square mile).

Proponents of the environmental racism argument point to controversial and unwanted facilities like nuclear power plants and airports located in areas with clusters of ethnic, racial, and religious minorities (Hurley 1995; Pastor, Sadd, and Hipp 2001). Such landscapes center on disadvantaged groups who bear the brunt of public bads. In the United States, for example, numerous waste repositories and incinerators are found in communities with large populations of African Americans, Native Americans, and Hispanics (Bullard 1994). A variety of community advocacy groups have formed to combat what they see as policies harmful to communities of people of color. Critics of the post-Katrina rebuilding have argued that the locations of temporary trailers reflect color lines within the city. Some studies have found statistically significant differences between African American and white communities in New Orleans in terms of the number of FEMA trailers (Craemer 2010). I measure this variable through the percentage of nonwhite residents in the zip code.

Another common explanation for the siting of public bads focuses on the economic conditions in local communities. Homeowners may be concerned about lowering of property values. Poorly educated, less wealthy individuals may be more comfortable with the idea of living near a trailer park than wealthier, more highly educated residents. For example, small towns in rural North Carolina view prisons as public goods because they bring jobs and other economic benefits (Hoyman 2002), despite fears of jailbreaks, riots, and other potential negative externalities. Others argue that we are likely to find facilities like industrial waste dumps and incinerators in communities with lower income levels (Mohai and Bryant 1992). However, studies of waste facility siting in Canada dismissed claims that siting was based on economic disadvantage, whether measured in terms of income or of unemployment (Castle and Munton 1996, 78). I measure socioeconomic conditions through income, unemployment, percentage of the population with income below the poverty line, education level, and house prices.

An alternative theory might posit that the number of trailers in an area is proportional to the damage the area received from Hurricane Katrina. A community with relatively little damage from flooding might have less demand for housing, and thus less interest in trailers for people internally displaced by the storm, while an area that suffered devastation would allow

or welcome trailer parks because of the large number of local residents affected. I tested three measures for floodwater depth after Hurricane Katrina
to model the amount of damage to each zip code block.

A final map of the siting landscape shows reservoirs of social capital. This
approach centers on the relative strength of horizontal associations, the ties
between individuals, and the depth of shared norms and behavior expectations. Research on siting in North America demonstrates that private developers avoid areas with greater potential for mobilizing against their projects
(Hamilton 1993). Similarly, local areas with more homogeneous constitu-
ents—that is, with stronger horizontal bonds between citizens—are more
likely than more heterogeneous areas to create zoning policies that exclude
unwanted group homes (Clingermayer 1994). In communities with more
social capital and better linkages, groups find it easier to organize against
unwanted projects (Aldrich 2008a, 2008b).

Research has shown that across nation-states and in a wide variety of
project types, both state authorities and private developers use pre-siting
surveys to gauge the strength of local civil society. For example, researchers
have found that many companies conduct a "windshield survey" by driving through potential host communities and noting signs of disconnected-
ness, low social capital, and poverty. In one notable case, court proceedings
showed that a surveyor had written "trailers everywhere" in his description of
a potential host of low-level radioactive waste, then designated the site as "in"
rather than "out" for siting future projects (Sherman 2006). Nations such as
the United Kingdom undertake similar investigations to estimate potential
opposition within civil society, sometimes through straightforward surveys
of local communities (Rüdig 1994, 84). French authorities may have selected
several localities in Normandy for nuclear power plants based on survey research that showed towns in that area more favorable to siting than those in
other regions (data reproduced in Hecht 1998, 248). Hence, in New Orleans
stronger bonds at the local level may mean that authorities sought to find
more acquiescent host communities for trailers elsewhere to avoid stalling
and delay in the rebuilding.

To test theories connecting the strength of civil society at the local level
with selection for trailer parks, I follow Hamilton (1993) and use voter turnout in recent presidential elections as a proxy for social capital and civic
engagement.[5] Research has long connected political participation through
initiatives like voting to broader engagement in citizen networks and activism (Verba and Nie 1972). Individuals who make the effort to vote—a costly
activity—demonstrate a stronger orientation to political and social issues
than nonvoters and a willingness to volunteer their time. Edward Walsh and

Rex Warland (1983), for example, interviewed close to seven hundred "activists" (those participating in antinuclear protests) and "free riders" (individuals expressing antinuclear sentiment but not actively participating) and found that activists were more likely to have voted in both the 1976 and 1980 presidential elections. Following the lead of previous scholarship in this area, I assume that this proxy of social capital is constant over time. That is, areas that demonstrated strong voter turnout in past presidential elections are assumed to be likely to do so in future ones, and those areas remain bastions of stronger civil society and interconnectedness.

I test the accuracy of these theories using data on the siting decisions for thousands of temporary trailers that the local and federal governments hoped to place in and around New Orleans after the devastation of Hurricane Katrina.

Data and Methodology

The universe of cases under study here includes all the potential zip codes in and around New Orleans where both FEMA and the city administration of New Orleans could have placed temporary housing units after Hurricane Katrina. I used the TAC-RC Master List, dated 29 June 2006, provided by the Governor's Hurricane Housing Task Force and New Orleans Housing Department, to create a comprehensive list, by zip code, of approved sites and trailers. With 114 zip codes in the data set, I need not use methods such as endogenous, choice-based sampling or weighting to make sure that the sample of cases closely matches the actual population. Rather, this data set captures all the areas in and around New Orleans where trailers could have been sited by city and federal authorities.

I have measures of two outcomes for my dependent variable: the number of trailers in a zip code, and the number of trailer parks. These are highly correlated (measured at close to 0.8), but nonetheless they are investigated in separate analyses because of their importance; an area may have more trailer parks but fewer overall trailers than comparable zip codes, and vice versa. Because the dependent variables involve count data (the number of trailer sites or trailers themselves per zip code block) and are bounded at zero, typical OLS regression analyses would be inappropriate. Additionally, zero truncated Poisson models involve assumptions about inaccurate nonzero counts within the dependent variable, which I do not believe are relevant here. This chapter uses the negative binomial model, which is a variant of the Poisson model but which overcomes its main problem—its assumption that the mean and variance are the same. The negative binomial allows for

mean-variance inequality. Multiple imputation filled in missing values (a total of five data points) across the data set.

This analysis cannot make inferences about the case-by-case heuristics
employed by decision makers such as Mayor Nagin and the New Orleans
Housing Department. Its strongest claims focus on the factors within zip
code blocks that are correlated with more or fewer temporary housing units.
Mayor Nagin and his team of advisers were the primary actors who selected
the final trailer park sites immediately after Hurricane Katrina. I assume that
decision makers' impressions of local-level social, racial, technocratic, and
civil society factors were based on available data that had been recorded or
intuited before the storm and based at broader spatial levels, such as the zip
code block level, as opposed to block-by-block or case-by-case. One potential obstacle to zip code–based analysis is spatial dependency; while various
technical fixes for issues of spatial dependency can be found in the epide-
miological literature, I assume that the placement of trailers in one zip code
block does not influence their placement (or lack thereof) in another block.
Given the small size of trailers vis-à-vis the available areas in typical zip codes,
I have no empirical or theoretical reason to believe that the number of trailers or trailer parks in one zip code interacts with or influences the number of
trailers in a neighboring one.

I use the percentage of a zip code block's voting age population that voted
in the 2004 presidential election as a proxy for the strength of local civil society, following previous scholars who have tied this measure to the potential
for collective action (Hamilton 1993). Furthermore, surveys of hundreds of
post-Katrina New Orleans residents carried out by the Student Hurricane
Network in 2006 and 2007 indicate strong correlations (chi-square values of
0.001 using cross-tabulation) between voting in presidential elections and
participating in local civil organizations. This proxy fits well with the indexes
of civil society created by such experts as Robert Putnam, who includes voting in national as well as local elections as a representative action of civic engagement (Putnam 2000). The Louisiana Secretary of State website provided
the number of voters that turned out for the 2004 presidential election for
each of the precincts which were laid over zip code boundaries. An archived
file, also provided by the secretary of state, listed registered voters.

I used a combined list of active and inactive registered voters as of 29
October 2004, the most recent data before the presidential election. Data on
socioeconomic indicators came from the 2000 United States national census, while information on water levels was taken from a number of sources,
including National Oceanic and Atmospheric Administration LIDAR plots
and local observers' estimations. Table 8 provides descriptive statistics about

the data set. Note the enormous variation across the variables. There were an average of 5 trailer sites, also known as trailer parks, per zip code, with some areas receiving only a single site and others receiving as many as 73. Furthermore, while the average zip code block was slated to receive more than 450 trailers, some had as few as 3 or as many as 3,800.

TABLE 8. Descriptive statistics of New Orleans data

Variable	Number of observations	Mean	Standard deviation	Minimum	Maximum
Dependent variables					
Number of trailer sites	114	5.64	10.49	1	73
Number of trailers	114	465	624.1	3	3787
Technocratic criteria					
Area {square miles}	114	75.6	98.1	0.4	445.7
Population density (people per square mile)	114	1676.1	2720.3	7.4	12,836.9
Discrimination against minorities					
Percentage of the population who are not white	114	42.9	26.1	2.4	98.5
Socioeconomic indicators					
Percentage of the population above 65	114	11.3	2.9	3.8	20.2
Percentage of the population who attended university	114	14.6	9.6	0	50.6
Percentage of population who attended high school	114	70	9.78	40.1	92.1
Income	114	30,544.7	8524.1	7448	52,375
House prices	114	79,577.1	25,839.1	42900	184,300
Percentage of the population beneath the poverty line	114	23.1	10.3	5.6	71.9
Percentage of population who are unemployed	114	4.5	1.9	1	10.3
Amount of damage					
Flood damage (calculated through raster image estimation)	114	0.72	1.65	0	8.5
Flood damage (calculated through fewer point estimates and maps)	114	0.74	1.65	0	8.22

(*continued*)

TABLE 8. (*continued*)

Variable	Number of observations	Mean	Standard deviation	Minimum	Maximum
Flood damage (calculated solely through LIDAR estimation)	114	0.60	1.53	0	8.117
Strength of social capital					
Voter turnout	114	0.60	0.06	0.39	0.77
General variables					
New Orleans (dummy variable)	114	0.1	0.366252	0	1
Population	114	17,426.12	13,516.77	472	57,638
Number of individuals of voting age	114	71.5421	6.457607	14.3	86.8

I used a VIF test to investigate the possibility of multicollinearity among these variables. Among the full list of variables within the data set there is considerable correlation, especially among the voting age population, income, and water level variables. Sophia Rabe-Hesketh and Brian Everitt (2007, 69) reported that "a mean of the VIF factors considerably larger than one suggests collinearity" and suggested that a value under 3 would be acceptable. Dropping factors with high levels of multicollinearity, the mean VIF value in the variables under study is under 2.45. I used skewness tests to investigate the distribution of my dependent variables (the number of trailer parks and the number of trailers) and found that they are positively skewed with kurtosis (thin tails in these measures). Given that my count data display a positive skew and thin tails, they do not fit the normal distribution. To correct for the heteroskedasticity of my dependent variable (White 1980), I used robust standard errors.

Results

I used a negative binominal regression using robust standard errors to analyze which factors influenced the number of trailers or trailer sites per zip code. Table A9 reports the coefficients from this model. A number of factors proved to be statistically significant at the 0.01 level, including whether the zip code was in New Orleans or outside it, population density, percentage unemployed, and voter turnout. Of these variables, those with the largest effect on the number of trailers per zip code (that is, with the absolute largest estimated coefficients) are the New Orleans dummy variable and the per-

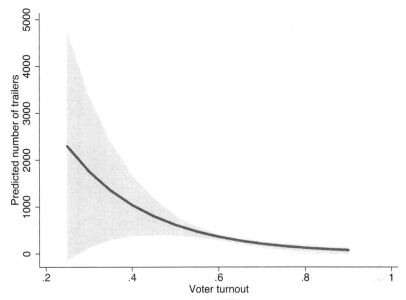

FIGURE 19. Connection between social capital and FEMA trailers per New Orleans zip code. $N =$ 114, simulations = 1,000. Simulations hold all other variables (area, population density, house prices, percentage of the population that attended high school, percentage of the population that is not white, percentage of the population that is unemployed, and flood damage) at their means, with voter turnout allowed to vary.

centage of eligible voters voting in past elections. Note that I cannot directly interpret these estimated coefficients as I might with a typical OLS regression owing to the structural form of the binomial model. While some analysts have used incidence rate ratios to understand the effects of negative binomial model coefficients, I instead provide simulations and confidence intervals that produce more intuitive displays of the variables (King, Tomz, and Wittenberg 2000, 341). Here, the quantity of interest is the number of trailers per zip code. The predicted number of trailers is displayed as a solid line bounded by a gray outline showing the 95 percent confidence intervals. For these simulations, I set all independent variables at their means except for the quantity of interest—social capital (measured through voter turnout).

Figure 19 demonstrates that locales with a more politically active citizenry received far fewer trailers than their less politically active counterparts. Setting all other variables at their means (employment levels, housing prices, education, population density, percentage nonwhite, etc.), the model predicts that an area where the vast majority (close to 80 percent) of the population voted would be slated to receive fewer than 100 trailers. On the other hand, a less active zip code area where only 30 percent of the eligible population showed

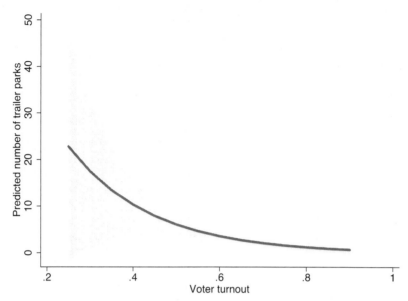

FIGURE 20. Relation between reservoirs of social capital and FEMA trailer parks per New Orleans zip code. $N = 114$, simulations $= 1,000$. Simulations hold all other variables (area, population density, house prices, percentage of the population that attended high school, percentage of the population that is not white, percentage of the population that is unemployed, and flood damage) at their means, with voter turnout allowed to vary.

up at election time would be chosen to receive as many as 1,200 trailers. Our uncertainty is greatest about the predictions concerning voter turnout levels of less than 40 percent; this can be seen in the width of the gray outline around these forecasts. Also, my model predicts that a zip code outside New Orleans would receive approximately 278 trailers (with a 95 percent confidence interval of 214 to 342), while one within the city limits would receive closer to 1,029 (with a larger confidence interval of 166 to 1,893). Hence, developers were more likely to concentrate trailers inside New Orleans, perhaps to ease access to grocery stores, medical services, and other needs.

To ensure that the results are not a function solely of the number of trailers, I also tested to see if these factors influenced the number of trailer sites. The coefficients from these regressions are available in table A10. Note here again that a number of factors were statistically significant, including the New Orleans dummy variable, high school education, and voter turnout. Those that both were significant at the 0.01 level or less and had a strong impact on the dependent variable (that is, a large estimated coefficient) were few: the presence or absence of the zip code within New Orleans itself, and voter turnout. As before, I used simulation and confidence techniques to demonstrate the effect of civil society on the quantity of interest, which in this case is the number of trailer sites (as opposed to trailers themselves).

Figure 20 displays more support for the argument that areas with stronger networks of politically active voters were not selected to host unwanted projects—in this case, trailer parks. My model predicts that an area where 80 percent of the voters turn out in elections would receive only a single trailer park, in contrast to an area where fewer than 40 percent did so, which would receive fifteen or more.

Discussion

Some observers might imagine that these results, which indicate that authorities took potential resistance seriously when selecting sites for trailers, were a function of the emergency conditions under which FEMA and the city of New Orleans sought to place temporary housing. After Hurricane Katrina, with an extreme shortage of housing, these government organizations may have used impressions and measurements to identify and avoid areas with high levels of social capital so as to respond quickly to the enormous disaster.

Such thinking would overlook other studies that have demonstrated that even in nonemergency settings, where siting procedures can take years, if not decades, authorities take seriously the potential for resistance from local communities. Research demonstrated that with controversial facilities such as nuclear power plants, dams, and airports, which can require up to three decades to site, Japanese authorities placed projects with an eye to the strength of local civil organizations (Aldrich 2008a, 2008b). Hamilton (1993) illuminated that private organizations seeking to expand existing controversial projects under normal decision-making conditions selected areas based on measures of social capital, which indicated to site planners the degree of potential resistance. Finally, Sherman (2006) revealed that siting authorities seeking new locations for radioactive waste took notice of social and demographic indicators that tied in to levels of social capital. In short, these results are not the function of an emergency situation: even when not pressed for time, authorities seek to place unwanted projects in backyards with weaker social ties and hence less potential for controversy.

Conclusions

Zip code–level data support arguments that decision makers within the New Orleans administration and FEMA took seriously the threat from well-organized and connected local areas when selecting sites for unwanted trailers. Edward Banfield and James Wilson (1963) set off a strong debate with their argument that certain urban-based ethnic communities were "private regarding," that is, concerned for private gain, as opposed to broader public gain, in contrast to "public regarding" worldviews that favored efficiency and good government. This chapter has gone beyond such binary categorizations to show that communities that are in fact public regarding in terms of turning out to vote may, deliberately or not, create outcomes that are private regarding in terms of unwanted facilities. My results fit with those of others scholars who emphasized the importance of civil society in siting divisive projects (Hamilton 1993; Clingermayer 1994; Sherman 2006; Aldrich 2008b). This chapter also supports past arguments that public policy outcomes in post-Katrina New Orleans are driven by voter turnout, so that neighborhoods with better turnout would have greater pull in coming battles over investment and development (Logan 2009, 258).

By avoiding potentially contentious areas, planners hope to speed up the recovery. Councilwoman Jacquelyn Clarkson, whose district includes Algiers and the French Quarter, spoke openly about her quest to ensure that any trailers placed in her district would be in locations that "don't intrude on our lifestyle." Seeing resistance to trailers as "common sense," not NIMBY politics, Clarkson predicted early on that attempts to site trailers in the area of the Lakewood Country Club would fail, since pressure from organized local residents would ensure that the club "was coming off that damn list [of potential sites]" (quoted in Nelson and Varney 2005). Her comment that politicians and decision makers should "know our districts better" fits well with the model predicted by the data. That is, savvy politicians—if not always the FEMA and city bureaucrats selecting locations for housing—may recognize the communities where stronger bonds between citizens bring them into active participation in politics and siting decisions and avoid those areas when selecting locations for controversial projects.

Given that New Orleans and FEMA officials evidently sought to avoid delay and controversy by selecting areas with less social capital for trailers, how can I explain the loud disagreements and protest over trailer sitings? Two explanations are possible. First, planners themselves may make forecast errors where they misjudge levels of local resistance. In many past conflicts between citizens and governments, officials underestimated the capability for local resistance (cf. Apter and Sawa 1984). Second, even if the individuals living near the planned site do not protest, extralocal individuals, civil rights and environmental groups, and other activists often take up the issue to raise its salience. Even the best-planned sites often end up embroiled in well-publicized contestation.

While scholars may continue to envision higher levels of social capital and civil society as inevitably leading to more efficient outcomes and enhanced governance, this book has given credence to the "counterweight" theories of civil society in which local citizens join together against state plans. Even after a disaster, tighter and deeper local networks have a double-edged quality, assisting those nearby but not necessarily those farther away.

Between State and Market:
The Way Forward

This book has provided qualitative and quantitative evidence of three ways that social resources have proved critical in building resilience following four disasters. After the 1923 Tokyo earthquake, population recovery levels across the thirty-nine police precincts in the capital city varied widely. Quantitative results using cross-tabulation, propensity score matching, and time series cross-sectional panel data supported the argument that social resources were the engine for recovery. When a number of variables including crime, factory workers, and trucks per capita, pawnbroker lending, quake damage, population density, and area of each precinct were held constant, the best predictors of strong population growth were the measures of social capital. Precincts across Tokyo that had higher turnout in the municipal elections of 1929 and 1933 and precincts that had more political rallies and demonstrations each year were the ones that demonstrated resilience. In these areas, citizens worked together not only in the political and social realms but also in achieving recovery. However, with the strong recovery of parts of the city came a strong negative externality: violence and attacks against racial minorities, with thousands of Korean residents murdered by mobs of survivors.

Next, I investigated the recovery from the 1995 Kobe earthquake. A qualitative case comparison of the very similar neighborhoods of Mano and Mikura showed that, despite identical problems of population decline, aging, and high population density, residents of Mano had deeper reservoirs of social capital, which allowed them to organize themselves and combat the fires that broke out after the quake. In Mikura, citizens lacked such coordination and could only watch as fires destroyed their neighborhoods. Then, using data on the nine wards of Kobe for eighteen years following the earthquake, I used quantitative analysis to show that holding constant population affected by the quake, welfare households per capita, population density, and socioeconomic inequality, the proxy for social resources again proved most important at bringing back population. In neighborhoods like Mano, where residents established NPOs to assist in the recovery, population growth rates were far higher than in wards where citizens did not.

In the case of the 2004 Indian Ocean, I began with qualitative case studies of six coastal villages affected by the tsunami, demonstrating that hamlets with higher levels of both bonding and linking social capital were more resilient than those with only one type or neither. Hamlets with uur panchayats effectively reached out to NGOs and government officials to ensure that their villages received food, shelter, and assistance, while those without such linking organizations were off the map of the recovery efforts. But with the strong bonding and linking capital came discrimination against out-groups, including Dalits, women, and other nonmembers of dominant local organizations, who were either deliberately or accidentally excluded from the lists of the needy. Next I used a quantitative analysis of sixty-two villages across Tamil Nadu to show that, holding constant economic, locational, and other factors, caste, wealth, and family structure strongly altered patterns of relief. I concluded the chapter with a large-N analysis of the survey results from 1,600 residents across the region, illuminating that—all other factors held constant—better-connected survivors were able to access more relief after the tsunami. Villagers who attended weddings and funerals were deeply embedded in social relationships that strengthened their resilience and gave them better access to resources after the devastating tsunami.

In the most recent disaster under study here, Hurricane Katrina in 2005, I showed how residents of zip codes across the city of New Orleans that were better organized and connected were able to avoid what they saw as "public bads" after the floods. Neighborhoods that turned out to vote—a costly initiative connected with trust in government and norms of civic participation—were the ones that, holding constant race, area, population density, age, income, house prices, unemployment, and damage—had to accept fewer FEMA trailers. Better able to coordinate their activities and display their intention to fight such temporary housing projects, these communities avoided having them in their backyards.

Despite different time periods, cultures, government capacities, and levels of development, all four cases showed that areas with more social capital made effective and efficient recoveries from crises through coordinated efforts and cooperative activities. These recoveries underscored the exact mechanisms through which social resources provide resilience before, during, and after a catastrophe. First, deep levels of social capital serve as informal insurance and promote mutual assistance after a disaster. As one observer argued after Hurricane Katrina, "The family networks that had remained strong in Louisiana were more important than any government aid in helping to ease the impact of the disaster" (Brinkley 2007, 435). By sharing tools, information, living space, and other scarce resources, networks of acquaintances and friends fill gaps left by the absence of state and private organizations. Citizens—not trained professionals such as police or firefighters—are most commonly the first responders to disaster (Zhao 2010).

Next, dense and numerous social ties help survivors solve collective action problems that stymie rehabilitation. Even in underdeveloped sections of Haiti, neighbors who trust each other set up spontaneous watch committees to deter looting and crime, work to remove debris and clean up public spaces, and provide clear signals to authorities about their needs. Neighbors coordinate the delivery of aid to members of their communities and structure demands to decision makers and NGOs, especially through focal points like the uur panchayats of southeast India. In areas of Kobe where condominium owners lacked these connections, they were unable to coordinate debris removal, whereas in the Village de L'Est neighborhood of New Orleans residents pushed local utilities to reactivate electrical power. In the New Orleans neighborhood of Lakeview, a civic leader reported, "We created a block captain network, where through everybody knowing somebody in Lakeview, we got somebody to volunteer to be the information officer for a particular block. And by doing that, we started our whole surveying process" (quoted in Weil 2010, 6).

Finally, strong social ties strengthen the voices of survivors and decrease the probability of their leaving. After tremendous tragedy, residents can choose to relocate or to rebuild their houses and lives in their hometowns despite steep costs. As one psychiatrist summarized the post-Katrina mood in New Orleans, "They're moving [out] because they're so discouraged by the situation. There's a lot of uncertainty about the future. It's not easy to live here" (quoted in McCulley 2006). Nossiter (2007) noted that it is "the network of friends, relations and acquaintances that often, in New Orleans, helps compensate for fragmentary families and neighborhoods that can be dangerous." Deeper local connections to friends, families, and institutions in the disaster-struck area motivate survivors to dig out, rebuild, and stay despite the incredible challenges. These embedded individuals speak out more forcefully to authorities and the media about their desires and goals; survivors turn their social capital into political capital (Birner and Wittmer 2003). Those with fewer ties can more seriously pursue starting over elsewhere, while those without local connections may impede recovery through crime and looting. Furthermore, relocating itself reduces social capital among survivors (Iuchi 2010, 215).

As with all resources, however, strong social capital brings with it negative externalities. One study found that residents with closer relationships with their neighbors and a higher propensity for volunteering were least likely to evacuate from hurricanes, perhaps because of they wanted to help others (Horney et al. 2010). Beyond such problems for well-connected individuals, disaster-affected residents and whole communities with fewer social resources may find themselves excluded from recovery lists (Kruks-Wisner 2011) and from receiving assistance, or they may be forced to host temporary housing and other unwanted projects that were rejected by better-organized neighborhoods. Attempts to meet the demands of well-organized citizens' groups can cause delays in implementing citywide plans (Edgington 2010, 173). In the worst scenario, peripheral social groups and ethnicities and those who have violated group norms may be the target of organized violence. Three of the four extended cases—Tokyo, Tamil Nadu, and New Orleans— brought clear evidence that individuals and neighborhoods with weaker ties had more difficulties because of problematic interactions with organized and mobilized groups.

This chapter builds on these arguments to explore three themes that flow from the ways social capital influences post-disaster recovery. I urge policy makers and NGOs to focus on evidence-based programs that incorporate social capital as a core factor in rebuilding. Broadly, I call for a reorientation of disaster recovery programs at all levels—local, national, and international— away from the standard fixes focused primarily on physical infrastructure and toward social infrastructure. Doing so will help build resilience in vulnerable communities around the world. Specifically, I make the arguments that centralized plans for recovery are ambitious and typically flawed; that existing recovery and mitigation plans at best ignore and at worst harm existing stocks of social capital; and that decision makers in the public and private sectors must design and apply new policy instruments that strengthen social capital before and after crises. These arguments take us between the typical institutions of the state and the market to focus instead on the role of social resources after crises.

Centralized Plans Are Ambitious and Flawed

James C. Scott, in showing how local, practical knowledge (*mētis* in Greek) inevitably trumps "state simplifications" and "utopian schemes," pointed out that "a mechanical application of generic rules that ignores these particularities is an invitation to practical failure, social disillusionment, or most likely both" (Scott 1998, 318). In almost all the cases under study here, government authorities saw megadisasters as opportunities to alter existing organizations and institute new and often controversial plans. Some planners hoped to reshape the physical space of their jurisdictions, while others hoped to change land use practices, along with cultures of work and play. In case after case, "local entities (nonprofit and local government agencies) were far more flexible and responsive than the federal government or national organizations" in responding to disaster (Appleseed 2006, 6).[1] Top-down, command-and-control frameworks for handling disaster through the North American emergency management system have proved less than ideal (United States Government Accountability Office 1991; Birkland 2009). Scholars have regularly criticized government schemes that involve centralized planning, standard operating procedures, and little flexibility in execution (Comfort 2005; Perrow 2007). While government planners in each of these disasters thought of these schemes as rational and practical, such top-down plans lacked popular support and almost inevitably fell apart or were challenged by residents.[2]

After the 1923 Tokyo earthquake, powerful politicians such as Shinpei Gotō stepped forward with plans to completely redo the capital city as a modern, safe metropolis. Gone would be the crooked, narrow alleys that served as roads throughout much of the city. Gone would be the older single-family wooden houses that survived the quake and the supposedly temporary barracks that had popped up like mushrooms after the tragedy (Seidensticker 1991). This ambitious plan would have required that municipal officials buy up all the damaged property and lands throughout Tokyo and then rationalize the space at a cost of 4 billion yen (an astronomical figure) (Schencking 2006, 836; Mochizuki 1993, 82–83; Hanes 2000, 132). Attacked by his political enemies and overpowered by other ministries that competed for the same funds, Gotō realized little of his ambitious scheme. Elites were not the only parties who objected to his proposals. Local residents protested plans for "necessary" post-quake projects, such as incinerators for burning debris and garbage, that they thought would worsen their quality of life (Yamada 1973).

Some seventy years later, Kobe's mayor hoped that a two-month moratorium on building would give planners a chance to design a city that would be more resilient to quakes and could be navigated by emergency workers after disasters. Kobe's recovery scheme was heavily weighted by a central planning procedure—controlled by the city planners in the mayor's office—but over time it became more interactive. The city provided broader strategies for potential recovery plans, then sent planners to each community to come up with counterproposals (Shigeo Tatsuki, pers. comm., 25 March 2010). The final plan—which put much of the onus for rebuilding on local neighbor-hoods—spurred many to create alternative strategies rather than accept ei-ther standard, large-scale public housing or individually owned homes. In Mano and other communities with high levels of social capital, survivors pooled resources to develop their own cooperative housing plans (Evans 2001; Nakagawa and Shaw 2004; Yasui 2007). These entrepreneurial groups collaborated to design earthquake- and fire-resistant condominiums with shared living and eating spaces but private sleeping quarters for each family (Sekikawa, Sakurai, and Song 2006). Local residents set up new nonprofit groups to coordinate their rebuilding, and they began to think about neigh-borhood planning not solely as owners of houses or condominiums, but rather as members of a larger community. Japan is not the only industrial-ized democracy whose national and political leaders have often ignored local residents in the drive to "build back better."

While most disaster management and recovery processes in the United States are bottom-up, the federal government has been deeply involved in distributing funds to affected communities on the Gulf Coast after Hurricane Katrina. Much of the money provided by the national government—$75 bil-lion out of $120.5 billion—went toward emergency relief efforts, not toward actual rebuilding (Ahlers, Plyer, and Weil 2008). The proportionally small amount of money focused on rebuilding has trickled through nine layers of subcontractors, leaving many local activists wondering exactly how much has worked its way down to the community (Frederick Weil, pers. comm., 25 March 2010). As one informant argued, "The usual suspects, including Halliburton and the Shaw Group, are getting the big contracts from FEMA and the Army Corps of Engineers" (quoted in King 2009, 170). Such prac-tices mesh heavily with criticisms of "disaster capitalism" (Klein 2007), in which large multinational corporations reap massive profits from disaster and crisis. Along with the disconnect between federal assistance and local needs, New Orleans city planners have struggled to produce a viable recovery plan embraced by both the administration and local residents.[3] The Bring New Orleans Back Commission was only one of several tries at formulating a "smaller, safer" city that would have applied financial resources and new infrastructure to areas thought viable for the long term; the New Orleans City Council itself initiated a separate procedure for analysis and neighbor-hood recovery planning in early 2006 (see Sanyika 2009 for a critical review of both). Federal dollars have gone into the Louisiana Recovery Authority's Road Home program,[4] which was the "primary grant for rebuilding perma-nent housing for uninsured or underinsured homeowners" (Bates and Green 2009, 236).

The most recent and comprehensive recovery scheme, known as the Unified New Orleans Plan (UNOP)—officially received by the city in June 2007 and involving roughly six months of work—sought to "ensure transparency and equity" in the planning through steering committees and various mechanisms to improve open decision making (Johnson 2007). Conferences and symposiums held across the Gulf Coast—a number of which allowed for public input—drew suggestions and plans from urban planners, architects, and civil engineers alike. The UNOP has proved to be a more collaborative effort, involving NGOs, neighborhood associations, consultants, and planners, but even these data-backed plans have lacked across-the-board support from residents. In some neighborhoods such as Broadmoor, for example, citizens' anger at top-down plans that would have reduced the city's footprint and increased green space spurred far more locals to join neighborhood associations than in the past (Warner and Darce 2006). Beyond the anger these plans generated, local residents in well-organized neighborhoods worked together to protest schemes to increase temporary housing (Davis and Bali 2008). In the end, many ignored directives, announcements, and statements from the city and instead focused on reading the signals from neighbors, friends, and relevant private institutions (Chamlee-Wright 2010). That is, "Much of the city's organic recovery took place in defiance of an engineered, top-down rebuilding plan that was proposed in the first few months after the storm, prompting a dispute that has never been resolved" (Robertson 2010).

Authorities in India similarly envisioned post-tsunami recovery as a chance to institute public policies that would be almost impossible in standard circumstances. The government sought to move coastal households inland from their vulnerable positions at the edge of the sea. This Coastal Regulation Zone (CRZ) policy was at odds with historical indigenous practice for fisher folk along the coast and had the potential to negatively affect those without proper documentation, who would not be included in rebuilding plans (HelpAge International 2005, 2). "Typically, the poorest in the village—single-woman-headed households, old and destitute people and crew members without assets—inhabit the houses close to the beach, while the boat- and other asset-owning, politically and socially powerful sectors of the village live farther away" (Salagrama 2006a, 45). Under the provisions of the 1986 Environment [Protection] Act, the CRZ notification was first issued in 1991 to allow the state to act "for the purpose of protecting and improving the quality of the environment and preventing, controlling and abating environmental pollution" (Sridhar 2005, 4).

In Government Order 172, dated 30 March 2005, the government of India backed away from harsher initial proposals to force the relocation of families who chose to continue inhabiting houses close to the waterline and altered the policy to punish such homeowners by denying them assistance for rebuilding (Tata Institute of Social Sciences 2005, 7). Homeowners within two hundred meters of the ocean's high tide line who were willing to relinquish their property would receive a new house—much farther from the beach, in most cases. Some villages accepted the terms of the policy across the board, while in others implementation has been mixed; for example, 646 out of 1,695 households in the village of Devanampattinam accepted the government's terms (Mahapatra 2005). Since many of the residents of coastal villages have no housing rights and lack proof of ownership, they have been viewed by the government as encroachers (Sudarshan Rodriguez, pers. comm., 25 March 2010). Critics have argued that large commercial properties, tourist hotels, and other institutions that "require access to the shoreline" (in the language of the regulation) have the most to gain—since they can stay close to the tide line—while the poorest local citizens are most likely to be relocated (Rodriguez 2008). Many fishermen on the Indian coast used the beach between their houses and the ocean for drying fish, spreading out nets for repair, and storing their fishing boats. The large tourist hotels hope to maintain beach access for their guests and have pressured regulators to allow them to stay close to the shore. "In effect, 16 years of active collusion between commercial interest lobbies and the government ensured repeated dilutions to this law" (Menon, Rodriguez, and Sridhar 2007, 5). The attempt to move native communities farther inland has resulted in the privatizing of what was traditionally communal space.[5]

Without the acceptance of local residents, top-down post-disaster plans will merely sit on the shelves gathering dust or will be implemented in the face of strong resistance from communities who feel ignored or harmed by such schemes.[6] What have these programs—intended to improve personal and community recovery—lacked?

Existing Programs Ignore or Damage Social Bonds

Top-down, government-driven rehabilitation plans inevitably overlook the role of social resources in rebuilding, assuming that money, infrastructure, and expert guidance will bring about the most efficient and effective recovery. Social capital and local networks are mentioned peripherally, if at all. For example, grants are available for post-disaster mental health programs in North America through the Crisis Counseling Assistance and Training Program (CCP), but they focus on treating individuals experiencing psychological distress, not on maintaining, restoring, or developing their social networks (United States Government Accountability Office 2006, 39). Furthermore, receiving federal assistance for this limited individual-level counseling requires strong justification: "A state's application for CCP funds must demonstrate that the need for crisis counseling in the affected area is beyond the capacity of state and local resources" (United States Government Accountability Office 2008b, 2–3).

The United Nations Team for Tsunami Recovery Support openly recognized the need for "social reintegration" of survivors but provided few details on how to achieve this (Office of the Secretary-General's Special Envoy for Tsunami Recovery 2005). Several US government committees have called on FEMA and the Department of Homeland Security to better integrate the resources and capabilities of civil organizations and NGOs such as the Red Cross, the Salvation Army, and Voluntary Organizations Active in Disaster into national disaster plans (United States Government Accountability Office 2008a). While there is some recognition of the role of such nonstate organizations, especially for their contribution after disasters, actual disaster plans may harm existing social networks.

A number of post-disaster schemes, such as the random assignment of survivors to nearby temporary shelters or permanent housing, damage existing stocks of social capital. All cases involving procedures to quickly relocate survivors had poor outcomes. While recovery coordinators may imagine that quick evacuation would somehow save more lives than a more methodical mass departure plan, their assumptions are often mistaken. Rapid, random evacuation places those citizens most in need of assistance after disasters in temporary housing where their social connections are limited at best and nonexistent at worst (Tsuji 2001). After the 1995 Kobe earthquake, for example, placing many senior citizens in huge, Soviet-style apartment blocks without attempting to resettle them near friends and family resulted in a number of "lonely deaths" (*kodoku shi*) where elders died without anyone's even knowing about it (*Mainichi Shinbun,* 17 January 1997, 4; Suga 2007). Many argued that these deaths were completely preventable; had they been placed near friends, acquaintances, or old neighbors, these seniors would have felt connected to the broader community; they would have had relatives to check on them and something to live for. On the whole, Kobe municipal officials made it difficult for those who actively sought to move together en masse to temporary or permanent housing (Yoshimune 1999). In site visits to affected communities in Tohoku, Japan, after the 11 March 2011 earthquake, I found a number of communities using lotteries to place elderly and special needs survivors in permanent housing.

In southeastern India after the 2004 tsunami, local residents complained bitterly that their random placement in resettlement communities severed connections to friends and family who often provided child care, informal job assistance, and help in daily living. Without these resources, tsunami survivors found themselves struggling to resume their normal lives. Studies have confirmed that random placement leads to poorer recovery (HelpAge International 2005, 12). Most recently, the buses leaving New Orleans for temporary shelters in August 2005 did not post signs to let survivors know where they were headed; for those leaving the state by aircraft, "evacuees often didn't even know where they were going until they were seated on a plane, listening to the captain describe the itinerary" (Brinkley 2007, 558).

Providing this simple information could have allowed New Orleans survivors to travel to cities and towns where they had family and friends. Many Katrina-affected residents were flown or bussed to new communities to which they had no connection, and their ability to maintain ties to their old networks was impaired by poor planning, disrupted communications, and new temporary addresses. Neighborhoods from the Big Easy that kept together after the storm—such as Village de L'Est—did so only by continuing to fight for that (Chamlee-Wright 2010). Survivors regularly told decision makers they wanted to rebuild homes near their old neighbors: one stated, "If you give us the money, we want to live near each other" (quoted in Krupa and Coleman 2006). The clearest lesson from these cases is the need to keep survivors connected during and after evacuation. This could be done by deliberately placing people from the same blocks, neighborhoods, and wards together. It could also be accomplished by making sure all shelter residents have access to e-mail, cell phones, or texting devices to allow them to stay in contact with their networks.[7] Evacuation plans[8] that take social networks into account are only the base of what could be more effective plans for recovery and mitigation.

The Way Forward: New Policies and Programs That Build Social Capital

The current situation in the field of disaster recovery is exactly parallel to 1950s-era beliefs about investment and foreign aid for developing nations. For years, Western bureaucrats and aid donors imagined that sending money and building physical infrastructure would somehow jump start the economies and development of poor nations in Southeast Asia, Africa, and South America. Driven by a belief that wealthy Western nations were morally obligated to provide resources to the poor (Singer 1972), many did so without considering the institutional and social resource context. As T. K. Ahn and Elinor Ostrom (2008, 89) explain, "For the past five decades, scholars and public officials have viewed investment in physical capital—roads, power plants, dams, and factories—as the essential missing factor in development. Hence, bilateral and multilateral donors have allocated billions of dollars to supply the 'missing capital,' thought to be essential in kick-starting development in the poorer countries of the world."

However, these bridges, roads, and other facilities did little to alter the productivity, skills, or entrepreneurial behavior of local residents. As scholars pointed out, "It soon became clear, however, that merely pumping physical and financial resources into poor countries was having, at best, a marginal positive impact" (Woolcock and Radin 2008, 415). In fact, aid—whether for development or for disaster recovery—often created perverse incentives in the recipients, undermining broader attempts at economic and social growth (Gibson et al. 2005). Several scholars have written books arguing that the typical development expert approach has failed and needs to be replaced by a more viable framework (Easterly 2001, 2006; Moyo 2009; see Coyne 2010 for a critical review of Graciana del Castillo's work on postwar reconstruction). In the mid-1990s the World Bank began to recognize that a focus on the social infrastructure in these nations had been missing from five decades of investment. Altering their underlying philosophy and creating a new perspective focused on building local trust, interconnectedness, and networks, the World Bank moved beyond physical infrastructure to include social infrastructure in its planning. Research showed that trust magnified the effectiveness of foreign aid; societies with more trust could more effectively utilize the new infrastructure to improve productivity, educational levels, and so on (see Woolcock 2002). In the field of disaster recovery, planners must similarly begin to place their actions in the context of social networks and resources and work to bring local citizens into the planning (Kondo 2008).

In the mid-1700s, advisers to the Portuguese king who had to deal with tremendous destruction wrought by the earthquakes and tsunami that had leveled much of Lisbon could only tell him, "Bury the dead and feed the living" (quoted in Shrady 2008, 24). Some two and a half centuries later, we can do much better. Experts have underscored that, when possible, we should mitigate the effects of future disasters, reducing the concentration of vulnerable targets (Perrow 2007) and implementing new financial and market-based schemes that will motivate citizens and businesses to use risk transfer mechanisms such as insurance, industry loss warranties, and catastrophe bonds (cf. Kunreuther and Useem 2010). Furthermore, given the vulnerability of critical infrastructure (such as the electrical power grid), the private sector[9] should take a more direct role in public security (Auerswald et al. 2006). These are all important and useful first steps, built on the premise that the decentralization of decision making and the shift of authority to local firms, communities, and residents are necessary.[10] For example, scholars have stressed the need for community-based laboratories that can better identify and propose solutions to the myriad environmental and health problems that threaten post-disaster recovery (Nance 2009). Many experts have already argued the need for community-managed health clinics (Banerjee, Deaton, and Duflo 2004), schools (King and Orazem 1999; Jimenez and Sawada 1999), and locally focused targeting of poverty (Galasso and Ravallion 2005), along with civilian-military joint community preparedness programs (Moore et al. 2010). Planners have emphasized the work carried out by the nonprofit and charitable sectors at the local, regional, and national levels through organizations such as the Red Cross, Jewish Family Services, and the YMCA (Boris and Steuerle 2006).

But, recognizing the implications of the empirical evidence brought together here from four megadisasters over time and space, planners and scholars alike should work to incorporate local social networks and social capital into schemes for both mitigation and recovery (Zhao 2010). As one disaster relief planner pointed out, "Recovery, here as in other disasters, will depend as much, if not more, on the support provided by neighbors and friends as on the help of strangers" (Darcy 2004, 5). Put another way, "Human recovery goes beyond infrastructure recovery to include restoring the social and daily routines and support networks that foster physical and mental health and promote well-being (Chandra and Acosta 2009, 1). Our job should be to "apply classic lessons in grassroots organizing in new ways to encourage participating and leading new and renewed civic institutions that tackle critical disaster recovery problems" (Berke and Campanella 2006, 205). To rebuild disaster-affected cities "physically without a concomitant commitment to recovering the social fabric and the human infrastructure" results in cities that are at best only shadows of their former selves (Lang and Danielson 2006, 247).

When dealing with disaster recovery, private and public sector decision makers should first recognize that stores of social capital—like other fungible assets—can be increased (or decreased) through both internal and external interventions (see also Tatsuki 2009). Thanks to maps that combine GIS data with past disaster outcomes and census data, we can clearly identify socially vulnerable locations (Cutter and Emrich 2006; Cutter and Finch 2008). The next step is to build up the trust and networks in these areas before and after crises. Hamlets, villages, and towns even in poor, developing nations can increase their stocks of structural and cognitive social capital. Scholars have carried out extensive research in rural Indian villages to demonstrate that trust, interactions, and informal networks can develop and strengthen over time because of self-initiated local organizations and local leaders (Krishna 2007). Further, external programs—not just locally initiated ones—can strengthen existing civil society and create new bonds between citizens. One study of two hundred households in post-conflict Nicaragua showed that targeted programs promoting management and leadership development improved both local trust and civic participation. Local residents in the program attended more community meetings, made larger contributions to local organizations, and were more likely than nonparticipants to take part in protests and mobilizations (Brune and Bossert 2009).

A similar two-year randomized field experiment in South Africa produced strong evidence that interventions can create higher levels of trust and community participation among residents. Using group-based microfinance practices along with workshops on trust building and HIV and gender training, the research team showed higher levels of collective action such as civic protests after a local injustice (Pronyk et al. 2008). In these studies, the communities under observation have not been wealthy and often have low levels of education, yet social capital proved effective even in these challenging environments.

Currently experimental methods for increasing social capital include policies that give incentives for community participation. In some programs in Japan and the United States, volunteers receive payment in currencies known as scrip, which they can exchange for services from local merchants (Lietaer 2004). Although these community currencies can take multiple forms—including paper, electronic, and "eco money" systems (Doteuchi 2002)—their goal is to bring more individuals into contact with each other and with local authorities in nonmarket activities such as attending town meetings and picking up litter. Encouraging citizens to serve food at homeless shelters or assist the weak at elder hostels, serve as Big Brothers, or work together pro bono on building new homes can increase stores of social capital and deepen trust. A survey of 1,200 people in Japan provided quantitative evidence that participating in community currency programs increased trust levels (Richey 2007). Further, children's participation in community service, Boys and Girls Clubs, and other events can speed up psychological and social network recovery after disasters (Pfefferbaum, Pfefferbaum, and Norris 2009). In another trial approach, one resident decided he would personally create stronger networks in his neighborhood in New York by asking twenty or so of his neighbors if he could sleep over at their houses to get to know them. Roughly half of them said yes, and as a result, the community supported a local woman with breast cancer who needed help (Lovenheim 2008).

Another mechanism for increasing social capital in vulnerable or disrupted areas is to create or reconstruct local institutions—such as children's halls, community development centers, and play schools—which provide residents with new sources of information along with links to each other and to external agencies. Many scholars have argued for the creation of these "neighborhood resilience centers," which provide information and resources and serve as the "point of entry for volunteer labor as well as philanthropic donations" (Vale 2006, 164). These organizations may be hosts for weekly, monthly, or annual festivals, which themselves have been shown to create deeper levels of trust and social capital in communities (Bhandari et al. 2010). Beyond such specialized groups, standard local institutions such as kindergartens, elementary schools (Ono 1998; Kobayashi 2006; Small 2009), faith-based organizations, and cooperative housing (Murosaki 1973; Sekikawa, Sakurai, and Song 2006) all play critical roles as repositories of and hubs for social networks. Such institutions serve as formal or informal community centers, offer a way to rebuild social networks, and provide a sense of normality and stability along with food, counseling, and support (Kilmer, Gil-Rivas, and MacDonald 2009). Synagogues, churches, and mosques can also reconnect families and congregation members to each other and thus help to repair and create social networks (Phillips and Jenkins 2009).

Urban and suburban infrastructure design itself can also influence levels of social capital (see Jacobs [1961] 1992). In designing new communities—whether as post-disaster housing or during noncrisis periods—we must alter their layout to increase interaction among residents. Oscar Newman's often-cited work on designing "defensible space" in urban communities underscored that the social fabric of the local community could be enhanced and extended through the deliberate design of residential environments. He advocated designing housing so that local residents adopt it as their own territory, enforcing their norms and creating respect for the property and security of neighbors (Newman 1972, 1996). Several studies argue broadly that that walkable, mixed-use neighborhoods (Leyden 2003), along with intentional communities and shared housing (Poley and Stephenson 2007), encourages the development of bonds among neighbors by creating areas where regular interactions are more likely (Putnam 2000; Williamson 2010; although see Freeman 2001 and Brueckner and Largey 2006 for opposing views). For example, "Homes punctuated by front porches and short setbacks from streets (not garages and long driveways) encourage street frontage spaces that are designed for people, not automobiles" (Berke and Campanella 2006, 197). Although real-world organizations and urban design have demonstrated their effectiveness at building bonds, virtual communities are the next frontier for social capital–based policies.

Communications technologies have changed dramatically over the past century; whereas residents of Tokyo in the 1920s used physical bulletin boards (*keijiban*) to diffuse information through the neighborhood, most residents in 2012 use mobile and smart phones to stay in contact with their networks of friends.[11] Internet-based frameworks for social networks are starting to come into their own during and after crisis situations in a variety of contexts.[12] Some researchers have experimented with using social networking services after disasters—similar to the well-known platforms Facebook, LinkedIn, Twitter, and Orkut—and reported mixed results, perhaps owing to a lack of support, lack of access to power or Internet-connected devices after crisis, or the newness of the technology (Schellong 2007). Other studies of networking technologies have suggested that they work well at disseminating information about emergencies when standard institutions are incapacitated (White et al. 2009). However, recent disasters have shown that these often unmoderated technologies can be used maliciously. Google set up a bilingual English/Japanese "Person Finder" website to help survivors locate each other after the March 2011 Tohoku earthquake and tsunami in Japan, and anecdotal evidence suggested that its 140,000 records provided assistance to many seeking lost family members. But at it was vulnerable to sick hoaxes and spam deliberately reporting the deaths of some who were still alive (*MetroNews UK*, 14 March 2011; *Japan Probe*, 14 March 2011).

The virtual organization Neighborhood Partnerships Network (NPN; online at npnnola.com) in New Orleans has worked to bring together the hundreds of local neighborhood associations, NGOs, volunteer groups, and faith-based organizations that seek to improve the quality of life since Katrina (Rick Weil, pers. comm., 25 March 2010). After the Haiti earthquake, many volunteer groups used GIS technology to speed up the delivery of aid, medical supplies, and food to victims throughout the country (Zook et al. 2010). For developing nations where cellular technology has less penetration, older technologies such as radios have proved effective. In Tamil Nadu, for example, local activists took the initiative to set up a low-power private community radio station (Radio Alaakal) to keep fishermen informed of day-to-day happenings and data (such as current weather conditions, fish prices, and events) and to issue alerts in the case of emergencies (such as future tsunami) (Nandakumar 2006). More research is necessary to see how effective virtual communities can be in creating and maintaining social ties and disseminating critical facts during disasters (Jaeger et al. 2007).

Most broadly, social capital thrives in a political and cultural environment where residents believe in their efficacy as citizens and trust each other and their representatives (Bailer, Bodenstein, and Heinrich 2007). When failing states such as Haiti undergo tragedy, donors and United Nation personnel should seek to go beyond simply delivering food, water, and medical supplies. Their ambition should stretch to helping overhaul governance mechanisms to build new institutions that will interact positively with social resources; some have argued that without an effective state it may be difficult to sustain strong civil society and resilience (Paker 2004; Savitch 2007). As seen in regions of Italy, stronger civic cultures themselves can influence governance, but frameworks and effective political institutions create virtuous cycles of reinforcement between the two (Putnam 1993). Recognizing the power and resources held by nation-states, scholars have strongly advocated that governments promote civic engagement and collaborative governance to enhance citizens' participation in policy making (Sirianni 2009), especially because typical "urban renewal" policies may in fact decrease the mobilization capacity of voluntary organizations (Widestrom 2008). All of these policy possibilities—from community currency to institutional reform—must be on the table if decision makers want to move beyond the outdated structures that continue to define our response to crises at home and abroad.

Finally, once planners have begun to incorporate social resources into their disaster mitigation and recovery plans, they also must recognize the potential downside of high levels of social capital. In India and other nations where caste systems remain strong (despite attempts within the legal system to eliminate them), planners must recognize the role of caste and look for its interaction with social capital. That is, "Discrimination in relief provision—on the basis of caste, gender and economic status—must be tackled" (Banerjee and Chaudhury 2005, 43). Based on the cases here, strong bonding social capital was most likely to create negative outcomes for peripheral groups in conditions of strong hierarchy (such as in India, with its caste system), high homogeneity (such as 1920s Japan, where Koreans and other non-Japanese were often viewed negatively), and broad inequality (such as late twentieth-century New Orleans, where historical legacies of racism and exclusion continue). Further studies should be done to pin down the exact conditions responsible for these outcomes, but with even a broad understanding of the problems, policy makers can start considering potential solutions.

Given extensive research showing that bonding social capital by itself cannot do more than help communities "get by," effective new programs seek to promote bridging and linking social capital along with deepening local connections (De Souza Briggs 1998, 178; Woolcock and Narayan 2000, 227; Elliott, Haney, and Sams-Abiodun 2010). Local residents who interact and enhance their relationships with government officials in recovery efforts create stronger community involvement; in China, such activities sped up returns to normality and strengthened feelings of efficacy (Chen et al. 2011). Institutions such as Mumbai's Tata Institute have set up training seminars in India for tribal groups and other minorities, who often lack the social resources and external connections found in other groups.

Dalits, women, and other often excluded groups may have a chance to access recovery materials and extralocal organizations through these new connections and skill sets. Scholars traced the important involvement of the Self Employed Women's Association both in post-disaster recovery and in generating self-reliance through programs focused on employing women and helping them with long-term planning and needs (Vaux and Lund 2003). Such programs hope to equalize social resources among groups that may see themselves as competing for assistance. In New Orleans and other North American cities, planners must think carefully about how to design schemes for recovery that can operate given the barriers of personal and institutional racism. Along with seeking to actively build stocks of social capital among groups who lack it, future policy work should follow up on initial studies (Djupe, Sokhey, and Gilbert 2007) and further illuminate the interaction between gender, social capital, and aid distribution.

A handful of innovators in some sectors have already taken notice of social infrastructure in post-crisis environments and have sought to incorporate it in their policies (Koh and Cadigan 2008). The United States Department of Agriculture published a report titled *Homeowners, Communities, and Wildfire: Science Findings from the National Fire Plan,* in which planners recognized the need to integrate social capital into plans for improving community preparedness for wildfires (Jakes 2002). Japanese law enforcement personnel have written openly about the critical post-crisis role for local volunteers who know disaster-struck neighborhoods and can respond more efficiently than centralized planners (Araki 2003). Officials within the Seattle Office of Emergency Management have set up a disaster response plan titled Seattle Neighborhoods Actively Prepare (SNAP), which describes explicit roles for local homeowners and residents. The SNAP guidelines point out, "Even without a plan, it is surprising how quickly communities with healthy institutions and effective leaders can organize. . . . Healthy communities will be able to quickly identify these resources and agree on how they should be distributed. They will be able to coordinate with the official response as it becomes available." The program helps local residents plan ways of coordinating their efforts and provides training in CPR, first aid, and other skills.

Several other cities and states—including Louisiana (with the Louisiana Family Recovery Corps [LFRC]), Florida, California, San Francisco, and Los Angeles—have disaster response plans that directly involve local residents and communities.[13] In San Francisco, the city government organized block parties on the anniversary of the 1989 Loma Prieta earthquake to help residents approach disaster preparedness through communal events (McKinley 2009). Social workers have emphasized the ways they can assist communities to locate "natural sources of positive social capital" internally as well as externally in the recovery (Hawkins and Maurer 2010). Similarly, the Tulane Community Organizing Research Project has sought to help nonprofits and volunteer groups in the city maximize their impact on the course of recovery (Pyles 2007).

International programs have also begun to incorporate social resources into their endeavors in a variety of programs intended to better integrate social networks into public policy programs. USAID, for example, has provided $140 million for the Iraq Community Action Program to mobilize local citizens for decision making and to strengthen local governance. Archaeologists struggling to protect national treasures from looters have described how local community members—not centralized law enforcement personnel—most effectively combat pillaging at archaeological sites in Peru, Iraq, and elsewhere (Atwood 2009). New research on recovery has focused explicitly on community level, not just individual, indicators, and it rests on recognizing the role of communities and NGOs as critical for rebuilding (Hyogo Earthquake Memorial Twenty-First Century Research Institute). These plans are few, far between, and only occasionally based on empirically supported theoretical foundations. Scholars of social capital must clearly articulate the role that networks and social resources can play in pre- and post-disaster planning.

There are visible signs of progress in the academic and public policy communities. In New Orleans, for example, new programs such as FastStart, working alongside legislative ethic reforms, have sought to create more viable social frameworks for recovery (*Economist*, 17 October 2009). A variety of NGOs and local civil society organizations including Mercy Corps, Kids with Cameras, Architecture for Humanity, and Global Green have sought to assist resource-poor residents in New Orleans in their recovery (Curtis 2007, 26). Other NPOs such as Roots of Music have created social frameworks for school-age children to engage with adult mentors and build not only musical talent but broader connections to local institutions (author interviews, 2010). Programs like these provide linking capital and new connections to survivors who otherwise may not come in regular positive contact with authority figures and decision makers.

While many decision makers and scholars still focus on physical structure, we now understand that "economic and social networks are more resilient than buildings. Buildings crumble, but human resources remain" (Olshansky 2006, 17). We must use our knowledge of the power of social networks to help survivors and planners build resilience through deliberate policies leveraging the power of people, not just physical infrastructure. Ensuring that social capital is on the agenda will create future plans that generate effective and efficient recovery and build resilient communities.

Appendix 1: Statistical Tables

TABLE A1. Means of treated and control groups and reduction in bias

Variable	Sample	Mean for treated	Mean for control	Percent bias	Percent reduction |bias|	t-test	p > t
Area of the precinct (square km)	Unmatched	2.1309	1.92	21.1		1.49	0.138
	Matched	1.8505	1.7306	12	43.1	0.03	0.977
Crime damage (in yen) per capita	Unmatched	14.97	2.7439	41.9		3.85	0.000
	Matched	3.0993	2.8058	1	97.6	−0.22	0.828
Factory workers per capita	Unmatched	0.1293	0.04819	58.2		5.34	0.000
	Matched	0.04215	0.05055	−6	89.6	−1.4	0.164
Number of commercial cars and trucks per capita	Unmatched	0.03411	0.00511	50.2		4.75	0.000
	Matched	0.00624	0.00628	−0.1	99.9	−1.54	0.125
Pawnbroker lending per capita	Unmatched	10.18	9.6944	10		0.7	0.482
	Matched	10.93	10.816	2.3	76.5	−1.22	0.223
Percentage of residents killed in the quake	Unmatched	0.01593	0.03279	−29.8		−1.8	0.073
	Matched	0.02183	0.02429	−4.3	85.4	0.74	0.461
Shitamachi dummy variable	Unmatched	0.55357	0.60112	−9.6		−0.63	0.530
	Matched	0.65789	0.60526	10.6	−10.7	0.74	0.460

TABLE A2. Average treatment effects for the social capital variables

Matching method	ATE for higher than average number of political gatherings	Number of observations on common support	ATE for higher than average voter turnout	Number of observations on common support
Kernel	0.019545	207	0.03337	53
Radius	0.020617	207	0.038703	55
Nearest neighbor without replacement	0.02391	76	0.037115	52
Nearest neighbor	0.02011	207	0.040164	55
Mahalanobis	0.02319	207	0.034442	55

Note: Matching was carried out on area of the precinct (square km), crime damage (in yen) per capita, factory workers per capita, number of commercial cars and trucks per capita, pawnbroker lending per capita, percentage of residents killed in the quake, and Shitamachi dummy variable.

TABLE A3. Estimated variable impact on population growth rate

Variable	Coefficients from TSCS model 1 (random effects, GLS)	Coefficients from TSCS model 2 (random effects, GLS)	Coefficients from TSCS model 3 (fixed effects)	Coefficients from TSCS model 4 (panel-corrected standard errors)
Area of the precinct	0.00306	.00126	...	.00126
(square km)	(0.0045)	(.0075)		(.0029)
Crime damage	−0.00014	−.00026	−.000143	−.00026
(in yen) per capita	(.0003)	(.0013)	(0.0004)	(.0016)
Factory workers per	−0.0424	−.0451	−.928	−.045
capita	(0.073)	(.126)	(0.35)	(.093)
Number of commercial	−0.0552	−.00835	−.243	−.00835
cars and trucks	(0.245)	(1.08)	(0.335)	(1.39)
per capita				
Pawnbroker lending	−0.00079	−.00059	−.003	−.00059
per capita	(0.00093)	(.0015)	(0.001)	(.001)
Percentage of residents	0.0876	.0889	...	.0889
killed in the quake	(0.0611306)	(.0979)		(.056)
Shitamachi	0.0208**	.0363**	...	.0363
dummy variable	(0.0098)	(.0176)		(.029)
Voter turnout in	...	.00165*	...	.00165***
municipal elections		(.00094)		(.0004)
(1929 and 1933)				
Higher than average	.0181**	.0209**	.0440***	.0209***
numbers of political	(0.0083)	(.011)	(0.012)	(.0085)
gatherings per year				
(dummy)				
_cons	0.0055	−.11	.104	−.11
sigma_u	0.0000	0.0000		
sigma_e	0.0490	0.0470		
Observations	234	78	234	78

Note: Standard errors are listed underneath the estimated coefficients. $*p < 0.1$, $**p < 0.05$, $***p < 0.01$.

TABLE A4. Coefficients for three models of population growth rate

Dependent variable: population growth rate	Model 1: fixed effects	Model 2: panel-corrected standard errors	Model 3: Prais-Winsten regression (panel-corrected standard errors with first-order autocorrelation)
Population growth rate (lagged)	0.131***	0.267***	0.230***
	0.042	0.063	0.059
Percentage of population affected by the earthquake	(dropped)	0.011**	0.011**
		0.004	0.005
Welfare-dependent households per capita	−0.983***	−1.73***	−1.69***
	0.334	0.388	0.414
NPOs created per capita (lagged)	43.01**	90.1***	84.7***
	20.950	27.700	28.00
Population density	−0.00001	−0.000008***	0.00***
	0.000	0.000	0.000
Socioeconomic inequality (lagged)	0.027	0.022***	0.021***
	0.018	0.006	0.005
_cons	0.074	0.035	0.035
	0.059	0.006	0.007
sigma_u	0.024		
sigma_e	0.003		
rho	0.989		0.215

Note: Standard errors are listed underneath the estimated coefficients. **$p < 0.05$, ***$p < 0.01$.

TABLE A5. Estimated coefficients for days spent in IDP camps

Dependent variable: days spent in IDP camps	Negative binomial (IRR)
Nagapattinam District (dummy)	0.314***
	0.13
Cuddalore District (dummy)	0.356***
	0.14
Thiruvallur District (dummy)	0.153***
	0.08
Scheduled Tribe percentage	1.24
	0.77
Scheduled Caste percentage	2.26**
	0.88
Most Backward Caste percentage	1.83
	0.83
Homes owned per family	2.34
	1.46
Percentage of families making between 0 and 500 rupees per week	1.33
	0.40
Contact only with the government of India	1.22
	0.48
Contact only with NGOs, private organizations, political parties, or the villagers themselves	1.85
	1.06
Contact with the government and at least one other group	2.31
	1.23
/lnalpha	−0.52
	0.20
alpha	0.59
	0.12
N	61

Note: Standard errors are listed underneath the estimated coefficients. ***$p < 0.01$, **$p < 0.05$, *$p < 0.1$.

TABLE A6. Estimated coefficients for percentage of eligible families receiving supplies

Dependent variable: percentage of eligible families receiving relief supplies	Two-limit tobit
Nagapattinam District (dummy)	0.206**
	0.091
Cuddalore District (dummy)	0.171*
	0.097
Thiruvallur District (dummy)	−0.157
	0.125
Homes owned per family	0.669***
	0.164
Percentage of families making between 0 and 500 rupees per week	0.003
	0.074
Contact only with the government of India	−0.032
	0.105
Contact only with NGOs, private organizations, political parties, or the villagers themselves	0.283**
	0.145
Contact with the government and at least one other group	0.224
	0.137
Constant	−0.099
	0.255
/sigma	0.217
	0.021
N	62

Note: Standard errors are listed underneath the estimated coefficients. ***$p < 0.01$, **$p < 0.05$, *$p < 0.1$.

TABLE A7. Estimated coefficients for percentage of eligible families receiving 4,000 rupees

Dependent variable: percentage of eligible families receiving 4,000 rupees	Two-limit tobit
Nagapattinam District (dummy)	0.839***
	0.32
Cuddalore District (dummy)	0.36
	0.36
Kanyakumari District (dummy)	1.348***
	0.52
Scheduled Caste percentage	−0.555*
	0.29
Percentage of families making 300 rupees per week or less	−0.10
	0.35
Homes owned per capita	5.3*
	2.72
Constant	−0.48
	0.77
/sigma	0.56
	0.14
N	43

Note: Standard errors are listed underneath the estimated coefficients. ***$p < 0.01$, **$p < 0.05$, *$p < 0.1$.

TABLE A8. Estimated coefficients for amount of relief aid

Outcome: amount of relief aid (rupees)	OLS standardized coefficient	Standard error
Age (at tsunami)	113.2983*	69.87
Education	531.3972**	215.89
Sex (male = 1)	1348.45	2336.88
Position in family (head, wife, child, parent, grandchild, grandparent, nephew, parent-in-law)	−462.69	1049.46
Marital status (1 = married, 2 = not married, 3 = divorced, 4 = widow)	3632.174*	2194.69
Family business/self-employed (dummy)	7508.94	6305.45
Hired worker (dummy)	3422.71	5098.57
Housewife/unpaid family worker (dummy)	2554.76	3823.82
Student (dummy)	2508.93	2972.72
Fisher (dummy)	−3765.36	5717.20
Farmer (dummy)	−5657.78	6096.20
Family lost house in tsunami (dummy)	63248.08***	4344.40
Family lost member in tsunami (dummy)	62705.87***	3858.21
Family's house or assets damaged by tsunami (dummy)	4774.193*	2600.10
Family Scheduled Caste	(dropped)	
Family Scheduled Tribe	(dropped)	
Family Backward Caste	19692.5***	5832.24
Family Most Backward Caste	24140.7***	5662.22
Family relief aid from government only	6630.818*	3955.60
Family relief aid from NGO sources only	12295.28**	5773.28
Family relief from government and NGO	6796.793*	3440.31
Family contact with government only (Dec.-Jan.)	−1923.06	2736.80
Family contact with government only (Jan.-Feb.)	−22514.87***	3092.38
Number of funerals family attended (Oct.–Dec. '04)	558.8231***	187.86
Amount of money family gave at weddings (Oct.–Dec. '04)	16.32697***	4.76
Constant	−27144.27	10009.67

Note: $*p < 0.1$, $**p < 0.05$, $**p < 0.01$.

TABLE A9. Negative binominal regression model coefficients

Dependent variable: number of trailer units (negative binomial model)	Co-efficient	Robust standard error	z	P > |z|	Low 95 percent confidence interval	High 95 percent confidence interval
New Orleans (dummy variable)	0.986198	0.412185	2.39	0.017	0.17833	1.794065
Area	−0.001488	0.001146	−1.3	0.194	−0.00374	0.000758
Population density	−0.000165	0.000044	−3.74	0.001	−0.00025	−7.8E-05
House prices	−8.72E-07	5.47E-06	−0.16	0.873	−1.2E-05	9.85E-06
Percentage of population who attended high school	0.033492	0.013797	2.43	0.015	0.006451	0.060533
Percentage of population who are not white	0.014204	0.005586	2.54	0.011	0.003255	0.025154
Percentage of population who are unemployed	−0.211801	0.064027	−3.31	0.001	−0.33729	−0.08631
Voter turnout	−5.26376	1.495056	−3.52	0.000	−8.19402	−2.3335
Flood damage	0.20741	0.085361	2.43	0.015	0.040106	0.374714
_cons	7.249693	1.08301	6.69	0	5.127032	9.372355
/lnalpha	/lnalpha	−0.127247	0.120351		−0.36313	0.108637
alpha	alpha	0.880516	0.105971		0.695496	1.114757

TABLE A10. Negative binominal regression model coefficients

Dependent variable: number of trailer parks (negative binomial model, robust standard errors)	Coefficient	Robust standard error	z	P > |z|	Low 95 percent confidence interval	High 95 percent confidence interval
New Orleans (dummy variable)	1.182	0.397	2.980	0.003	0.405	1.959
Area	−0.001	0.001	−1.210	0.224	−0.003	0.001
Population density	0.000	0.000	−0.210	0.835	0.000	0.000
House prices	0.000	0.000	−0.940	0.347	0.000	0.000
Percentage of population who attended high school	0.038	0.010	3.670	0.000	0.018	0.059
Percentage of population who are not white	0.006	0.005	1.380	0.168	−0.003	0.016
Percentage of population who are unemployed	−0.078	0.052	−1.490	0.135	−0.181	0.024
Voter turnout	−5.278	1.460	−3.610	0.000	−8.140	−2.416
Flood damage	0.186	0.096	1.920	0.054	−0.003	0.374
_cons	2.115	0.897	2.360	0.018	0.358	3.873
/lnalpha	−1.109	0.190			−1.482	−0.736
alpha	0.330	0.063			0.227	0.479

Appendix 2: Interviewees

India

(twenty-seven individual interviews)

NONGOVERNMENTAL ORGANIZATIONS

NGO Coordination and Resource Center (NGOCRC)
South Indian Federation of Fishermen Societies
People's Watch

ACADEMIC INSTITUTIONS

Tata Institute of Social Sciences
Jawaharlal Nehru University
Dakshin Foundation
M. S. Swaminathan Research Foundation

Japan

(twenty individual interviews)

LOCAL GOVERNMENT

Kobe Institute of Urban Research

NONGOVERNMENTAL ORGANIZATIONS

Shibafu Spirit
NGO Collaboration Center for Hanshin Quake Rehabilitation
Nakayoshikai
Kobe Shimin Koryukai
Higashi-Nada Chiiki Tasukeai Nettowa-ku

ACADEMIC INSTITUTIONS

Kobe University
Tokyo University
Tokyo Metropolitan University
Ishinomaki Senshu University

New Orleans

(thirty individual interviews)

LOCAL GOVERNMENT

New Orleans City Hall

NONGOVERNMENTAL ORGANIZATIONS

Bywater Neighborhood Association
Central City Partnership
Chabad Lubavitch of New Orleans
Committee for a Better New Orleans (CBNO)
East New Orleans Neighborhood Advisory Commission
Gentilly Terrace and Gardens Improvement Association
Holy Cross Neighborhood Association
Jewish Federation of New Orleans
Kid Camera Project
Louisiana Association of Nonprofit Organizations (LANO)
Louisiana Family Recovery Corps
Mary Queen of Vietnam Catholic Church and Community Development
    Center
Roots of Music
Touro Bouligny Neighborhood Association

Trinity Christian Community
United Jewish Communities

ACADEMIC INSTITUTIONS

Tulane University
University of New Orleans

CONSULTANTS AND PLANNING FIRMS

AFL-CIO Investment Trust
Concordia, LLC

Notes

Chapter One

1. Using the language of "collective efficacy," Daniel Alesch, Lucy Arendt, and James Holly (2009, 50) similarly point out the importance of community mobilization, coordination, and collective action in disaster recovery.

2. Owing to a lack of consistent neighborhood-level data on insurance, this book does not test the role of private insurance (or its absence) on recovery. However, available information on these four disasters indicates that many victims did not have insurance, and it is unlikely that insurance itself serves as a critical engine for recovery. In Kobe, for example, "only 3 percent of property in the Kobe area was covered by earthquake indemnity" (Edgington 2010, 10). With America's market-based approach to recovery, authorities assume that individuals will receive necessary assistance from private insurance. Yet observers estimated that fewer than half of the homes affected by Hurricane Katrina had federal flood coverage (Taylor 2006, 26), while only one-third of Lower Ninth Ward households had coverage under the National Flood Insurance Program (Bates and Green 2009). Others have stated that an exceptionally high number of Louisiana residents were uninsured (New Orleans Health Disparities Initiative 2007, 2). Broadly, North American homeowners display similar risk strategies: of the more than 1,500 victims of floods in Vermont in 1998, more than 80 percent of homeowners in the flood areas did not hold insurance (despite laws mandating coverage) (Kunreuther 2010, 243), and this was similar to the level of the uninsured among West Virginia homeowners living in floodplains (*State Journal*, 18 June 2009). Few of the Indian residents in coastal villages in Tamil Nadu had insurance on their boats, nets, or homes (author interviews, 2008). Some have called this lack of adoption of cost-effective, loss-reduction measures *natural disaster syndrome* (Kunreuther 2007); it is well established empirically that disaster victims themselves are actually less likely to adopt risk mitigation measures after experiencing crisis (Lin, Shaw, and Ho 2008).

3. Albala-Bertrand further distinguishes between "complex humanitarian emergencies" (such as civil unrest and civil war) and natural disasters, arguing that the effects of complex emergencies are primarily institutional and fully endogenous, while those of natural disasters are random and only partially endogenous (2000).

4. Many have pointed out that the "sinking of New Orleans was a man-made debacle" (Brinkley 2007, 426).

5. For an update of the work done by Dacy and Kunreuther, see Okuyama 2003.

6. Some observers labeled the crisis the worst since Chernobyl (*ABC News,* 15 March 2011), while Germany's chancellor Angela Merkel called it a turning point in the history of the industrial world (*Economist,* 15 March 2011).

7. One study of villagers in Tamil Nadu after the Indian Ocean tsunami showed that women were more likely than men to suffer from posttraumatic stress disorder (Kumar et al. 2007). (For a study of how levels of social capital correlate with stress post-disaster, see Weil, Shihadeh, and Lee 2006, and for psychological perspectives on disaster recovery see Golec 1980; Silberbauer 2003; Capewell 2004; and Kilmer et al. 2009.)

8. Takashima and Hayashi (1999) even used consumption of electricity to measure recovery after the 1995 Kobe earthquake. Perhaps because of these varying approaches, scholars have warned about the difficulties in generalizing about the course of recovery (Bates and Peacock 1989).

9. Peacock and Ragsdale (2000, 25) point out that community recovery occurs when local groups "attempt to re-establish social networks to carry out the routines of daily life." Other scholars have similarly emphasized that "disaster and dislocation are not events but *processes* that unfold over time" (Elliott, Haney, and Sams-Abiodun 2010, 628).

10. Recognizing that bringing back pre-catastrophe conditions is unlikely, Alesch, Arendt, and Holly define community recovery as having occurred when the community "repairs or develops social, political, and economic processes, institutions and relationships that enable it to function in the new context within which it finds itself" (2009, 36).

11. The United Nations International Strategy for Disaster Reduction defined resilience as "the capacity of a system, community or society potentially exposed to hazards to adapt, by resisting or changing in order to reach and maintain an acceptable level of functioning and structure. This is determined by the degree to which the social system is capable of organising itself to increase this capacity for learning from past disasters for better future protection and to improve risk reduction measures" (2005, 4n7).

12. For an extended critique of FEMA, see Perrow 2007, chaps. 3 and 4; Brinkley (2007) has sharp words for FEMA and also criticizes Ray Nagin, then mayor of New Orleans. Other observers have listed flaws with FEMA's process for paying for repairs under its "public assistance" program (Eaton 2007b).

13. The Japanese government learned from its experiences with temporary housing, so when the Chūetsu earthquake struck Niigata Prefecture a decade or so later in 2004, neighbors were placed together in community housing as opposed to being randomly relocated (Yasu Sawada, pers. comm., 25 March 2010).

14. For a detailed overview of federal disaster programs, see Syzerhans 2006.

15. Similarly, quantitative studies of foreign aid have found very limited conditions under which such financial assistance improves the income growth of the recipient (Burnside and Dollar 2000), and later economic studies have found even less evidence of actual progress (Roodman 2007).

16. According to experts, the average period of education provided for girls working in agriculture in rural India was only two years (Ramakumar 2008).

17. For a discussion of the difficulties caused by the initial introduction of motorized fishing boats into the Tamil Nadu fishing community, see Bavinck (1997). After the tsunami, some hamlets saw the number of fishing boats double, creating a shortage of manpower and pulling

children out of school to help their fathers in the industry. To understand the problems associated with the overprovision of boats, see Daniel 2005.

18. Jane Jacobs makes a similar argument in her classic work on American cities, where she points out that billions of dollars in urban development have not rebuilt cities, but rather have sacked them (Jacobs [1961] 1992, 4).

19. For a comparative perspective on the need for affordable housing, see Daniels and Steinberg 2006.

20. As Putnam pointed out (2000, 136), trusting one other person by itself is not sufficient to build generalized expectations of reciprocity and influence broader social behavior in a community or society. Rather, residents must have the broader capability of being able to trust others whom they may not know well at all; this norm is most efficacious when widespread at the community level.

21. A new study of Kobe's post-earthquake reconstruction similarly underscores the role played by "local community attitudes and relationships with governments" (Edgington 2010, 22).

22. Social scientists recognize that measurement is a perennial problem with concepts such as social capital, and I understand that not all readers will be convinced that the measures used here accurately capture norms of trust and the exchange of information. While the community and individual proxies that I use, such as mass mobilization, connections with translocal NGOs, and voter turnout, have been relied on by past scholars, other experts may disagree about their interpretation. However, even with different measures of social capital, these quantitative analyses show that densely connected communities recover more effectively after disaster. I return to the issue of measurement in chapter 2.

23. One observer of post-Katrina New Orleans described reasons that people exited the Big Easy to settle elsewhere: "The old house was gone. The neighborhood was empty. The friends were missing" (quoted in Nossiter 2007). In interviews, a Japanese community organizer argued that "people returned to the damaged neighborhood because they wanted to maintain their relationship with their neighbors" (15 February 2008).

24. This is similar to economic arguments about the "fallacy of composition" (Fafchamps 2006) in that strongly connected individuals and groups benefit from higher levels of social capital, but other groups and perhaps society as a whole may not. Some have labeled this condition "individually remunerative yet socially unproductive" (Yasuyuki Sawada, pers. comm., 25 March 2010).

25. Kruks-Wisner refers to these groups instead as "traditional panchayats" (2011).

26. For a discussion of the role of citizen expectations after disaster, see Chamlee-Wright and Storr 2010.

27. "In Kobe, as elsewhere in Japan, there was no general compensation system to allow households to recover after a disaster" (Edgington 2010, 214). Initially, two Japanese laws were relevant to survivors: the Core Law for Countermeasures against Great Disasters (Saigai taisaku kihon hō) and the Livelihood Assistance Act (Saigai kyūjo hō); neither allowed compensation for loss of personal assets. In 1998, some three years after the Kobe earthquake, the national government passed the Livelihood Recovery Support Act (Hisaisha seikatsu saiken shien hō) and further amended the law in 2004. While this law created a fund for compensating victims of disasters, it was not retroactive for victims of earlier disasters (Sawada, Ichimura, and Shimizutani 2008).

28. Putnam has argued that neighborhoods with greater diversity display less cooperation and trust (Putnam 2007).

Chapter Two

1. George Simmel was among the first to mention a form of bridging or linking social capital, in his writings about the existence of brokers—that is, individuals who connect cliques and groups that otherwise share no direct ties (see Simmel [1908] 1950).

2. Clifford Geertz (1962) was among the first to point out the role of rotating credit associations (also known as mutual lending societies, pooling clubs, and thrift groups). More recently, social science has focused on microfinance and microcredit, in which small loans and grants are provided to residents of developing nations (see, for example, Tedeschi 2008 and Yunus 2008).

3. The standard trust game consists of two players; each individual is given money and a chance to send it anonymously to the other. Player A can choose to give none, some, or all of her money to player B; player B then decides how much to send back (if she received anything). While the predicted Nash equilibrium is that the first player would give nothing to player B and that player B, if she receives anything, would hold it all, that result is actually rare. In thousands of games, players given ten dollars turned roughly half of it over to the other player, who then generally returned 90 percent of what she received.

4. These tribal or caste councils should not be confused with the institutions making up the official local tier of the Indian government known as the *panchayati raj* (see Johnson 2003 for a full discussion).

5. As another scholar argued, "One of the major decisions that communities encounter is between relocation and return—a decision between the opportunity of starting a new life in a new location or sustaining their pre-disaster livelihood" (Iuchi 2010, ii).

6. See the NGO *Coordination and Resource Center Newsletter* issue of 5 January 2006 for a discussion of the ways the minority status of Dalits in Tamil Nadu has made them an excluded community.

7. After the earthquake, the Communications Ministry sped up the licensing of radio stations throughout Japan, which would help stop the spread of rumors in the future (Kasza 1986, 750). And after the 1995 Kobe earthquake, activists set up the multilingual Radio FMYY in Kobe's Nagata Ward to provide information to minorities and foreigners in the area.

8. In communitarian perspectives, residents seek to collaborate collectively to solve problems, initiate conversations with others, and find a balance between group and individual rights and needs.

Chapter Three

1. Tokyo is in the region known as Kanto, and Japanese researchers refer to the 1923 quake as the Great Kanto Earthquake. For consistency, however, I refer to the disaster as the Tokyo earthquake. This chapter builds (with permission) on my article "Social, Not Physical, Infrastructure: The Critical Role of Civil Society in Disaster Recovery," *Disasters: The Journal of Disaster Studies, Policy and Management* 36, 3 (2012): 398–419.

2. Detailed photographs of the damage done to Tokyo can be found at the Brown University Library Center for Digital Initiatives, which houses the Dana and Vera Reynolds Collection; they are accessible online through http://dl.lib.brown.edu/repository2/repoman.php. Masuo Ogawa also documented the destruction in *Tōkyō shōshitsu—Kantō Daishinsai no hiroku* [The disappearance of Tokyo—Confidential papers on the Great Kanto Earthquake] (1973).

3. For technical details on the seismicity and geographic efforts of these massive tremors, see Takemura 2003.

4. The 1666 London fire, for example, burned only 1.8 million square meters, the 1871 Chicago fire burned 8.6 million, and the 1906 San Francisco fire destroyed 12.1 million. Tokyo had close to 33.5 million square meters burned (Tokyo Municipal Office 1930).

5. For a detailed study of the reconstruction of Kanazawa after the 1927 Hikoso fire, see Phillipps 2008. The 9.0 quake off Japan's northeastern shore in March 2011, which generated a twenty-five-foot tsunami, has claimed close to 10,000 lives.

6. Charles Fritz is said to have stated that "disasters are natural laboratories for studying underlying social processes" (Miller and Simile 1992).

7. Given the extreme kurtosis in the distribution of the number of political gatherings per precinct per year—with many having none and others having hundreds—I dichotomize this measure at its mean of sixty-seven demonstrations to measure whether having more rallies, marches, and demonstrations than average has an effect on population change.

8. Additional requirements for voting included living in the district for a year before the election and not receiving social welfare (Narita 2007, 194).

9. Observers may wonder if the rallies and marches in a community were, in fact, made up principally of local residents or of outsiders; perhaps certain neighborhoods, such as Hibiya, served as focal points for protest during this period. Historical studies show that during the 1920s and 1930s many neighborhoods actively protested specific local events—such as the plans by city authorities to place an incinerator in their backyard (Yamada 1973). Furthermore, tests of Hibiya and other popular gathering spots show that overall population growth in these areas was negative, not positive; hence we need not worry that this independent variable biases our estimates.

10. Additional merits of matching methods are their transparency in statistical identification (Angrist and Krueger 1999, 1315), fewer assumptions about model fit, less model dependence, less bias (Ho et al. 2007), and the observation that nontechnical audiences often find it "a persuasive method of adjusting for imbalances in observed covariates" (Rosenbaum and Rubin 1985, 33).

11. For technical details of the mathematics of matching, see Ho et al. 2007.

12. Nearest neighbor matching chooses the observation with the closest propensity score as a match; radius matching sets a limit on the gap distance between the matched propensity scores; kernel matching uses the averages of observations in the control group to create a match; and Mahalanobis matching randomly orders the observations and determines the propensity score gap between treated groups and controls. Allowing replacement in matching means that an observation can be matched more than once.

Chapter Four

1. This chapter uses (with permission) material from my article "The Power of People: Social Capital's Role in Recovery from the 1995 Kobe Earthquake," *Natural Hazards* 56, 3 (2010): 595–611.

2. Akira Nakamura (2000, 24-25) claims that the SDF remained at standstill for four hours after the crisis because of bureaucratic entanglement and concerns about who would pay for its operations. Kathleen Tierney and James Goltz (1997, 6) suggested that the lack of an official request from the governor, devastation of communications networks, logistical problems, the size of the event, and ambivalent attitudes toward the role of military in society were also responsible for the SDF's sluggish reaction (see also Yasui 2007, 97).

3. In many cases local residents had trained and served as volunteer firefighters in local fire

brigades. See Konishi 1998 and Haddad 2007, 2010 for details on these embedded volunteer groups.

4. According to Katsuji Tsuji (2001, 218, figs. 9-1 and 9-2), the Nagata District had 35 percent of its population in emergency housing after the earthquake, and it took a full year for them to return to permanent housing. In a similar-sized district of Fukushima, 70 percent of the population moved into emergency shelters, but all had moved out within one hundred days.

5. These organizations—composed of local volunteers who had been professionally trained as firefighters—are discussed by Konishi (1998) and Haddad (2010).

6. In the case of New Orleans, "proposals for a building moratorium were almost universally rejected by residents" (Kates et al. 2006, 14656). As a result, New Orleans has seen a "hasty, haphazard aesthetic that some planners warned would emerge unless officials seized on Katrina as an opportunity to rethink the Crescent City in a more systematic fashion" (Pogrebin 2007).

7. Since ADL models often create high levels of multicollinearity, I tested the data using the VIF approach and found relatively low levels of interaction among the variables (with a VIF of less than 7 for all models) (Rabe-Hesketh and Everitt 2007, 69). A second concern for ADLs is that variables within them remain strictly stationary. A multivariate augmented Dickey-Fuller test indicated that we can reject the null hypothesis that the processes for one-, two-, and three-period lags are nonstationary (that is, lack equilibrium). Further, the Hausman specification test determines whether a fixed or random effects model is more appropriate when using time series data, and it indicated that in this case a fixed effects model fit more closely (chi-square value of 0.0001).

8. The Sichuan earthquake in China similarly "strengthened civil society through increased capacity, publicity, and interaction with local government" (Teets 2009, 330).

Chapter Five

1. This chapter draws (with permission) on my articles "Separate and Unequal: Post-Tsunami Aid Distribution in Southern India," *Social Science Quarterly* 91, 4 (2010): 1369–89, and "The Externalities of Social Capital: Post-Tsunami Recovery in Southeast India," *Journal of Social Capital* 8, 1 (2011): 81–99.

2. For an extended description of the multiple forms of discrimination against Dalits, see Navsarjan Trust and RFK Center for Justice and Human Rights 2008.

3. I traveled to the urban areas to meet with several NGO leaders and scholars who worked with tsunami-affected residents in villages in rural Tamil Nadu but had offices in nearby cities; these cities themselves are not the focus of the study.

4. Communities where fishing is the core livelihood will elevate the caste of that demographic group above normally higher castes. Thus, in a fishing community the Pattinavars would be the dominant caste, although the same village might have representatives of the higher castes like Brahmins (Venkatesh Salagrama, pers. comm., 29 July 2009). See also Srinivas 1987 and Norr 1975.

5. A full description of India's caste system is beyond the scope of this chapter, but broadly, Dalits (also known as "outcastes" or "untouchables") stand outside the standard four-tier caste system. They cannot marry those within the system and "are considered spiritually and physically unclean, and in the caste system must live in a separate colony, must use separate water and eating facilities, must never come in contact with caste Hindus, must call out an identifying greeting to ensure everyone knows they are 'untouchable' and must perform the tasks considered too unclean for caste Hindus to do. These jobs include removing carcasses of dead animals,

working with leather, performing midwifery duties, cleaning toilets, giving news of death and working with particular metals" (Gill 2007, 20). The Indian Constitution set up official categories for the population groups previously known as untouchables (with Scheduled Castes often referred to as Dalits and Scheduled Tribes as *adivasis*). The government reserves a certain proportion of positions in public sector employment for these groups, and some Indian states (such as Tamil Nadu) provide them with educational programs, uniforms, and other services (Ramachandran 2010). For an ethnographic view of the caste system see Natrajan 2005, and for a broader overview see Bayly 2001.

6. Similarly, among coastal dwellers in the Andaman and Nicobar Islands, strong social ties enabled rapid in-group assistance to tsunami-affected villagers and children. "The social capital of the tuhets is so strong that there is no need for any external aid agencies to assist orphaned children from any tribal community—the tuhet treats the children as its family children" (Gupta and Sharma 2006, 74). For more on the resilience of the Nicobarese communities, see Mehta 2007.

7. Similarly, in Banda Aceh, community organizations bridged the gap between the world of NGOs and individual survivors (Tanaka 2007).

8. In another case recorded by social workers with the Tata Institute, Dalit families who lost their houses were "completely cut off from the village, and no one, neither NGOs nor the government came" to assist. Only after the foreign NGO ActionAid identified these victims did the eighty-four families receive any help.

9. Some might argue that the existence of "social development advisers" with organizations such as Britain's Joint Funding Scheme with Official Development Assistance (Wallace 1997, 42) and the Department for International Development is evidence that foreign donors recognize that aid provision and receipt has not been sufficiently "objective." Whether this is also the pattern post-tsunami requires empirical investigation.

10. These villages may indeed define communities "sidelined" in the relief process; exactly who received what in these marginalized, peripheral hamlets has not yet been investigated quantitatively, and data on these outcomes provide empirical evidence for broader patterns of aid delivery.

11. The relief packet included saris, bedsheets, rice, kerosene, turmeric, salt and other condiments, and money for purchasing utensils and a stove (Government Order 57 dated 4 February 2005).

12. For a discussion of the growing competition in the institutional environment of international NGOs, see Cooley and Ron 2002, and for a brief discussion of the competition among NGOs in post-tsunami India, see Gauthamadas n.d.

13. As methodologists regularly point out, we cannot infer individual-level activities from communal or aggregate data. That is, we cannot make assumptions about how individuals within villages were able to access aid packages based solely on information about their village or hamlet. While aggregate data on villages have provided important insights into how factors such as caste and linking social capital affected village outcomes as a whole, we need individual-level data to talk precisely about individual-level outcomes.

Chapter Six

1. This chapter uses (with permission) material from my article (coauthored with Kevin Crook) "Strong Civil Society as a Double-Edged Sword: Siting Trailers in Post-Katrina New Orleans," *Political Research Quarterly* 61, 3 (2008): 379–89.

2. See Polidori 2006 for a visual tour of the damage to the city.

3. Respondents from the Lower Ninth Ward knew more of their neighbors by name and had longer tenure in their current residence than the primarily white and affluent area of Lakeview (Elliott, Haney, and Abidoun 2010, 631).

4. Local opposition to post-disaster housing plans is all too common. St. Charles County, Missouri, has flooded repeatedly, yet in 1994 when officials proposed a subdivision that would be built "in a safer spot not too far from where the old mobile home parks existed," local residents protested and shut down the plan (Steinberg 2000, 114).

5. Some observers might think that local elections, such as those for mayoral races, would better capture levels of social capital. I tested this theory using data from the most recent run-off mayoral election in New Orleans on 20 May 2006, which was won by incumbent mayor Ray Nagin. However, out of the 114 zip codes, only 17 had voting districts in the city of New Orleans itself, and attempts at integrating this small number of observations into my large-scale quantitative analysis resulted in incredibly high levels of multicollinearity along with far less analytic efficiency (since I was forced to drop close to one hundred observations to match the in-city blocks). Further, turnout for the mayoral election itself did not measurably affect the number of trailers per zip code, while the percentage of voters from the zip code voting for Mayor Nagin was only somewhat significant (p value of 0.014). Furthermore, based on coefficient estimates of these seventeen data points, zip codes that voted for Mayor Nagin were *more likely* to be slated as hosts for trailer parks, an outcome that seems counterintuitive (since Nagin would not want to punish his supporters after a close election with a four-point spread). As a result of these tests, I rely instead on presidential voter turnout. For a perspective on race relations and the 2006 mayoral election, see Cecil 2009.

Chapter Seven

1. In post-Katrina New Orleans, for example, local nonprofit organizations and NGOs documented tremendous work being carried out by their volunteers (Bradley Center for Philanthropy and Civic Renewal 2006).

2. For a positive review of the impact of relief agencies and government assistance in India, see Kapur (2009).

3. As researchers have pointed out, the regulations connected with the Stafford Act (which structures federal aid to local and state governments after disaster) "can become roadblocks that hamper both the initial response and long-term human recovery in large-scale disasters" (Chandra and Acosta 2009, 8).

4. Scholars have branded the Road Home program a failure because "money did not get to homeowners in a timely fashion" (Whelan and Strong 2009, 198; see also Burns and Thomas 2008 for an overview of the obstacles to its timely implementation). In interviews, activists within the Vietnamese community in Village de L'Est argued that "they took too much time, so we used our own savings instead" (author interview, 12 May 2010).

5. Critics of the recovery have pointed to other cases where tourist hotels have gained at the expense of local villagers; in the state of Kerala, for example, officials sought to siphon off funds slated for local tsunami rehabilitation to construct an offshore artificial reef for foreign tourists (Shaji 2008, 18).

6. In a number of post-tsunami reconstruction sites, NGOs and contractors ignored local requests to tailor homes to their needs and created houses without critical necessities such as prayer rooms, kitchens, and connections to septic tanks (*Hindu*, 18 December 2006). In villages

where relief agencies and the government interacted with the community to determine local needs, residents have reported much higher rates of satisfaction with new homes.

7. Military bases overseas, for example, regularly provide service people with free phone calls and Internet access to allow them to connect with family and friends back home.

8. Various studies have shown that local-level plans focused on disaster preparedness have a positive outcome on overall recoveries (Wu 2003).

9. Observers have argued that private sector firms—such as Walmart—are better positioned to respond to disasters than the federal government (Cosh 2008; Horwitz 2008).

10. For an investigation of the legal and political responses to catastrophe, see Sarat and Lezaun 2009.

11. However, pictures from the March 2011 Tohoku tsunami did show Japanese residents in the damaged prefectures of Fukushima and Miyagi using notes pinned on bulletin boards to seek information on missing loved ones, and site visits in one summer confirmed this.

12. The Internet and mobile communications devices have proved critical in increasing government transparency even in developing nations (Auletta 2011) and in coordinating antiestablishment movements. Egyptian authorities, for example, under strain from nationwide protests against the government, used a "kill switch" to effectively cut off access to the Internet in late January 2011; this was clearly an attempt to diminish the opposition's ability to mobilize on platforms like Facebook. While the 55 million Egyptians with cell phones and 20 million Internet users keenly felt the impact of this policy, in the end it was ineffective at dispersing the protestors (*Economist*, 12 February 2011).

13. The LFRC's stated mission was to "coordinate and mobilize a network of providers, organizations, and government agencies to deliver aid and services to displaced Louisiana families in transitional housing throughout the state" (Louisiana Family Recovery Corps 2005); it disbanded within three years of Hurricane Katrina.

References

Acheson, James. 1981. Anthropology of Fishing. *Annual Review of Anthropology* 10:275–316.

Adger, W. Neil. 2003. Social Capital, Collective Action, and Adaptation to Climate Change. *Economic Geography* 79 (4): 387–404.

Adger, W. Neil; Hughes, Terry P.; Folke, Carl; Carpenter, Stephen R.; and Rockström, Johan. 2005. Social-Ecological Resilience to Coastal Disasters. *Science* 309:1036–1039.

Agrawal, Arun. 2005. Environmentality: Community, Intimate Government, and the Making of Environmental Subjects in Kumaon, India. *Current Anthropology* 46 (2): 161–190.

Ahern, Jennifer, and Galea, Sandro. 2006. Social Context and Depression After a Disaster: The Role of Income Inequality. *Journal of Epidemiology and Community Health* 60 (9): 766–770.

Ahlers, Douglas; Plyer, Allison; and Weil, Frederick. 2008. Where Is the Money? Presentation downloaded from http://gnocdc.s3.amazonaws.com/reports/HurricaneFundingGap.pdf.

Ahn, T. K., and Ostrom, Elinor. 2008. Social Capital and Collective Action. In Dario Castiglione, Jan W. van Deth, and Guglielmo Wolleb, eds., *The Handbook of Social Capital*, 70–100. New York: Oxford University Press.

Albala-Bertrand, J. M. 1993. *Political Economy of Large Natural Disasters: With Special Reference to Developing Countries*. Oxford: Clarendon Press.

———. 2000. Complex Emergencies versus Natural Disasters: An Analytical Comparison of Causes and Effects. *Oxford Development Studies* 28 (2): 187–204.

Aldrich, Daniel P. 2005. Controversial Facility Siting: Bureaucratic Flexibility and Adaptation. *Journal of Comparative Politics* 38 (1): 103–123.

———. 2008a. Location, Location, Location: Selecting Sites for Controversial Facilities. *Singapore Economic Review* 53 (1): 145–172.

———. 2008b. *Site Fights: Divisive Facilities and Civil Society in Japan and the West*. Ithaca, NY: Cornell University Press.

———. 2008c. The Crucial Role of Civil Society in Disaster Recovery and Japan's Emergency Preparedness. *Japan aktuell* [Journal of current Japanese affairs] 3 (September): 81–96.

———. 2011. Between Market and State: Directions in Social Science Research on Disaster. *Perspectives on Politics*. 9 (1): 61–68.

Aldrich, Daniel P., and Crook, Kevin. 2008. Strong Civil Society as a Double-Edged Sword: Siting Trailers in Post-Katrina New Orleans. *Political Research Quarterly* 61 (3): 378–389.

Aldrich, Daniel P., and Kage, Rieko. 2003. Mars and Venus at Twilight: A Critical Investigation of Moralism, Age Effects, and Sex Differences. *Political Psychology* 24 (1): 23–40.

Alesch, Daniel; Arendt, Lucy A.; and Holly, James. 2009. *Managing for Long Term Community Recovery in the Aftermath of Disaster.* Fairfax, VA: Public Entity Risk Institute.

Alexander, Rajan. 2006. *Tsunami—Build Back Better: Mantra Aside, an Aid Gone Wrong Story?* Bangalore: Development Consultancy Group.

Almond, Gabriel A., and Verba, Sidney. 1963. *The Civic Culture: Political Attitudes and Democracy in Five Nations.* Princeton, NJ: Princeton University Press.

Anderson, Mary, and Woodrow, Peter. 1998. *Rising from the Ashes: Development Strategies in Times of Disaster.* Boulder, CO: Lynne Rienner.

Angrist, Joshua D., and Krueger, Alan B. 1999. Empirical Strategies in Labor Economics, In Orley Ashenfelter and David Card, eds., *Handbook of Labor Economics,* 3:1277–1366. Amsterdam: North-Holland.

Appleseed. 2006. *A Continuing Storm: The On-going Struggles of Hurricane Katrina Evacuees.* Washington, DC: Appleseed.

Apter, David, and Sawa, Nagayo. 1984. *Against the State: Politics and Social Protest in Japan.* Cambridge, MA: Harvard University Press.

Araki, Jiro. 2003. Shōnen to boranteia [Youth and volunteering]. *Keisatsugaku ronshū* [Journal of police science] 56 (3):10.

Arrow, Kenneth. 1999. Observations on Social Capital. In Partha Dasgupta and Ismail Serageldin, eds., *Social Capital: A Multifaceted Perspective.* Washington, DC: World Bank.

Arvin, Mak; Piretti, Anna; and Lew, Byron. 2002. Biases in the Allocation of Foreign Aid: The Case of Italy. *Review of Economic Conditions in Italy,* no. 2 (May–August): 305–312.

Arya, Anand; Mandal, G. S.; and Muley, E. V. 2006. Some Aspects of Tsunami Impact and Recovery in India. *Disaster Prevention and Management* 15 (1): 51–66.

Athukorala, Prema-Chandra, and Resosudarmo, Budy P. 2006. The Indian Ocean Tsunami: Economic Impact, Disaster Management and Lessons. *Asian Economic Papers* 4 (1): 1–39.

Atkinson, Matthew, and Fowler, Anthony. 2010. The Effect of Social Capital on Voter Turnout: Evidence from Saint's Day Fiestas in Mexico. Working paper available at http://papers.ssrn.com/sol3/papers.cfm?abstract_id=1808110.

Atwood, Roger. 2009. To Catch a Looter. *New York Times,* 13 October.

Auerswald, Philip; Branscomb, Lewis; La Porte, Todd; and Michel-Kerjan, Erwann, eds. 2006. *Seeds of Disaster, Roots of Response: How Private Action Can Reduce Public Vulnerability.* New York: Cambridge University Press.

Auletta, Ken. 2011. The Dictator Index: A Billionaire Battles a Continent's Legacy of Misrule. *New Yorker,* 7 March, 42–55.

Axelrod, Robert. 1984. *The Evolution of Cooperation.* New York: Basic Books.

Bailer, Stefanie, Bodenstein, Thilo, and Heinrich, V. Finn. 2007. What Makes Civil Society Strong? Testing Bottom-Up and Top-Down Theories of a Vibrant Civil Society. Paper presented at Effective and Legitimate Governance Conference, 13–14 July, Darmstadt, Germany.

Bakewell, Oliver. 2001. Refugee Aid and Protection in Rural Africa: Working in Parallel or Cross-Purposes? Working Paper no. 35, United Nations High Commission for Refugees.

Baltagi, Badi. 2005. *Econometric Analysis of Panel Data.* 3rd ed. West Sussex, UK: John Wiley.

Banerjee, Abhijit; Deaton, Angus; and Duflo, Esther. 2004. Health Care Delivery in Rural Rajasthan. *Economic and Political Weekly* 39 (9): 944–949.

Banerjee, Paula, and Chaudhury, Sabyasachi Basu Ray. 2005. Report on a Symposium on Tsunami and the Issues of Relief, Rehabilitation and Resettlement. *Forced Migration Review* (special issue), 42–43.

Banfield, Edward, and James Wilson. 1963. *City Politics.* New York: Vintage Press.

Bankston, Carl, and Zhou, Min. 2002. Social Capital as Process: The Meanings and Problems of a Theoretical Metaphor. *Sociological Inquiry* 72 (2): 285–317.

Bates, Frederick, and Peacock, Walter Gilis. 1989. Long Term Recovery. *International Journal of Mass Emergencies and Disasters* 7 (3): 349–366.

Bates, Lisa, and Green, Rebekah. 2007. Misuses of Data: What Counts as Damage in Post-Katrina New Orleans Recovery Planning. Working paper, University of Illinois, Urbana-Champaign.

———. 2009. Housing Recovery in the Ninth Ward: Disparities in Policy, Process, and Prospects. In Robert Bullard and Beverly Wright, eds., *Race, Place, and Environmental Justice after Hurricane Katrina,* 229–245. Philadelphia: Westview Press.

Baum, Dan. 2006. Deluged: When Katrina Hit, Where Were the Police? *New Yorker,* 9 January, 50–63.

Bavinck, Maarten. 1997. Changing Balance of Power at Sea: Motorisation of Artisanal Fishing Craft. *Economic and Political Weekly* 32 (5): 198–200.

———. 2001. Caste Panchayats and the Regulation of Fisheries along Tamil Nadu's Coromandel Coast. *Economic and Political Weekly* 36 (13): 1088–1094.

———. 2003. The Spatially Splintered State: Myths and Realities in the Regulation of Marine Fisheries in Tamil Nadu, India. *Development and Change* 34 (4): 633–657.

———. 2005. Understanding Fisheries Conflict in the South—a Legal-Pluralist Perspective. *Society and Natural Resouces* 18 (9): 805–820.

———. 2008. Collective Strategies and Windfall Catches: Fisher Responses to Tsunami Relief Efforts in South India. *Transforming Cultures Ejournal* 3 (2): 76–92.

Bayley, David. 1991. *Forces of Order: Policing Modern Japan.* Berkeley: University of California Press.

Bayly, Susan. 2001. *Caste, Society, and Politics in India from the Eighteenth Century to the Modern Age.* New York: Cambridge University Press.

Beck, Nathaniel, and Katz, Jonathan. 2004. Time-Series Cross-Section Issues: Dynamics. Draft paper available at http://polmeth.wustl.edu/mediaDetail.php?docId=36.

———. 2009. Modeling Dynamics in Time-Series Cross-Section Political Economy Data. Working paper available at http://ideas.repec.org/p/clt/sswopa/1304.html.

Becker, Gary. 2005. And the Economics of Disaster Management. *Wall Street Journal* (Eastern edition), 4 January, A12.

Beggs, John; Haines, Valerie; and Hurlbert, Jeanne. 1996a. Situational Contingencies Surrounding the Receipt of Informal Support. *Social Forces* 75 (1): 201–222.

———. 1996b. The Effects of Personal Network and Local Community Contexts on the Receipt of Formal Aid during Disaster Recovery. *International Journal of Mass Emergencies and Disasters* 14:57–78.

Begley, Sharon, and McKillop, Peter. 1995. Lessons of Kobe. *Newsweek,* 30 January, 24.

Bellah, Robert; Madsen, Richard; Sullivan, William; Swidler, Ann; and Tipton, Steven. 1985. *Habits of the Heart: Individualism and Commitment in American Life.* New York: Harper and Row.

Benning, Tom. 2010. Katrina Population May Help Texas Gain 4th U.S. House Seat. *Dallas Morning News* 20 January.

Benson, Charlotte, and Clay, Edward. 2004. *Understanding the Economic and Financial Impacts of Natural Disasters*. Washington, DC: World Bank.

Berke, Philip; Beatley, Timothy; and Feagin, Clarence. 1993. *Hurricane Gilbert Strikes Jamaica: Linking Disaster Recovery to Development*. HRRC Article 89A. College Station: Texas A&M University, Hazard Reduction and Recovery Center.

Berke, Philip, and Campanella, Thomas. 2006. Planning for Postdisaster Resiliency. *Annals of the American Academy of Political and Social Science* 604:192–207.

Berman, Sheri. 1997. Civil Society and the Collapse of the Weimar Republic. *World Politics* 49 (3): 401–429.

Bhandari, Roshan; Yokomatsu, Muneta; Okada, Norio; and Ikeo, Hitoshi. 2010. Analyzing Urban Rituals with Reference to Development of Social Capital for Disaster Resilience. *IEEE Systems, Man, and Cybernetics Conference Proceedings*, 10–13 October, 3477–3482.

Bhavnani, Ravi, and Backer, David. 2007. Social Capital and Political Violence in Sub-Saharan Africa. Paper presented at the 1 September annual meeting of the American Political Science Association, Chicago.

Bindra, Satinder. 2005. *Tsunami: 7 Hours That Shook the World*. New Delhi: HarperCollins.

Birkland, Thomas. 2006. *Lessons of Disaster: Policy Change after Catastrophic Events*. Washington, DC: Georgetown University Press.

———. 2009. Disasters, Catastrophes, and Policy Failure in the Homeland Security Era. *Review of Policy Research* 26 (4): 423–438.

Birner, Regina, and Wittmer, Heidi. 2003. Using Social Capital to Create Political Capital: How Do Local Communities Gain Political Influence? A Theoretical Approach and Empirical Evidence from Thailand. In Nives Dolsak and Elinor Ostrom, eds., *The Commons in the New Millennium: Challenges and Adaptations*, 291–334. Cambridge, MA: MIT Press.

Blomkvist, Hans. 2003. Social Capital, Political Participation, and the Quality of Democracy in India. Paper presented at the annual meeting of the American Political Science Association, 28–31 August.

Blumenthal, Ralph. 2007. Stalled Health Tests Leave Storm Trailers in Limbo. *New York Times*, 18 October.

Boin, Arjen; McConnell, Allan; and 'T Hart, Paul. 2008. *Governing after Crisis*. New York: Cambridge University Press.

Boix, Carles, and Posner, Daniel. 1998. Social Capital: Explaining Its Origins and Effects on Government Performance. *British Journal of Political Science* 28 (4): 686–693.

Boris, Elizabeth, and Steuerle, C. Eugene. 2006. *After Katrina: Public Expectation and Charities' Response*. Urban Institute and the Hauser Center for Nonprofit Organizations. Cambridge, MA: Harvard University.

Borland, Janet. 2005. Stories of Ideal Japanese Subjects from the Great Kantō Earthquake of 1923. *Japanese Studies* 25 (1): 21–34.

———. 2006. Capitalising on Catastrophe: Reinvigorating the Japanese State with Moral Values through Education following the 1923 Great Kantō Earthquake. *Modern Asian Studies* 40 (4): 875–907.

Bourdieu, Pierre. 1986. Forms of Capital. In John Richardson, ed., *Handbook of Theory and Research for the Sociology of Education*, 241–60. Westport, CT: Greenwood Press.

Bourne, Joel. 2004. Gone with the Water. *National Geographic Magazine*, October. Accessible at http://ngm.nationalgeographic.com/ngm/0410/feature5.

Bowden, Martyn; Pijawka, David; Roboff, Gary; Gelman, Kenneth; and Amaral, Daniel. 1977.

Reestablishing Homes and Jobs: Cities. In J. Eugene Haas, Robert Kates, and Martyn Bowden, eds., *Reconstruction following Disaster*, 69–145. Cambridge MA: MIT Press.

Bowman, Michael. 2010. Obama Calls New Orleans a "Symbol of Resilience" on Katrina Anniversary. *Voice of America*, 29 August.

Bradley Center for Philanthropy and Civic Renewal. 2006. Service in the Storm. Transcript from 20 September conference, Hudson Institute, Washington, DC.

Breiger, Ronald. 2004. The Analysis of Social Networks. In Melissa Hardy and Alan Bryman, eds., *Handbook of Data Analysis*, 505–526. London: Sage.

Brinkley, Douglas. 2007. *The Great Deluge: Hurricane Katrina, New Orleans, and the Mississippi Gulf Coast*. New York: Harper.

Brookings-Bern Project on Internal Displacement. 2008. *Human Rights and Natural Disasters: Operational Guidelines and Field Manual on Human Rights Protection in Situations of Natural Disaster*. Washington, DC: Brookings Institution.

Brueckner, Jan, and Largey, Ann. 2006. Social Interaction and Urban Sprawl. Working paper 1843, Center for Economic Studies and the Ifo Institute.

Brune, Nancy, and Bossert, Thomas. 2009. Building Social Capital in Post-conflict Communities: Evidence from Nicaragua. *Social Science and Medicine* 68:885–893.

Buckland, Jerry, and Rahman, Matiur. 1999. Community Based Disaster Management during the 1997 Red River Flood in Canada. *Disasters* 23 (2): 174–191.

Bullard, R. D. 1994. *Dumping in Dixie: Race, Class, and Environmental Quality*. Boulder, CO: Westview Press.

Bullard, Robert, and Wright, Beverly, eds. 2009. *Race, Place, and Environmental Justice* after *Huricane Katrina*. Philadelphia: Westview Press.

Bunch, Martin J.; Franklin, Beth; Morley, David; Kumaran, T. Vasantha; and Suresh, V. Madha. 2005. Research in Turbulent Environments: Slums in Chennai, India and the Impact of the December 2004 Tsunami EcoHealth Project. *Ecohealth* 2:1–5.

Burnett, John. 2010. Haitian Communities Set Up Neighborhood Watches. National Public Radio, *Morning Edition*, 22 January.

Burns, Peter, and Thomas, Matthew. 2008. The Fiscal Politics of Reconstruction: The Case of New Orleans. Paper presented at the annual meeting of the American Political Science Association, 27–31 August, Boston.

Burnside, Craig, and Dollar, David. 2000. Aid, Policies, and Growth. *American Economic Review* 90 (4): 847–868.

Busch, Noel. (1962) 2005. *Shōgo nipun mae* [Two minutes to noon]. Tokyo: Hakakawa.

Bryant, Bunyan, and Mohai, Paul, eds. 1992. *Race and the Incidence of Environmental Hazards: A Time for Discourse*. Boulder, CO: Westview Press.

Callahan, William A. 2005. Social Capital and Corruption: Vote Buying and the Politics of Reform in Thailand. *Perspectives on Politics* 3 (3): 495–508.

Capewell, Elizabeth. 2004. Working with Disaster: Transforming Experence into a Useful Practice. PhD diss., University of Bath.

Caputo, Marc. 2010. New Orleans Is Recovering, and Offering Lessons for Haiti. *Miami Herald*, 21 February.

Cardinas, Juan Camilo, and Carpenter, Jeffrey. 2008. Behavioral Development Economics: Lessons from Field Labs in the Developing World. *Journal of Development Studies* 44 (3): 337–364.

Case, Donald O. 2002. *Looking for Information: A Survey of Research on Information Seeking, Needs, and Behavior*. Amsterdam, NY: Academic Press.

Castiglione, Dario; van Deth, Jan W.; and Wolleb, Guglielmo, eds. 2008. *The Handbook of Social Capital.* New York: Oxford University Press.

Castle, Geoffrey, and Don Munton. 1996. Voluntary Siting of Hazardous Waste Facilities in Western Canada. In Don Munton, ed., *Hazardous Waste Siting and Democratic Choice.* Washington, DC: Georgetown University Press.

Cavallo, Eduardo; Powell, Andrew; and Becerra, Oscar. 2010a. Estimating the Direct Economic Damages of the Earthquake in Haiti. *Economic Journal* 120 (546): F298–F312.

———. 2010b. Catastrophic Natural Disasters and Economic Growth. Working paper, Inter-American Development Bank, Washington, DC.

Cave, Damien. 2010. Fighting Starvation, Haitians Learn to Share Portions. *New York Times,* 25 January.

Cecil, Katherine. 2009. Race, Representation, and Recovery: Documenting the 2006 New Orleans Mayoral Elections. Master's thesis, University of New Orleans.

Chambers, Simone, and Kopstein, Jeffrey. 2001. Bad Civil Society. *Political Theory* 29 (6): 837–865.

Chamlee-Wright, Emily. 2008. Signaling Effects of Commercial and Civil Society. *International Journal of Social Economics* 35 (7/8): 615–626.

———. 2010. *The Cultural and Political Economy of Recovery: Social Learning in a Post-disaster Environment.* New York: Routledge.

Chamlee-Wright, Emily, and Rothschild, Daniel. 2007. *Disastrous Uncertainty: How Government Disaster Policy Undermines Community Rebound.* Mercatus Policy Series, Policy Comment no. 9. Arlington, VA: Mercatus Center at George Mason University.

Chamlee-Wright, Emily, and Storr, Virgil. 2009a. Club Goods and Post-disaster Community Return. *Rationality and Society* 21 (4): 429–458.

———. 2009b. There's No Place Like New Orleans: Sense of Place and Community Recovery in the Ninth Ward after Hurricane Katrina. *Journal of Urban Affairs* 31 (5): 615–634.

———. 2010. Expectations of Government Response to Disaster. *Public Choice* 144 (1): 253–274.

Chandra, Anita, and Acosta, Joie. 2009. The Role of Nongovernmental Organizations in Long-Term Human Recovery after Disaster. RAND Occasional Paper.

Chandra, Anita; Acosta, Joie; Meredith, Lisa; Sanches, Katherine; Stern, Stefanie; Uscher-Pines, Lori; Williams, Malcolm; and Yeung, Douglas. 2010. Understanding Community Resilience in the Context of National Health Security: A Literature Review. Rand Working Paper WR-737-DHHS.

Chandran, P. n.d. Role of National Disaster Management System in the Context of South Asia Tsunami 2004. Accessed at http://info.worldbank.org/etools/docs/library/239529/Best%20 End%20of%20Course%20Project-P%20Chandran.pdf.

Chandrasekhar, Divya. 2010. Understanding Stakeholder Participation in Post-disaster Recovery (Case Study: Nagapattinam, India. PhD diss., University of Illinois at Urbana-Champaign.

Chang, Stephanie. 2000. Disasters and Transport Systems: Loss, Recovery and Competition at the Port of Kobe after the 1995 Earthquake. *Journal of Transport Geography* 8:53–65.

———. 2001. Structural Change in Urban Economies: Recovery and Long-Term Impacts in the 1995 Kobe Earthquake. *Kokumin keizai zasshi* [Journal of economics and business administration] 183 (1): 47–66.

Chen, Yi Feng; Yi, Kang; Tjosvold, Dean; and Guo, Cathy Yang. 2011. Recovery from the 2008 Great Sichuan Earthquake in China: Constructive Controversy and Relationships. Paper presented at the annual meeting of the Academy of Management, 12–16 August, San Antonio, TX.

Chenoweth, Erica, and Stephan, Maria. 2011. *Why Civil Resistance Works: The Strategic Logic of Nonviolent Conflict*. New York: Columbia University Press.

Christakis, Nicholas, and Fowler, James. 2007. The Spread of Obesity in a Large Social Network over 32 Years. *New England Journal of Medicine* 357 (4): 370–379.

Clancey, Gregory. 2006a. *Earthquake Nation: The Cultural Politics of Japanese Seismicity, 1868–1930*. Berkeley: University of California Press.

———. 2006b. The Meiji Earthquake: Nature, Nation, and the Ambiguities of Catastrophe. *Modern Asian Studies* 40 (4): 909–951.

Clark, George E. 2001. Vulnerability to Coastal Flood Hazards in Revere, Massachusetts: A Social Component of Risk. PhD diss., Clark University.

Clarke, Lee. 1999. *Mission Improbable: Using Fantasy Documents to Tame Disaster*. Chicago: University of Chicago Press.

Clingermayer, James. 1994. Electoral Representation, Zoning Politics, and the Exclusion of Group Homes. *Political Research Quarterly* 47 (4): 969–984.

Coffé, Hilde, and Geys, Benny. 2005. Institutional Performance and Social Capital: An Application to the Local Government Level. *Journal of Urban Affairs* 27 (5): 485–501.

Cohen, Charles, and Werker, Eric. 2008. The Political Economy of "Natural" Disasters. *Journal of Conflict Resolution* 52 (6): 795–819.

Cohen, Jean, and Arato, Andrew. 1992. *Civil Society and Political Theory*. Cambridge, MA: MIT Press.

Cohen, Joshua, and Rogers, Joel, eds. 1995. *Associations and Democracy*. New York: Verso Books.

Coleman, James S. 1988. Social Capital in the Creation of Human Capital. *American Journal of Sociology* 94, suppl., Organizations and Institutions: Sociological and Economic Approaches to the Analysis of Social Structure, S95–S120.

———. 1990, *Foundations of Social Theory*. Cambridge, MA: Harvard University Press.

Comfort, Louise K. 2005. Fragility in Disaster Response: Hurricane Katrina, 29 August 2005. *Forum* 3 (3): 1–8.

Committee on Homeland Security and Governmental Affairs. 2008. Hearing before the Ad Hoc Subcommittee on Disaster Recovery of the Committee on Homeland Security and Governmental Affairs, United States Senate, 110th Congress, 23 September.

Cooley, Alexander, and Ron, James. 2002. The NGO Scramble: Organizational Insecurity and the Political Economy of Transnational Action. *International Security* 27 (1): 5–39.

Cosh, Colby. 2008. In Wal-Mart We Trust. *National Post*, 1 April.

Cox, Kevin R. 1982. Housing Tenure and Neighborhood Activism. *Urban Affairs Review* 18 (1): 107–129.

Coyne, Christoper. 2010. Critical Dialogue: Review of Graciana del Castillo's Rebuilding War-Torn States. *Perspectives on Politics* 8 (1): 302–304.

Craemer, Thomas. 2010. Evaluating Racial Disparities in Hurricane Katrina Relief Using Direct Trailer Counts in New Orleans and FEMA Records. *Public Administration Review* 70 (3): 367–377.

Cuaresma, Jesus; Hlouskova, Jaroslava; and Obersteiner, Michael. 2008. Natural Disasters as Creative Destruction? Evidence from Developing Countries. *Economic Inquiry* 46 (2): 214–226.

Curtis, Donald E.; Hlady, Chris; Pemmaraju, Sriram; Segre, Alberto; and Polgreen, Phil. 2010. Social Network Influence on Vaccination Uptake among Healthcare Workers. Paper presented at the 5th Decennial International Conference on Healthcare-Associated Infections, Atlanta.

Curtis, Wayne. 2007. Block by Block. *Preservation*, September/October, 22–37.

Cutter, Susan; Boruff, Bryan; and Shirley, W. Lynn. 2003. Social Vulnerability to Environmental Hazards. *Social Science Quarterly* 84 (2): 242–261.

Cutter, Susan, and Emrich, Christopher. 2006. Moral Hazard, Social Catastrophe: The Changing Face of Vulnerability along the Hurricane Coasts. *Annals of the American Academy of Political and Social Science* 604:102–112.

Cutter, Susan, and Finch, Christina. 2008. Temporal and Spatial Changes in Social Vulnerability to Natural Hazards. *Proceedings of the National Academy of Sciences* 105 (7): 2301–2306.

DaCosta, Elsa, and Turner, Sarah. 2007. Negotiating Changing Livelihoods: The Sampan Dwellers of Tam Giang Lagoon, Viet Nam. *Geoforum* 38:190–206.

Dacy, Douglas, and Kunreuther, Howard. 1969. *The Economics of Natural Disasters: Implications for Federal Policy.* New York: Free Press.

Dahal, Ganga Ram, and Adhikari, Krishna. 2008. Bridging, Linking, and Bonding Social Capital in Collective Action: The Case of Kalahan Forest Reserve in the Philippines. CAPRI Working Paper 79, Washington, DC.

Dahlmann, Joseph. 1924. *The Great Tokyo Earthquake: September 1, 1923: Experiences and Impressions of an Eye-Witness.* Translated by Victor Gettelman. New York: America Press.

Daniel, Sam. 2005. Tsunami Relief: Tranquebar Faces Problem of Plenty. New Delhi Television, 24 December.

Daniels, Thomas, and Steinberg, Harris. 2006. Lessons from Sri Lanka. In Eugenie Birch and Susan Wachter, eds., *Rebuilding Urban Places after Disaster: Lessons from Hurricane Katrina*, 244–255. Philadelphia: University of Pennsylvania Press.

Darcy, James. 2004. The Indian Ocean Tsunami Crisis: Humanitarian Dimensions. Working paper, Humanitarian Policy Group.

Dash, Nicole; Peacock, Walter; and Morrow, Betty. 2000. And the Poor Get Poorer: A Neglected Black Community. In Walter Peacock, Betty Morrow, and Hugh Gladwin, eds., *Hurricane Andrew: Ethnicity, Gender, and the Sociology of Disasters*, 206–225. Miami: International Hurricane Center.

Davis, Belinda, and Bali, Valentina. 2008. Examining the Role of Race, NIMBY, and Local Politics in FEMA Trailer Park Placement. *Social Science Quarterly* 89 (5): 1175–1194.

Davis, Donald R., and Weinstein, David E. 2002. Bones, Bombs, and Break Points: The Geography of Economic Activity. *American Economic Review* 92 (5): 1269–1289.

De Allesi, Louis. 1975. Towards an Analysis of Postdisaster Cooperation. *American Economic Review* 65 (1): 127–138.

DeFilippis, James. 2001. The Myth of Social Capital in Community Development. *Housing Policy Debate* 12 (4): 781–806.

de Hart, Joep, and Dekker, Paul. 2003. A Tale of Two Cities: Local Patterns of Social Capital. In Marc Hooghe and Dietlind Stole, eds., *Generating Social Capital: Civil Society and Institution in Comparative Perspective*, 153–169. New York: Palgrave.

De Souza Briggs, Xavier. 1998. Brown Kids in White Suburbs: Housing Mobility and the Many Faces of Social Capital. *Housing Policy Debate* 9 (1): 177–221.

Diez de Ulzurrun, Laura Morales. 2002. Associational Membership and Social Capital in Comparative Perspective: A Note on the Problems of Measurement. *Politics and Society* 30 (3): 497–523.

Djupe, Paul; Sokhey, Anand; and Gilbert, Christopher. 2007. Present but Not Accounted For? Gender Differences in Civic Resource Acquisition. *American Journal of Political Science* 51 (4): 906–920.

Donner, William, and Rodriguez, Havidan. 2008. Population Composition, Migration and Inequality: The Influence of Demographic Changes on Disaster Risk and Vulnerability. *Social
Forces* 87 (2): 1089–1114.

Dorairaj, S. 2005. Critical Gaps in Rebuilding Tsunami Hit Villages. *Hindu*, 23 October, 1.

————. 2009. Spreading Menace. *Frontline* 26 (8): 11–24.

Doteuchi, Akio. 2002. Community Currency and NPOs—a Model for Solving Social Issues in
the 21st Century. Research Paper 163, NLI Research Institute.

Dow, Kirstin. 1999. The Extraordinary and the Everyday in Explanations of Vulnerability to an
Oil Spill. *Geographical Review* 89 (1): 74–93.

Dowling, J. M., and Hiemenz, Ulrich. 1985. Biases in the Allocation of Foreign Aid: Some New
Evidence. *World Development* 13 (4): 535–541.

Dueñas-Osorio, Leonardo; Buzcu-Guven, Birnur; Stein, Robert; and Subramanian, Devika.
2011. Engineering-Based Hurricane Risk Estimates and Comparison to Perceived Risks in
Storm-Prone Areas. *Natural Hazards Review* 1 (28): ••–••.

Dynes, Russell. 1989. Conceptualizing Disaster in Ways Productive for Social Science Research.
Seminar on Research in Socio-economic Aspects of Disaster, Bangkok, Thailand, 22–24
March.

————. 2005. Community Social Capital as the Primary Basis of Resilience. Preliminary Paper
344, University of Delaware Disaster Research Center.

Dynes, Russell, and Quarantelli, E. L. 2008. A Brief Note on Disaster Restoration, Reconstruction, and Recovery: A Comparative Note Using Post Earthquake Observations. Preliminary
Paper 359, University of Delaware Disaster Research Center.

Easterly, William. 2001. *The Elusive Quest for Growth: Economists' Adventures and Misadventures
in the Tropics*. Cambridge, MA: MIT Press.

————. 2006. *The White Man's Burden: Why the West's Efforts to Aid the Rest Have Done So
Much Ill and So Little Good*. New York: Penguin Books.

Eaton, Leslie. 2007a. New Orleans Recovery Is Slowed by Closed Hospitals. *New York Times*,
24 July.

————. 2007b. Critics Cite Red Tape in Rebuilding of Louisiana. *New York Times*, 6 November.

Edgington, David. 2010. *Reconstructing Kobe: The Geography of Crisis and Opportunity*. Toronto:
UBC Press.

Eisenstadt, S. N. 1951. The Place of Elites and Immigrant Groups in the Absorption of new Im-
migrants in Israel. *American Journal of Sociology* 57 (3): 222–231.

Elliott, James R.; Haney, Timothy J.; and Sams-Abiodun, Petrice. 2010. Limits to Social Capital:
Comparing Network Assistance in Two New Orleans Neighborhoods Devastated by Hurricane Katrina. *Sociological Quarterly* 51 (4): 624–648.

Elliott, James R., and Pais, Jeremy. 2006. Race, Class, and Hurricane Katrina: Social Differ-
ences in Human Responses to Disaster. *Social Science Research* 35:295–321.Elster, Jon. 1990.
Selfishness and Altruism. In Jane J. Mansbridge, ed., *Beyond Self-Interest*, 44–53. Chicago:
University of Chicago Press.

EM-DAT. 2010. International Disaster Database. http://www.emdat.be/.

Enarson, Elaine, and Morrow, Betty. 2000. A Gendered Perspective: The Voices of Women.
In Walter Peacock, Betty Morrow, and Hugh Gladwin, eds., *Hurricane Andrew: Ethnicity,
Gender, and the Sociology of Disasters*, 116–140. Miami: International Hurricane Center.

Enia, Jason. 2008. Shaking the Foundations: The Effects of Disasters and Institutional Quality
on Violent Civil Conflict. Paper presented at annual meeting of the American Political Science Association, 28–31 August, Boston.

Eoh, Min Sun. 1998. A Comparative Study of Recovery Time between Counties That Experience Floods Frequently and Infrequently. PhD diss., Texas A&M University.

Erikson, Kai. 1976. *Everything in Its Path: Destruction of Community in the Buffalo Creek Flood.* New York: Simon and Schuster.

Erselcuk, Muzaffer M. 1947. Electricity in Japan. *Far Eastern Quarterly* 6 (3): 283–293.

Etzioni, Amitai. 1988. *The Moral Dimension: Toward a New Economics.* New York: Free Press.

Evans, Neil. 2001. Community Planning in Japan: The Case of Mano, and Its Experience in the Hanshin Earthquake. PhD. diss., School of East Asian Studies, University of Sheffield.

———. 2002. Machi-zukuri as a New Paradigm in Japanese Urban Planning: Reality or Myth? *Japan Forum* 14 (3): 443–464.

Faciane, Valerie. 2007. Vietnamese Community Thriving in Eastern New Orleans. *New Orleans Times-Picayune*, 23 April.

Fafchamps, Marcel. 2006. Development and Social Capital. *Journal of Development Studies* 42 (7): 1180–1198.

Farr, James. 2004. Social Capital: A Conceptual History. *Political Theory* 32 (1): 6–33.

Farrell, Henry, and Knight, Jack. 2003. Trust, Institutions, and Institutional Change: Industrial Districts and the Social Capital Hypothesis. *Politics and Society* 31 (4): 537–566.

Field, John. 2003. *Social Capital.* London: Routledge.

Fine, Ben. 2001. *Social Capital versus Social Theory: Political Economy and Social Science at the Turn of the Millennium.* London: Routledge.

Fischer, Henry W. 1998. *Response to Disaster: Fact versus Fiction and Its Perpetuation.* Lanham, MD: University Press of America.

Flanagan, Barry; Gregory, Edward; Hallisey, Elaine; Heitgerd, Janet; and Lewis, Brian. 2011. A Social Vulnerability Index for Disaster Management. *Journal of Homeland Security and Emergency Management* 8 (1): article 3.

Fletcher, Michael. 2010. Uneven Katrina Recovery Efforts Often Offered the Most Help to the Most Affluent. *Washington Post,* 27 August.

Foley, Michael W., and Edwards, Bob. 1996. The Paradox of Civil Society. *Journal of Democracy* 7 (3): 38–52.

Foner, Nancy, ed. 2005. *Wounded City: The Social Impact of 9/11.* New York: Russell Sage Foundation.

Food and Agricultural Organization of the United Nations. 2006. *Report of the Regional Workshop on Rehabilitation in Tsunami Affected Areas.* Bangkok: FAO UN.

Freeman, Lance. 2001. The Effects of Sprawl on Neighborhood Social Ties: An Explanatory Analysis. *Journal of the American Planning Association* 67 (1): 69–77.

Frey, Bruno; Oberholzer-Gee, Felix; and Eichenberger, Reiner. 1996. The Old Lady Visits Your Backyard: A Tale of Morals and Markets. *Journal of Political Economy* 104 (6): 1297–1313.

Fritz Institute. 2005a. *Recipient Perceptions of Aid Effectiveness: Rescue, Relief, and Rehabilitation in Tsunami Affected Indonesia, India, and Sri Lanka.* San Francisco: Fritz Institute.

———. 2005b. *Lessons from the Tsunami: Survey of Affected Families in India and Sri Lanka.* San Francisco: Fritz Institute.

Fukkōkyoku [Reconstruction Bureau], ed. 1930. *Fukkō kansei kinen Tōkyō shigai chizu* [Tokyo city map celebrating the completion of its recovery]. Tokyo: Tokyo Nichinichi Shinbun.

Fukuyama, Francis. 1999. Social Capital and Civil Society. Paper presented at the IMF Conference on Second Generation Reforms, 8–9 November, Washington, DC.

———. 2001. Social Capital, Civil Society and Development. *Third World Quarterly* 22 (1): 7–20.

Galasso, Emanuela, and Ravallion, Martin. 2005. Decentralized Targeting of an Antipoverty Program. *Journal of Public Economics* 89 (4): 705–727.

Galster, George; Cutsinger, Jackie; and Lim, Up. 2007. Are Neighborhoods Self-Stabilising? Exploring Endogeneous Dynamics. *Urban Studies* 44 (1): 167–185.

Gangadharan, Nipin. 2006. Homeless Blues. *Tsunami Response Watch*, 12 January.

Garvin, Glenn. 2010. Managua a Model of How Not to Rebuild after Quake. *Miami Herald*, 14 February.

Gauthamadas, Udipi. n.d. Social Transformation of the Tsunami Affected Fishing Community: The Concept and the Need. Working paper, Academy for Disaster Management Education Planning and Training.

Geertz, Clifford. 1962. The Rotating Credit Association: A "Middle Rung" in Development. *Economic Development and Cultural Change* 10 (3): 241–263.

George, Alexander, and Bennett, Andrew. 2004. *Case Studies and Theory Development in the Social Sciences.* Cambridge MA: MIT Press.

Gerring, John. 2004. What Is a Case Study and What Is It Good For? *American Political Science Review* 98 (2): 341–354.

Gibson, Clark C.; Andersson, Krister; Ostrom, Elinor; and Shivakumar, Sujai. 2005. *The Samaritan's Dilemma: The Political Economy of Development Aid.* New York: Oxford University Press.

Gilbert, Roy, and Kreimer, Alcira. 1999. Learning from the World Bank's Natural Disaster Related Assistance. Working paper 2, World Bank, Washington, DC.

Gill, Timothy. 2007. Making Things Worse: How "Caste Blindness" in Indian Post-tsunami Disaster Recovery Has Exacerbated Vulnerability and Exclusion. Dalit Network, Netherlands.

Girard, Chris, and Peacock, Gillis. 2000. Ethnicity and Segregation: Post-hurricane Relocation. In Walter Peacock, Betty Morrow, and Hugh Gladwin, eds., *Hurricane Andrew: Ethnicity, Gender, and the Sociology of Disasters,* 191–205. Miami: International Hurricane Center.

Giroux, Henry. 2006. *Stormy Weather: Katrina and the Politics of Disposability.* Boulder, CO: Paradigm.

Goffman, Erving. 1959. *The Presentation of Self in Everyday Life.* New York: Anchor Books.

Golec, Judith Ann. 1980. Aftermath of Disaster: The Teton Dam Break. PhD diss., Ohio State University.

Gomathy, N. B. 2006a. Pattinavar Panchayats 2: Post Tsunami. Presentation at TRINet Workshop, 15 February.

———. 2006b. Pattinavar Panchayats 1. Presentation TRINet Workshop, 15 February.

———. 2006c. The Role of Traditional Panchayats in Coastal Fishing Communities in Tamil Nadu, with Special Reference to Their Role in Mediating Tsunami Relief and Rehabilitation. Presented at ICSF Post-tsunami Rehab Workshop, 18–19 January.

Granovetter, Mark. 1973. The Strength of Weak Ties. *American Journal of Sociology* 78 (6): 1360–1380.

Grenier, Paola, and Wright, Karen. 2004. Social Capital in Britain: An Update and Critique of Hall's Analysis. Working paper 14, London School of Economics, Centre for Civil Society.

Grootaert, Christiaan; Narayan, Deepa; Jones, Veronica; and Woolcock, Michael. 2003. World Bank Social Capital Thematic Group: Integrated Questionnaire for the Measurement of Social Capital (SC-IQ). World Bank, Washington, DC.

Grootaert, Christian, and van Bastelaer, Thierry. 2002. Understanding and Measuring Social Capital. Paper for The Institutional Approach to Donor-Facilitated Economic Development: Session on Social Capital, 11 January, Washington, DC.

Gupta, Manu, and Sharma, Anshu. 2006. Compounded Loss: the Post Tsunami Recovery Experience of Indian Island Communities. *Disaster Prevention and Management* 15 (1): 67–78.

Haas, J. Eugene; Kates, Robert W.; and Bowden, Martyn J., eds. 1977. *Reconstruction following Disaster*. Cambridge, MA: MIT University Press.

Haas, J. Eugene; Trainer, Patricia; Bowden, Martyn; and Bolin, Robert. 1977. Reconstruction Issues in Perspective. In J. Eugene Haas, Robert Kates, and Martyn Bowden, eds., *Reconstruction following Disaster*, 25–68. Cambridge MA: MIT Press.

Haas, Peter. 2004. When Does Power Listen to Truth? A Constructivist Approach to the Policy Process. *Journal of European Public Policy* 11 (4): 569–592.

Haddad, Mary Alice. 2007. *Politics and Volunteering in Japan: A Global Perspective*. Cambridge: Cambridge University Press.

———. 2010. From Undemocratic to Democratic Civil Society: Japan's Volunteer Fire Departments. *Journal of Asian Studies* 69 (1): 33–56.

Hagiwara, Taiji, and Jinushi, Toshiki. 2005. Hanshin Awaji Daishinsai no higai to fukkō—chiiki-teki bunseki [Damage and reconstruction of the Hanshin—Awaji Earthquake: A Spatial Analysis]. Paper presented at the 10th anniversary of Hanshin-Awaji Earthquake Memorial Academic Symposium, Kobe University.

Hamilton, James. 1993. Politics and Social Costs: Estimating the Impact of Collective Action on Hazardous Waste Facilities. *RAND Journal of Economics* 24 (1): 101–125.

Hammer, Joshua. 2006. *Yokohama Burning: The Deadly 1923 Earthquake and Fire That Helped Forge the Path to World War II*. New York: Free Press.

Hanes, Jeffrey. 2000. Urban Planning as an Urban Problem: The Reconstruction of Tokyo after the Great Kanto Earthquake. *Seisaku kagaku* [Policy science] 7 (3): 123–137.

Haque, C. Emidad. 2003. Perspectives of Natural Disasters in East and South Asia, and the Pacific States. *Natural Hazards* 49:465–483.

Hardin, Garrett. 1968. The Tragedy of the Commons. *Science* 162 (3859): 1243–1248.

Hastings, Sally Ann. 1995. *Neighborhood and Nation in Tokyo, 1905–1937*. Pittsburgh: University of Pittsburgh Press.

Hattori, Kumie. 2003. Reconstruction of Disaster and Recreation of Local Heritage. Presented at International Symposium on Asian Heritage, 22 August to 10 September, Malaysia.

Havens, Thomas. 1977. Japan's Enigmatic Election of 1928. *Modern Asian Studies* 2 (4): 543–555.

Hawkins, Robert, and Maurer, Katherine. 2010. Bonding, Bridging, and Linking: How Social Capital Operated in New Orleans following Hurricane Katrina. *British Journal of Social Work* 40 (6): 1777–1793.

Hayes, Alan; Gray, Matthew; and Edwards, Ben. 2008. Social Inclusion: Origins, Concepts, and Key Themes. Working paper, Social Inclusion Unit, Department of the Prime Minister and Cabinet, Australia.

Heath, Chris. 2006. 1 Block, 1 Year, 13 Houses. *GQ*, December, 341–354.

Hecht, Gabrielle. 1998. *The Radiance of France: Nuclear Power and National Identity after World War II*. Cambridge, MA: MIT Press.

HelpAge International. 2005. *The Impact of the Indian Ocean Tsunami on Older People: Issues and Recommendations*. London: HelpAge International.

Hill, Peter. 2003. *The Japanese Mafia: Yakuza, Law, and the State*. Oxford: Oxford University Press.

Hirschman, Albert. 1970. *Exit, Voice, and Loyalty: Responses to Decline in Firms, Organizations, and States*. Cambridge, MA: Harvard University Press.

Ho, Daniel; Imai, Kosuke; King, Gary; and Stuart, Elizabeth. 2007. Matching as Nonparametric

Preprocessing for Reducing Model Dependence in Parametric Causal Inference. *Political Analysis* 15:199–236.

Horie, Kei; Maki, Norio; Kohiyama, Masayuki; Lu, Hengjian; Tanaka, Satoshi; Hashitera, Shin; Shigekawa, Kishie; and Hayashi, Haruo. 2003. Process of Housing Damage Assessment: The 1995 Hanshin-Awaji Earthquake Disaster Case. *Natural Hazards* 29:341–370.

Horne, Jed. 2005. Carving a Better City. *New Orleans Times-Picayune*, 13 November.

Horney, Jennifer; MacDonald, Pia; Willigen, Marieke Van; Berke, Philip; and Kaufman, Jay. 2010. Factors Associated with Risk of Evacuation Failure from Hurricane Isabel in North Carolina, 2003. *International Journal of Mass Emergencies and Disasters* 28 (1): 33–58.

Horwich, George. 2000. Economic Lessons of the Kobe Earthquake. *Economic Development and Cultural Change* 48 (3): 521–542.

Horwitz, Steven. 2008. *Making Hurricane Response More Effective: Lessons from the Private Sector and the Coast Guard during Katrina.* Mercatus Policy Series. Policy Comment no. 17. Arlington, VA: Mercatus Center at George Mason University.

Hoyman, Michele. 2002. Prisons in N.C.: Are They a Rational Strategy for Rural Economic Development? *International Journal of Economic Development* 4, no. 1.

Hoyois, P.; Below, R.; Scheuren, J.-M.; and Guha-Sapir, D. 2007. *Annual Disaster Review: Numbers and Trends.* Brussels: Centre for Research on the Epidemiology of Disasters.

Human Rights Watch. 2007. Hidden Apartheid: Caste Discrimination against India's "Untouchables." Center for Human Rights and Global Justice 19 (3), downloadable at http://www.chrgj.org/docs/IndiaCERDShadowReport.pdf.

Hurlbert, Jeanne S.; Haines, Valerie A.; and Beggs, John J. 2000. Core Networks and Tie Activation: What Kinds of Routine Networks Allocate Resources in Nonroutine Situations? *American Sociological Review* 65 (4): 598–618.

Hurley, Andrew. 1995. *Environmental Inequalities: Class, Race, and Industrial Pollution in Gary, Indiana, 1945–1980.* Chapel Hill: University of North Carolina Press.

Hutton, David. 2001. Psychosocial Aspects of Disaster Recovery: Integrating Communities into Disaster Planning and Policy Making. Paper 2, Institute for Catastrophic Loss Reduction, Toronto.

Hyogo Earthquake Memorial 21st Century Research Institute. 2009. *Joint Research on the Assessment Methodology for Recovery Community Development.* Kobe, Japan: United Nations Center for Regional Development.

Hyōgo Ken [Hyogo Prefecture]. 2003. Saigai fukkō kōei jutaku danchi komyuniti chōsa hōkokusho [Report on the survey of the community in post-disaster public housing]. Hyogo Prefecture.

Hyōgoken Kendo Seiribu Fukkōkyoku Fukkō Suishinka [Hyogo Prefecture, Land Development Department, Reconstruction Bureau, Reconstruction Promotion Division]. 2007. Fukkō monitā chōsa 2006 hōkokusho [Report on reconstruction monitor survey 2006]. Hyogo Prefecture.

Ikeda, Hirotaka. 2004. Comparative Study of Housing Recovery Measures Taken after the 1999 Kocaeli Earthquake and the 1995 Hanshin-Awaji Earthquakes. In Itsuki Nakabayshi, ed., *A Comparative Study of Urban Reconstruction Processes after Earthquakes in Turkey, Taiwan, and Japan*, 33–38. Tokyo: Graduate School of Urban Science, Tokyo Metropolitan University.

Ikeda, Ken'ichi, and Richey, Sean. 2005. Japanese Network Capital: The Impact of Social Networks on Political Participation. *Political Behavior* 37 (3): 239–260.

Imai, Kosuke. 2005. Do Get-Out-the-Vote Calls Reduce Turnout? The Importance of Statistical Methods for Field Experiments. *American Political Science Review* 99 (2): 283–300.

International Collective in Support of Fishworkers. 2006. Regional Workshop on Post-tsunami Rehabilitation of Fishing Communities and Fisheries-Based Livelihoods. Chennai, India, 18–19 January.

Inui, Koh. 1998. Sanka ni okeru gōi/kettei to wa nanika [What is an agreement/decision in participation?], in Hanshin-Awaji Daishinsai Fukkō ni kansuru Tokubetu Chousa Kenkyu Purojekuto [The Great Hanshin-Awaji Earthquake Reconstruction Reseach Project], ed., *Hanshin-Awaji* Daishinsai *sougo kenkyu ronbunsyu* [The great Hanshin-Awaji Earthquake comprehensive study report], 243–249. Kyoto: Ritsumeikan University.

Ishise, Hirokazu, and Sawada, Yasuyuki. 2006. Aggregate Returns to Social Capital. Working paper F-413, Center for International Research on the Japanese Economy.

Iuchi, Kanako. 2010. Redefining a Place to Live: Decisions, Planning Processes, and Outcomes of Resettlement after Disasters. PhD diss., University of Illinois at Urbana-Champaign.

Jacobs, Jane. (1961) 1992. *The Death and Life of Great American Cities.* New York: Vintage Books.

Jackman, Robert, and Miller, Ross. 1998. Social Capital and Politics. *Annual Review of Political Science,* 1:47–73.

Jaeger, Paul; Shneiderman, Ben; Fleischmann, Kenneth; Preece, Jennifer; Qu, Yan; and Wu, Philip. 2007. Community Response Grids: E-Government, Social Networks, and Effective Emergency Management. *Telecommunications Policy* 31 (10–11): 592–604.

Jakes, Pamela, ed. 2002. *Homeowners, Communities, and Wildfire: Science Findings from the National Fire Plan.* Proceedings of the Ninth International Symposium on Society and Resource Management Bloomington, Indiana, June 2–5. St. Paul, MN: Forest Service, US Department of Agriculture.

James, Charles D., and Cameron, Carol. 2002. *The Earthquake Engineering Online Archive: The 1923 Tokyo Earthquake and Fire.* National Information Service for Earthquake Engineering. http://nisee.berkeley.edu/kanto/tokyo1923.pdf.

Jimenez, Emmanuel, and Sawada, Yasuyuki. 1999. Do Community-Managed Schools Work? An Evaluation of El Salvador's EDUCO Program. *World Bank Economic Review* 13:415–441.

Johnson, Craig. 2003. Decentralization in India: Poverty, Politics, and Panchayati Raj. Working paper 199, Department of Political Science, University of Guelph, Ontario.

Johnson, Laurie A. 2007. New Orleans' Recovery following Hurricane Katrina: Observations on Local Catastrophe Recovery Management. *Journal of Disaster Research* 2 (6): 517–529.

Joiner, Lottie. 2010. *New Orleans' "Black Mayberry" Looks for a Second Act.* New York: New York Times Student Journalism Institute.

Kage, Rieko. 2010a. Making Reconstruction Work: Civil Society and Information after War's End. *Comparative Political Studies* 43 (2): 163–187.

———. 2010b. Rebuilding from War in Japan: Information and Coordination, 1945–55. Paper presented at the annual Association for Asian Studies conference, Philadelphia.

———. 2011. *Civic Engagement in Postwar Japan: The Revival of a Defeated Society.* New York: Cambridge University Press.

Kamel, Nabil, and Loukaitou-Sideris, Anastasia. 2004. Residential Assistance and Recovery following the Northridge Earthquake. *Urban Studies* 41 (3): 533–562.

Kannan, Ramya. 2005. A Community on the Way to Recovery. *Hindu,* 25 December.

Kantō Daishinsai Hachishūnenkinen Gyōji Jikkō Iinkai [Great Kanto Earthquake 80th Anniversary Commemoration Committee], ed. 2004. *Rekishi to shite no* Kantō Daishinsai—*Ajia, Kokka, minshū* [The great Kanto earthquake as history—Asia, Japan, and the people]. Tokyo: Nihon Keizai Hyoronsha.

Kapur, Akash. 2009. Letter from India: Changed Forever by Disaster. *New York Times*, 29 December.

Karatani, Yuka, et al. 2000. Seikatsu saiken shihyō kara mita Hanshin-Awaji Daishinsai go no Kobeshi no seikatsu saiken katei [The process of recovery in Kobe City after the Hanshin-Awaji Earthquake as analyzed through a "recovery index"]. Paper presented at the 55th annual Academic Conference of Japan Society of Civil Engineers, September.

Karlan, Dean. 2005. Using Experimental Economics to Measure Social Capital and Predict Financial Decisions. *American Economic Review* 95 (5): 1688–1699.

Kasza, Gregory J. 1986. Democracy and the Founding of Japanese Public Radio. *Journal of Asian Studies* 45 (4): 745–767.

Kates, R. W.; Colten, C. E.; Laska, S.; and Leatherman, S. P. 2006. Reconstruction of New Orleans after Hurricane Katrina: A Research Perspective. *Proceedings of the National Academy of Sciences* 103 (40): 14653–14660.

Kates, Robert, and Pijawka, David. 1977. From Rubble to Monument: The Pace of Reconstruction. In J. Eugene Haas, Robert Kates, and Martyn Bowden, eds., *Reconstruction following Disaster*, 1–23. Cambridge, MA: MIT Press.

Katz, Bruce. 2006. The Material World: Concentrated Poverty in New Orleans and Other American Cities. *Chronicle of Higher Education*, 1 August.

Kaur, Naunidhi. 2003. Rebuilding Mutual Trust. *Frontline* 20 (14): 5–18.

Keele, Luke. 2007. Social Capital and the Dynamics of Trust in Government. *American Journal of Political Science* 51 (2): 241–254.

Keele, Luke, and Kelly, Nathan. 2005. Dynamic Models for Dynamic Theories: The Ins and Outs of Lagged Dependent Variables. *Political Analysis* 14 (2): 186–205.

Keishichō Kanbō Bunshoka Tōkei Henshū [Tokyo Metropolitan Police Department, Archives Section, Statistics Committee]. *Keishichō tōkeisho* [Police statistics] (various years). Tokyo: Keishichō.

Keishichō Shi Hensan Iinkai [Tokyo Metropolitan Police History Editing Committee]. 1960. *Keishichō shi Taishōhen* [Taisho period history of the Tokyo Metropolitan Police]. Tokyo: Keishichō Shi Hensan Iinkai.

Kilmer, Ryan P.; Gil-Rivas, Virginia; and MacDonald, Jacqueline. 2009. Implications of Major Disaster for Educators, Administrators, and School-Based Mental Health Professionals: Needs, Actions, and the Example of Mayfair Elementary. In Ryan P. Kilmer, Virginia Gil-Rivas, Richard G. Tedeschi, and Lawrence G. Calhoun, *Helping Families and Communities Recover from Disaster*, 167–191. Washington DC: American Psychological Association.

Kilmer, Ryan P.; Gil-Rivas, Virginia; Tedeschi, Richard G.; and Calhoun, Lawrence G., eds. 2009. *Helping Families and Communities Recover from Disaster*. Washington DC: American Psychological Association.

Kimbara, Samon. 1994a. Kindai sekai no tenkan to Taishō demokurashii [Taisho democracy and changes in the modern world]. In Samon Kimbara, ed., Taishō demokurashī: Kindai nihon no kiseki [Taishō democracy: The trajectory of modern Japan], 4:1–27. Tōkyō: Yoshikawa Kōbunkan.

———, ed. 1994b. *Taishō demokurashī: Kindai nihon no kiseki* [Taishō democracy: The trajectory of modern Japan], vol. 4. Tōkyō: Yoshikawa Kōbunkan.

Kimura, Reo. 2007. Recovery and Reconstruction Calendar. *Journal of Disaster Research* 2 (6): 465–474.

King, Elizabeth M., and Orazem, Peter F. 1999. Evaluating Education Reforms: Four Cases in Developing Countries. *World Bank Economic Review* 13:409–441.

King, Gary. 1995. Replication, Replication. *PS: Political Science and Politics* 28 (3): 443–499.

―――. 1997. *A Solution to the Ecological Inference Problem*. Princeton, NJ: Princeton University Press.

King, Gary; Keohane, Robert; and Verba, Sidney. 1994. *Designing Social Inquiry: Scientific Inference in Qualitative Research*. Princeton, NJ: Princeton University Press.

King, Gary; Tomz, Michael; and Wittenberg, Jason. 2000. Making the Most of Statistical Analyses: Improving Interpretation and Presentation. *American Journal of Political Science* 44 (2): 341–355.

King, Gary, and Zeng, Lanche. 2001. Logistic Regression in Rare Events Data. *Political Analysis* 9 (2): 137–163.

King, Rita. 2009. Post-Katrina Profiteering: The New Big Easy. In Robert Bullard and Beverly Wright, eds. *Race, Place, and Environmental Justice after Hurricane Katrina*, 169–182. Philadelphia: Westview Press.

Kingston, Christopher. 2005. Social Capital and Corruption: Theory and Evidence from India. Working paper, Amherst College.

Klein, Naomi. 2007. *The Shock Doctrine: The Rise of Disaster Capitalism*. Toronto: Alfred A. Knopf.

Knack, Stephen. 2002. Social Capital and Quality of Government: Evidence from States. *American Journal of Political Science* 46 (4): 772–785.

Knowles, Robin; Sasser, Diane D.; and Garrison, M. E. Betsy. 2009. Family Resilience and Resiliency following Hurricane Katrina. In Ryan P. Kilmer, Virginia Gil-Rivas, Richard G. Tedeschi, and Lawrence G. Calhoun, *Helping Families and Communities Recover from Disaster*, 97–115. Washington DC: American Psychological Association.

Kobayashi, Masahiro. 2006. Kantō Daishinsai go no shōgakkō kenchiku: "Fukkō shōgakkō" no zenyō to tōkyōshi kenchikukyoku ni yoru gakkō sekkei [A study on the building of elementary schools after the Great Kanto Earthquake: A broader view of the "reconstructed elementary school" and its planning by the city of Tokyo Construction Bureau]. *Bulletin of the Graduate School of Education, the University of Tokyo* 46:21–30.

Kobe City NPO Database. http://www.kobenpomap.com/photo/hojin/120080129130902.xls.

Kōbe Shi Senkyo Kanri Iinkai [Kobe City Election Committee]. n.d. Kakushu senkyo no tōhyō titsu: Kekka nado [The rates and results of various elections]. Available online at http://www.city.kobe.jp/cityoffice/60/06.html.

Kōbe Shi Sōmukyoku Tōkeika [Kobe City General Affairs Bureau, Statistics Department]. 1990–2005. *Kōbe Shi tōkeisho* [Kobe City Statistics], various years. Kobe: Kobe Shi.

Koh, Howard, and Cadigan, Rebecca. 2008. Disaster Preparedness and Social Capital. In Ichiro Kawachi, S. V. Subramanian, and Daniel Kim, eds., *Social Capital and Health*, 273–285. New York: Springer.

Kohnert, Dirk. 2009. Review Article: New Nationalism and Development in Africa. *Africa Spectrum* 1:111–123.

Kolbert, Elizabeth. 2006. Can Southern Louisiana Be Saved? *New Yorker*, February.

Kondo, Naoki; Minai, Junko; Imai, Himashi; and Yamagata, Zentaro. 2007. Engagement in a Cohesive Group and Higher-Level Functional Capacity in Older Adults in Japan: A Case of the Mujin. *Social Science and Medicine* 64:2311–2323.

Kondo, Tamiyo. 2008. Planning for Post-disaster Recovery in New Orleans after Hurricane Katrina. Paper presented at International Symposium on City Planning, Tokyo.

Konishi, Satchio. 1998. Kōkyūzai no shiteki kyōkyū shisutemu toshite no shōbōdan no kenkyū [The private supply of public goods: Research on fire brigades]. *Sanken Ronshū*, no. 25:13–27.

Krishna, Anirudh. 2001. Moving from the Stock of Social Capital to the Flow: The Role of Agency. *World Development* 29 (6): 925–943.

———. 2002. *Active Social Capital: Tracing the Roots of Democracy and Development*. New York: Columbia University Press.

———. 2003. Understanding, Measuring, and Utilizing Social Capital: Clarifying Concepts and Presenting a Field Application from India. Working paper 28, CGIAR Systemwide Program on Collective Action and Property Rights, CAPRI, Washington, DC.

———. 2007. How Does Social Capital Grow? A Seven-Year Study of Villages in India. *Journal of Politics* 69 (4): 941–956.

———. 2008. Social Capital and Economic Development. In Dario Castiglione, Jan W. van Deth, and Guglielmo Wolleb, eds., *The Handbook of Social Capital*, 438–466. New York: Oxford University Press.

———. 2009. Can We Bank upon Social Capital? Comparing Levels across Seven Years in 61 Villages of Rajasthan, India. Working paper, Duke University.

Kruks-Wisner, Gabrielle. 2011. Seeking the Local State: Gender, Caste, and the Pursuit of Public Services in Post-tsunami India. *World Development* 39 (7): 1143–1154.

Krupa, Michelle. 2011. New Orleans Neighborhoods That Suffered Worst Flooding Lost Most Residents, Census Data Show. *New Orleans Times-Picayune*, 6 February.

Krupa, Michelle, and Coleman, Warner. 2006. Across South, Displaced Chime in with Own Ideas for Rebuilding New Orleans. *New Orleans Times-Picayune*, 3 December.

Kumar, Krishan. 1993. Civil Society: An Inquiry into the Usefulness of an Historical Term. *British Journal of Sociology* 44 (3): 375–395.

Kumar, M. Suresh; Murhekar, Manoj; Hutin, Yvan; Subramanian, Thilagavathi; Ramachandran, Vidya; and Gupte, Mohan. 2007. Prevalence of Posttraumatic Stress Disorder in a Coastal Fishing Village in Tamil Nadu after the December 2004 Tsunami. *American Journal of Public Health* 97 (1): 99–101.

Kunreuther, Howard. 2007. Catastrophe Insurance Challenges for the U.S. and Asia. Paper presented at Asian Catastrophe Insurance Innovation and Management, Kyoto University 3–4 December.

———. 2010. Long Term Contracts for Reducing Losses from Future Catastrophes. In Howard Kunreuther and Michael Useem, eds., *Learning from Catastrophes: Strategies for Reaction and Response*, 235–248. Saddle River, NJ: Wharton School.

Kunreuther, Howard, and Useem, Michael, eds. 2010. *Learning from Catastrophes: Strategies for Reaction and Response*. Saddle River, NJ: Wharton School.

Kweit, Mary, and Kweit, Robert. 2004. Citizen Participation and Citizen Evaluation in Disaster Recovery. *American Review of Public Administration* 34 (4): 354–373.

———. 2006. A Tale of Two Disasters. *Publius: The Journal of Federalism* 36 (3): 375–392.

Lang, Robert. 2006. Measuring Katrina's Impact on the Gulf Megapolitan Area. In Eugenie Birch and Susan Wachter, eds., *Rebuilding Urban Places after Disaster: Lessons from Hurricane Katrina*, 89–102. Philadelphia: University of Pennsylvania Press.

Lang, Robert, and Danielsen, Karen. 2006. Review Roundtable: Is New Orleans a Resilient City? *Journal of the American Planning Association* 72 (2): 245–257.

Large, Stephen. 1972. *The Rise of Labor in Japan: The Yūaikai, 1912–19*. Tokyo: Sophia University Press.

LaRose, Greg. 2006. Asian Businesses Drive Eastern New Orleans Recovery. *New Orleans City Business*, 2 October.

Lee, Matthew, and Bartkowski, John. 2004. Love Thy Neighbor? Moral Communities, Civic Engagement, and Juvenile Homicide in Rural Areas. *Social Forces* 82 (3): 1001–1035.

Lee, Matthew; Weil, Frederick; and Shihadeh, Edward. 2007. The FEMA Trailer Parks: Negative Perceptions and the Social Structure of Avoidance. *Sociological Spectrum* 27:741–766.

Leong, Karen; Airriess, Christopher; Li, Wei; Chen, Angela; and Keith, Verna. 2007. Resilient History and the Rebuilding of a Community: The Vietnamese Community in New Orleans East. *Journal of American History* 94:770–779.

Lesbirel, S. Hayden. 1998. *NIMBY Politics in Japan: Energy Siting and the Management of Environmental Conflict.* Ithaca, NY: Cornell University Press.

Levitt, Steven, and List, John. 2009. Field Experiments in Economics: The Past, the Present, and the Future. *European Economic Review* 53:1–18.

Levy, Jonah. 1999. *Tocqueville's Revenge: State, Society, and Economy in Contemporary France.* Cambridge, MA: Harvard University Press.

Lewis, Michael. 1990. *Rioters and Citizens: Mass Protest in Imperial Japan.* Berkeley: University of California Press.

Leyden, Kevin. 2003. Social Capital and the Built Environment: The Importance of Walkable Neighborhoods. *American Journal of Public Health* 93 (9): 1546–1551.

Lietaer, Bernard. 2004. Complementary Currencies in Japan Today: History, Originality and Relevance. *International Journal of Community Currency Research* 8:1–23.

Lin, Nan. 2008. A Network Theory of Social Capital. In Dario Castiglione, Jan W. van Deth, and Guglielmo Wolleb, eds., *The Handbook of Social Capital,* 50–69. New York: Oxford University Press.

Lin, Shuyeu; Shaw, Daigee; and Ho, Ming-Chou. 2008. Why Are Flood and Landslide Victims Less Willing to Take Mitigation Measures Than the Public? *Natural Hazards* 44:305–314.

Liu, Amy; Fellowes, Matt; and Mabanta, Mia. 2006. *A One-Year Review of Key Indicators of Recovery in Post-storm New Orleans.* Washington, DC: Brookings Institution.

Liu, Baodong; Austin, Sharon D. Wright; and Orey, Byron D'Andrá. 2009. Church Attendance, Social Capital, and Black Voting Participation. *Social Science Quarterly* 90 (3): 576–592.

Lochner, Kimberly; Kawachi, Ichiro; Brennan, Robert; and Buka, Stephen. 2003. Social Capital and Neighborhood Mortality Rates in Chicago. *Social Science and Medicine* 56:1797–1805.

Logan, John. 2009. Unnatural Disaster: Social Impacts and Policy Choices after Katrina. In Robert Bullard and Beverly Wright, eds., *Race, Place, and Environmental Justice after Hurricane Katrina: Struggles to Rebuild, Reclaim, and Revitalize New Orleans and the Gulf Coast,* 249–264. Boulder, CO: Westview Press.

Long, J. Scott. 1997. *Regression Models for Categorical and Limited Dependent Variables.* Thousand Oaks, CA: Sage.

Louis, M. 2005. *Study on Discrimination and Exclusion in State Relief.* Madurai, India: People's Watch-Tamil Nadu.

Louisiana Family Recovery Corps. 2005. Louisiana Family Recovery Corps (home page). http://www.recoverycorps.org/.

Lovenheim, Peter. 2008. Won't You Be My Neighbor? *New York Times*, 23 June.

MacTavish, Katherine. 2006. We're Like the Wrong Side of the Tracks: Upscale Suburban Development, Social Inequality, and Rural Mobile Home Park Residence. Working paper 06-03, Rural Poverty Research Center of the University of Missouri.

Maeda, Kiyoshi. 2007. Twelve Years since the Great Hanshin Awaji Earthquake, a Disaster in an Aged Society. *Psychogeriatrics* 7:41–43.

Maggi, Laura. 2006. Seven New Orleans Cops Indicted in Killings on Bridges. *New Orleans Times-Picayune*, 29 December.

Mahapatra, Anirban Das. 2005. Old Man and the Sea. *Telegraph* (Calcutta), 19 August.

Maloney, William; Smith, Graham; and Stoker, Gerry. 2000. Social Capital and Urban Governance: Adding a More Contextualized "Top Down" Perspective. *Political Studies* 48: 802–820.

Marcelo, Ray. 2005. India Seeks Aid for Long-Term Rehabilitation. *Financial Times* (London), 12 January.

Martin, Max. 2005. A Voice for Vulnerable Groups in Tamil Nadu. *Forced Migration Review*, July, 44–45.

Mathbor, Golam. 2007. Enhancement of Community Preparedness for Natural Disasters: The Role for Social Work in Building Social Capital for Sustainable Rrelief and Management. *International Social Work* 50 (3): 357–369.

Matsuda, Yoko, et al. 2002. Jikūkan tokei shuhō ni yoru Hanshin-Awaji Daishinsai go no jinkō kaihuku katei ni kansuru bunseki [Analysis on the population recovery process after the Hanshin-Awaji Earthquake through conditional spatial autoregression]. Paper presented at the Fifty-seventh Annual Academic Conference of Japan Society of Civil Engineers, September.

Matsuo, Takayoshi. 1990. *Taishō demokurashī no gunzō* [Forms of Taishō democracy]. Tokyo: Iwanami Shoten.

Mattingly, Shirley. 2000. Public Support for Livelihood Reconstruction. In Committee for Global Assessment of Earthquake Countermeasures, Hyogo Prefectural Government, ed., *Assessment Reports of the Global Assessment of Earthquake Countermeasures*, vol. 4, *Support of Disaster Victims*, 179–186. Hyogo Prefecture: Hyogo Prefectural Government.

May, Peter. 1985. *Recovering from Catastrophes: Federal Disaster Relief Policy and Politics.* London: Greenwood Press.

McCreight, Robert. 2010. Resilience as a Goal and Standard in Emergency Management. *Journal of Homeland Security and Emergency Management* 7 (1): 1–7.

McCulley, Russell. 2006. Is New Orleans Having a Mental Health Breakdown? *Time*, 1 August.

McKinley, Jesse. 2009. Celebrate a Quake? Why Shouldn't We? *San Francisco Journal*, 17 October.

McLaren, Lauren, and Baird, Vanessa. 2006. Of Time and Causality: A Simple Test of the Requirement of Social Capital in Making Democracy Work in Italy. *Politics Studies* 54: 889–897.

McQuaid, John, and Schleifstein, Mark. 2002. Washing Away. *New Orleans Times-Picayune*, 23–27 June.

Mehta, Neha. 2007. Great Indian Family's Mind Balm. *Hindustan Times*, 11 March.

Menon, Manju; Rodriguez, Sudarshan; and Sridhar, Aarthi. 2007. *Coastal Zone Management Notification '07—Better or Bitter Fare?* Bangalore: Post-tsunami Environment Initiative Project, Ashoka Trust for Research in Ecology and the Environment.

Menon, Sudha Venu. 2007. Grass Root Democracy and Empowerment of People: Evaluation of Panchayati Raj in India. MPRA Paper 3839, ICFAI Business School, Ahmedaba.

Mercks, Eva. 2007. Caste Cloud over Tsunami Relief and Rehabilitation. MA thesis, ISHSS, University of Amsterdam.

Mildenberg, David. 2011. Census Finds Hurricane Katrina Left New Orleans Richer, Whiter, Emptier. *Bloomberg News*, 4 February.

Miller, Kristen, and Simile, Catherine. 1992. They Could See the Stars from Their Beds: The Plight of the Rural Poor in the Aftermath of Hurricane Hugo. Paper presented at the annual meeting of the Society for Applied Anthopology, March, Memphis.

Mills, C. Wright. 1959. *The Sociological Imagination*. New York: Grove Press.

Mochizuki, Masashi. 1993. Kantō Daishinsai kenkyū wo meguru shoronten-gyakusatsu jiken to fukkōron [Various issues concerning research on the Great Kanto Earthquake: Massacres and reconstruction theory]. *Rekishi Hyoron* 521:74–83.

Moore, Melinda; Wermuth, Michael; Castaneda, Laura; Chandra, Anita; Noricks, Darcy; Resnick, Adam; Chu, Carolyn; and Burks, James. 2010. *Bridging the Gap: Developing a Tool to Support Local Civilian and Military Disaster Preparedness*. Santa Monica, CA: RAND Corporation.

Morrow, Betty. 2000. Stretching the Bonds: The Families of Andrew. In Walter Peacock, Betty Morrow, and Hugh Gladwin, eds., *Hurricane Andrew: Ethnicity, Gender, and the Sociology of Disasters*, 141–170. Miami: International Hurricane Center.

———. 2005. Recovery: What's Different, What's the Same? Paper presented at National Academies of Science Disaster Roundtable, 8 March.

Moyo, Dambisa. 2009. *Dead Aid: Why Aid Is Not Working and How There Is a Better Way for Africa*. New York: Farrar, Straus and Giroux.

Murakami, Suminao. 2000. Support for Home Reconstruction. In Committee for Global Assessment of Earthquake Countermeasures, Hyogo Prefectural Government, ed., *Assessment Reports of the Global Assessment of Earthquake Countermeasures*, vol. 4, *Support of Disaster Victims*, 219–250. Hyogo Prefecture: Hyogo Prefectural Government.

Murosaki, Masuteru. 1973. Kantō Daishinsai to toshi keikaku [The Kanto Earthquake and city planning]. *Reikishi Hyōron* 281:12–20.

Murosaki, Yoshiteru. 2007. The Great Hanshin Earthquake and Fire. *Journal of Disaster Research* 2 (4): 298–302.

Murray, Brendan. 2006. Katrina's Damage to Bush's Standing Still Haunts His Presidency. *Bloomberg News*, 25 August.

Nagar, Na'ama, and Rethemeyer, R. Karl. 2007. Do Good Neighbors Make Good Terrorists? The Dark Side of Civil Society. Paper presented at annual meeting of the American Political Science Association, Chicago.

Naimushō Shakaikyoku [Bureau of Social Affairs, Home Office]. 1926. *The Great Earthquake of 1923 in Japan*. Tokyo: Sanshusha Press.

Nakabayashi, Itsuki. 2004. Research Framework of International Comprehensive Studies. In Itsuki Nakabayshi, ed., *A Comparative Study of Urban Reconstruction Processes after Earthquakes in Turkey, Taiwan, and Japan*, 1–4. Tokyo: Graduate School of Urban Science, Tokyo Metropolitan University.

Nakabayashi, Itsuki, and Ichiko, Taro. 2004. A Comparative Study of Built Up Reconstruction Measures and Strategy among Earthquake Disasters of Hanshin Awaji, East Marmar, and 921 Chi-chi. In Itsuki Nakabayshi, ed., *A Comparative Study of Urban Reconstruction Processes after Earthquakes in Turkey, Taiwan, and Japan*, 5–14. Tokyo: Graduate School of Urban Science, Tokyo Metropolitan University.

Nakagawa, Yuko, and Shaw, Rajib. 2004. Social Capital: A Missing Link to Disaster Recovery. *International Journal of Mass Emergencies and Disasters* 22 (1): 5–34.

Nakajima, Yōichirō. 1973. *Kantō Daishinsai—Sono jissō to rekishiteki igi* [The Kanto Earthquake—Its realities and historical significance]. Tokyo: Yūzankaku.

Nakamura, Akira. 1982. Shinsai fukkō no seijigaku-shiron, teito fukkō keikaku no shōchō [The politics of earthquake reconstruction: An essay on the rise and fall of the great city reconstruction plan]. *Seikei ronsō* [Essays on politics and economics] 50 (3): 295–388.

———. 2000. The Need and Development of Crisis Management in Japan's Public Administration: Lessons from the Kobe Earthquake. *Journal of Contingencies and Crisis Management* 8 (1): 23–29.

Namboothri, Naveen;, Subramanian, Devi; Muthuraman, B.; Sridhar, Aarthi; Rodriguez, Sudarshan; and Shanker, Kartik. 2008. *Beyond the Tsunami: Coastal Sand Dunes of Tamil Nadu, India—an Overview.* Bangalore: UNDP/UNTRS, Chennai and ATREE.

Nance, Earthea. 2009. Making the Case for Community-Based Laboratories. In Robert Bullard and Beverly Wright, eds., *Race, Place, and Environmental Justice after Huricane Katrina*, 153–166. Philadelphia: Westview Press.

Nandakumar, T. 2006. Community Radio for Fisherfolk Set to Take Off. *Hindu*, 26 April.

Narita, Ryuichi. 2007. *Taishō demokurashi* [Taisho democracy]. Tokyo: Iwanami Shoten.

Natrajan, Balmurli. 2005. Caste, Class, and Community in India: An Ethnographic Approach. *Ethnology* 44 (3): 227–241.

Navsarjan Trust and RFK Center for Justice and Human Rights. 2008. *Understanding Untouchability.* Washington, DC: Robert F. Kennedy Center for Justice and Human Rights.

Nel, Philip, and Righarts, Marjolein. 2008. Natural Disasters and the Risk of Violent Civil Conflict. *International Studies Quarterly* 52:159–185.

Nelson, Rob, and Varney, James. 2005. Not in My Back Yard Cry Holding up FEMA trailers. *New Orleans Times-Picayune*, 26 December.

Nelson, Stephanie C. 2007. Small-Scale Aid's Contribution to Long Term Tsunami Recovery. *Carolina Papers on International Development*, no. 18.

Newman, Oscar. 1972. *Defensible Space: Crime Prevention through Urban Design.* New York: Macmillan.

———. 1996. *Creating Defensible Space.* Washington, DC: US Department of Housing and Urban Development, Office of Policy Development and Research.

New Orleans Health Disparities Initiative. 2007. *After Katrina: Rebuilding a Healthy New Orleans.* Washington, DC: Health Policy Institute of the Joint Center for Political and Economic Studies.

Newton, Kenneth. 2001. Trust, Social Capital, Civil Society, and Democracy. *International Political Science Review* 22:201–214.

Nidhiprabha, Bhanupong. 2007. *Adjustment and Recovery in Thailand Two Years after the Tsunami.* ADB Institute Discussion Paper 72. Tokyo: Asian Development Bank Institute.

Nigg, Joanne; Barnshaw, John; and Torres, Manuel. 2006. Hurricane Katrina and the Flooding of New Orleans: Emergent Issues in Sheltering and Temporary Housing. *Annals of the American Academy of Political and Social Science* 604:113–128.

Nolte, Isabella, and Boenigk, Silke. 2011. Public-Private Partnership Performance in a Disaster Context: The Case of Haiti. *Public Administration Review.* Available at doi: 10.1111/j.1467-9299.2011.01950.x.Nordahl, Peter. 1995. New Fires in Kobe Challenge Rescuers. *Christian Science Monitor*, 20 January.

Nordlinger, Eric. 1981. *On the Autonomy of the Democratic State.* Cambridge, MA: Harvard University Press.

Norr, Kathleen. 1975. The Organization of Coastal Fishing in Tamil Nadu. *Ethnology* 14 (4): 357–371.

Norris, Fran; Stevens, Susan; Pfefferbaum, Betty; Wyche, Karen; and Pfefferbaum, Rose. 2008.

Community Resilience as a Metaphor, Theory, Set of Capacities, and Strategy for Disaster Readiness. *American Journal of Community Psychology* 41:127–150.

Nossiter, Adam. 2007. With Regrets, New Orleans Is Left Behind. *New York Times*, 18 December.

Nossiter, Adam, and Eaton, Leslie. 2007. Violent Protest over Housing in New Orleans. *New York Times*, 21 December.

Obinata, Sumio. 2000. *Kindai nihon no keisatsu to chiiki shakai* [Modern Japan's police and local ommunities]. Tokyo: Chikuma Shobo.

Office of the Secretary-General's Special Envoy for Tsunami Recovery. 2005. *Tsunami Recovery: Taking Stock after 12 Months.* New York: United Nations.

Ogasawara, Haruno. 1999. Living with Natural Disasters: Narratives of the Great Kanto and Great Hanshin Earthquakes. PhD diss., Northwestern University.

Ogawa, Masuo, ed. 1973. *Tōkyō shōshitsu—Kantō Daishinsai no hiroku* [The disappearance of Tokyo—Confidential papers on the Great Kanto Earthquake]. Tokyo: Kōsaidō.

Ohlemacher, Thomas. 1996. Bridging People and Protest: Social Relays of Protest Groups against Low-Flying Military Jets in West Germany. *Social Problems* 43 (2): 197–218.

Okuyama, Yasuhide. 2003. Economics of Natural Disasters: A Critical Review. Paper presented at the 50th North American Meeting, Regional Science Association International, 20–22 November, Philadelphia.

Oliver-Smith, Anthony, and Hoffman, Susanna. 1999. *The Angry Earth: Disaster in Anthropological Perspective.* New York: Routledge.

Olshansky, Robert. 2006. San Francisco, Kobe, New Orleans: Lessons for Rebuilding. *Social Policy* 36 (2): 17–19.

Olshansky, Robert; Johnson, Laurie; and Topping, Kenneth. 2005. *Opportunity in Chaos: Rebuilding after the 1994 Northridge and 1995 Kobe Earthquakes.* Urbana-Champaign: University of Illinois Department of Urban and Regional Planning.

Olshansky, Robert; Kobayashi, Ikuo; and Ohnishi, Kazuyoshi. 2005. The Kobe Earthquake, Ten Years Later. *Planning* 71 (9): 36.

Olson, Mancur. 1965. *The Logic of Collective Action: Public Goods and the Theory of Groups.* Cambridge, MA: Harvard University Press.

Ono, Masāki. 1998. Kantō Daishinsai to gakkō no fukkō-Tōkyōshi no fukkō katei wo jirei to shite [The restoration of schools and the Great Kanto Earthquake: A case study of the process of rebuilding Tokyo]. *Bulletin of Universities and Institutes* (Institute of Humanities and Social Sciences, Nihon University), 56119–135.

Ōoka, Satoshi. 2001. Senkanki Tokyoshino chiiki to seiji [Regions and politics in Tokyo during the interwar period]. *Nihonshi kenkyū* [Journal of Japanese history], no. 464188–212.

Ordeshook, Peter. 1995. *Game Theory and Political Theory.* New York: Cambridge University Press.

Ostrom, Elinor. 1990. *Governing the Commons: The Evolution of Institutions for Collective Action.* New York: Cambridge University Press.

———. 2000. The Danger of Self-Evident Truths. *PS: Political Science and Politics* 33 (1): 33–44.

Ouma, Emily, and Abdulai, Awudu. 2009. Contributions of Social Capital Theory in Predicting Collective Action Behavior among Livestock Keeping Communities in Kenya. Paper presented at the International Association of Agricultural Economists Conference, 16–22 August, Beijing.

Ovalle, David. 2010. Haiti Could Learn from Mexico's Earthquake Recovery. *Miami Herald*, 17 February.

Özerdem, Alpaslan, and Jacoby, Tim. 2006. *Disaster Management and Civil Society: Earthquake Relief in Japan, Turkey and India*. New York: I. B. Tauris.

Pais, Jeremy, and Elliott, James R. 2008. Places as Recovery Machines: Vulnerability and Neighborhood Change after Major Hurricanes. *Social Forces* 86 (4): 1415–1453.

Paker, Hande. 2004. Social Aftershocks: Rent Seeking, State Failure, and State–Civil Society Relations in Turkey. PhD diss., McGill University.

Paruchuri, Srikanth. 2011. Natural Disasters, Community Distress and Church Foundings. Paper presented at the annual Academy of Management conference, 12–16 August, San Antonio, TX. Pastor, Manuel; Sadd, Jim; and Hipp, John. 2001. Which Came First? Toxic Facilities, Minority Move Up, and Environmental Justice. *Journal of Urban Affairs* 23 (1): 1–21.

Paxton, Pamela. 2002. Social Capital and Democracy: An Interdependent Relationship. *American Sociological Review* 67 (2): 254–277.

Peacock, Walter; Dash, Nicole; and Zhang, Yang. 2006. Sheltering and Housing Recovery following Disaster. In Havidán Rodríguez, Enrico L. Quarantelli, and Russell R. Dynes, eds., *Handbook of Disaster Research*, 258–274. New York: Springer.

Peacock, Walter, and Girard, Chris. 2000. Ethnic and Racial Inequalities in Hurricane Damage and Insurance Settlements. In Walter Peacock, Betty Morrow, and Hugh Gladwin, eds., *Hurricane Andrew: Ethnicity, Gender, and the Sociology of Disasters*, 171–190. Miami: International Hurricane Center.

Peacock, Walter; Morrow, Betty; and Gladwin, Hugh. 2000. *Hurricane Andrew: Ethnicity, Gender, and the Sociology of Disasters*. Miami: International Hurricane Center.

Peacock, Walter, and Ragsdale, Kathleen. 2000. Social Systems, Ecological Networks and Disasters. In Walter Peacock, Betty Morrow, and Hugh Gladwin, eds., *Hurricane Andrew: Ethnicity, Gender, and the Sociology of Disasters*, 20–35. Miami: International Hurricane Center.

Pekkanen, Robert. 2000. Japan's New Politics: The Case of the NPO Law. *Journal of Japanese Studies* 26 (1): 111–146.

People's Watch. 2007. *Compounding Disaster: Conformability of Post–Natural Disaster Relief and Rehabilitation Process with Human Rights Standards*. Tamil Nadu; People's Watch.

Perrow, Charles. 2007. *The Next Catastrophe*. Princeton, NJ: Princeton University Press.

Pfefferbaum, Betty; Pfefferbaum, Rose L.; and Norris, Fran H. 2009. Community Resilience and Wellness for Children Exposed to Hurricane Katrina. In Ryan P. Kilmer, Virginia Gil-Rivas, Richard G. Tedeschi, and Lawrence G. Calhoun, *Helping Families and Communities Recover from Disaster*, 265–288. Washington, DC: American Psychological Association.

Phillipps, Jeremy. 2008. Creating Modern Cityscapes and Modern Civilians: The Urban Planning Law and the 1927 Hikoso Fire Reconstruction in Kanazawa. *Japan Review* 20:157–188.

Phillips, Brenda, and Jenkins, Pamela. 2009. The Roles of Faith-Based Organizations after Hurricane Katrina. In Ryan P. Kilmer, Virginia Gil-Rivas, Richard G. Tedeschi, and Lawrence G. Calhoun, *Helping Families and Communities Recover from Disaster*, 215–238. Washington, DC: American Psychological Association.

Pilling, David. 2005. Tokyo Prepares for "the Big One." *Financial Times* (London), January 17, 10.

Pittman, Cassi. 2008. The Use of Social Capital in Borrower Decision-Making. Working paper, Joint Center for Housing Studies of Harvard University.

Pogrebin, Robin. 2007. Rebuilding New Orleans, Post-Katrina Style. *New York Times*, 6 November.

Poley, Lisa, and Stephenson, Max. 2007. Community and the Habits of Democratic Citizenship: An Investigation into Civic Engagement, Social Capital and Democratic Capacity-Building in U.S. Cohousing Neighborhoods. Paper presented at the 103rd annual meeting of the American Political Science Association, Chicago.

Polidori, Robert. 2006. Waste Land. *New Yorker*, 9 January.

Poortinga, Wouter. 2006. Social Relations or Social Capital? Individual and Community Health Effects of Bonding Social Capital. *Social Science Medicine* 63 (1): 255–270.

Portes, Alejandro. 1998. Social Capital: Its Origins and Applications in Modern Sociology. *Annual Review of Sociology* 24:1–24.

Portes, Alejandro, and Vickstrom, Erik. 2011. Diversity, Social Capital, and Cohesion. *Annual Review of Sociology* 37:461–479.

Praxis Institute for Participatory Practices. 2006. *Village Level People's Plans: Realities, Aspirations, Challenges.* New Delhi: Praxis Institute.

Pronyk, Paul M.; Harpham, Trudy; Busza, Joanna;, Phetla, Godfrey; Morison, Linda A.; Hargreaves, James R.; Kim, Julia C.; Watts, Charlotte H.; and Porter, John. 2008. Can Social Capital Be Intentionally Generated? A Randomized Trial from Rural South Africa. *Social Science and Medicine* 67:1559–1570.

Putnam, Robert. 1993. *Making Democracy Work: Civic Traditions in Modern Italy.* Princeton, NJ: Princeton University Press.

———. 1995. Bowling Alone: America's Declining Social Capital. *Journal of Democracy* 6 (1): 65–78.

———. 2000. *Bowling Alone: The Collapse and Revival of American Community.* New York: Simon and Schuster.

———. 2007. E Pluribus Unum: Diversity and Community in the Twenty-First Century. *Scandinavian Political Studies* 30 (2): 137–174.

Pyles, Loretta. 2007. Research in Post-Katrina New Orleans: Recommendations from Community Organizations. Working paper, Tulane University September.

Quarantelli, Enrico L. 1999. The Disaster Recovery Process: What We Know and Do Not Know from Research. Preliminary Paper 286, University of Delaware Disaster Research Center.

Rabe-Hesketh, Sophia, and Everitt, Brian. 2007. *A Handbook of Statistical Analyses Using Stata,* 4th ed. New York: Chapman and Hall.

Rahn, Wendy, and Rudolph, Thomas. 2005. A Tale of Political Trust in American Cities. *Public Opinion Quarterly* 69 (4): 530–560.

Ramachandran, Sanjeev. 2006. SIFFS Rehab of Tsunami Hit Fishermen Earns Laurels. *Business Standard*, 25 April.

Ramachandran, Thiru. 2010. *Backward Classes, Most Backward Classes, and Minorities.* Welfare Department Demand no. 9 Policy Note. Tamil Nadu: Government of Tamil Nadu.

Ramakumar, R. 2008. Contextualizing Disaster Studies: Socioeconomic Vulnerabilities in India. Paper presented at Researching Disasters Conference, Tata Institute, 4 February, Mumbai.

Reiter, Bernd. 2009. Civil Society and Democracy: Weimar Reconsidered. *Journal of Civil Society* 5 (1): 21–34.

Reuter, Peter, and Truman, Edwin. 2004. *Chasing Dirty Money: The Fight against Money Laundering.* Washington, DC: Institute for International Economics.

Richardson, James. 2006. What's Needed for Post-Katrina Recovery. Working paper, Financial Services Roundtable.

Richey, Sean. 2007. Manufacturing Trust: Community Currencies and the Creation of Social Capital. *Political Behavior* 29:69–88.

Roberts, Patrick. 2007. Was It the Plans, the Leaders, or the System? Hurricane Katrina and the

Difficulty of Reform in the American Political System. Paper presented at the annual meeting of the American Political Science Association, Chicago.

Robertson, Campbell. 2010. On Anniversary of Katrina, Signs of Healing. *New York Times*, 27 August.

Robison, Lindon; Schmid, A. Allan; and Siles, Marcelo. 2002. Is Social Capital Really Capital? *Review of Social Economy* 60 (1): 1–21.

Rodriguez, Havidan; Wachtendorf, Tricia; Kendra, James; and Trainor, Joseph. 2006. A Snapshot of the 2004 Indian Ocean Tsunami: Societal Impacts and Consequences. *Disaster Prevention and Management* 15 (1): 163–177.

Rodriguez, Sudarshan. 2008. Push Out Fisherfolk, Make Room for Water Sports? *Tehelka*, 9 February, 53.

Rodriguez, Sudarshan; Balasubramanian, Gomathy; Shiny, M. P.; Mohanambigai, D.; and Jaiprakash, P. 2008. *Beyond the Tsunami: Community Perceptions of Resources, Policy and Development, Post-tsunami Interventions and Community Institutions.* Bangalore: UNDP/ UNTRS, Chennai and ATREE.

Rogers, Elizabeth S. Cousins, and Rogers, Walter. 1965. Riding the Nightmare Express: New Orleans' Betsy Hurricane-Flood. Photocopy. Available online at http://hurricanearchive .org/object/26649.

Rohe, William, and Basolo, Victoria. 1997. Long-Term Effects of Homeownership on the Self-Perceptions and Social Interaction of Low-Income Persons. *Environment and Behavior* 29 (6): 793–819.

Roodman, David. 2007. The Anarchy of Numbers: Aid, Development, and Cross-Country Empirics. *World Bank Economic Review* 21 (2): 255–277.

Rosenbaum, Paul R., and Rubin, Donald B. 1983. The Central Role of the Propensity Score in Observational Studies for Causal Effects. *Biometrika* 70 (1): 41–55.

———. 1985. Constructing a Control Group Using Multivariate Matched Sampling Methods That Incorporate the Propensity Score. *American Statistician* 39 (1): 33–38.

Rosenzweig, Mark, and Wolpin, Kenneth. 2000. Natural "Natural Experiment" in Economics. *Journal of Economic Literature* 38 (4): 827–874.

Rosett, Richard N., and Nelson, Forrest D. 1975. Estimation of the Two-Limit Probit Regression Model. *Econometrica* 43 (1): 141–146.

Rossi, Ino. 1993. *Community Reconstruction after an Earthquake: Dialectical Sociology in Action.* New York: Praeger.

Rovai, Eugenie. 1994. The Social Geography of Disaster Recovery: Differential Community Responses to the North Coast Earthquakes. *Association of Pacific Coast Geographers Yearbook* 56:49–74.

Rubin, Claire, and Barbee, Daniel. 1985. Disaster Recovery and Hazard Mitigation: Bridging the Intergovernmental Gap. *Public Administration Review* 45:57–63.

Rüdig, Wolfgang. 1994. Maintaining a Low Profile: The Anti-nuclear Movement and the British State. In Helena Flam, ed., *States and Anti-nuclear Movements*, 70–100. Edinburgh: Edinburgh University Press.

Rural Education and Development Society. 2006. *Tsunami: Competition, Conflict, and Cooperation.* Tamil Nadu: REDS.

Russell, Gordon. 2006. Inspiration for Rebuilding. *New Orleans Times-Picayune*, 5 December, 1.

Sakurai, Ryoju. 2002. 1920 Nendai Tōkyō ni okeru chiiki seiji kōzō no henka [Shifts in the structure of regional politics in Tokyo in the 1920s]. In Hiroshi Onishi and Sadahiro Umeda, eds., *Dai Tōkyō kūkan no seijishi, 1920–1930 nendai* [The history of politics in the greater sphere of Tokyo: 1920s–1930s], chap. 6. Tokyo: Nihon Keizai Hyoronsha.

Salagrama, Venkatesh. 2006a. *Trends in Poverty and Livelihoods in Coastal Fishing Communities of Orissa State, India.* Technical Paper 490. Rome: Food and Agriculture Organization of the United Nations.

———. 2006b. *Post-tsunami Rehabilitation of Fishing Communities and Fisheries Livelihoods in Tamil Nadu, Kerala, and Andra Pradesh.* Andra Pradesh: Integrated Coastal Management.

Santha, Sunil D. 2007a. Conflicts in Fish Trade: A Study among the Riverine Fishing Communities in Kerala, India. *International Sociological Bulletin,* no. 8:22–35.

———. 2007b. State Interventions and Natural Resource Management: A Study on Social Interfaces in a Riverine Fisheries Setting in Kerala, India. *Natural Resources Forum* 31:61–70.

Sanyika, Mtangulizi. 2009. Katrina and the Condition of Black New Orleans: The Struggle for Justice, Equity, and Democracy. In Robert Bullard and Beverly Wright, eds., *Race, Place, and Environmental Justice after Hurricane Katrina,* 87–111. Philadelphia: Westview Press.

Sarat, Austin, and Lezaun, Javier, eds. 2009. *Catastrophe: Law, Politics, and the Humanitarian Impulse.* Amherst: University of Massachusetts Press.

Savitch, H. V. 2007. *Cities in a Time of Terror: Space, Territory, and Local Resilience.* Armonk, NY: M. E. Sharpe.

Sawada, Yasuyuki. 2010. How Do Households Cope with Natural and Man-Made Disasters? Paper presented at Building Resilience Conference, 25 March, Purdue University.

Sawada, Yasuyuki; Ichimura, Hidehiko; and Shimizutani, Satoshi. 2008. The Economic Impacts of Earthquakes on Households: Evidence from Japan. Paper presented at Centre for Research on the Epidemiology of Disasters Workshop, 28 April.

Sawada, Yasuyuki; Sarath, Sanga; and Shoji, Masahiro. 2006. University of Tokyo–Tamil Nadu Agricultural University (UT-TNAU Dataset).

Sawada, Yasuyuki, and Shimizutani, Satoshi. 2007. Consumption Insurance and Risk-Coping Strategies under Non-separable Utility: Evidence from the Kobe Earthquake. Working paper F-512, CIRJE. Faculty of Economics, Tokyo University.

———. 2008. How Do People Cope with Natural Disasters? Evidence from the Great Hanshin-Awaji (Kobe) Earthquake in 1995. *Journal of Money, Credit and Banking* 40 (2–3): 463–488.

Schellong, Alexander. 2007. Increasing Social Capital for Disaster Response through Social Networking Services in Japanese Local Governments. Working paper 07-005, National Center for Digital Government.

Schencking, J. Charles. 2006. Catastrophe, Opportunism, Contestation: The Fractured Politics of Reconstructing Tokyo following the Great Kantō Earthquake of 1923. *Modern Asian Studies* 40 (4): 833–873.

Schneider, Mark; Teske, Paul; Marschall, Melissa; Mintrom, Michael; and Roch, Christine. 1997. Institutional Arrangements and the Creation of Social Capital: The Effects of Public School Choice. *American Political Science Review* 91 (1): 82–93.

Schneider, Saundra. 1990. FEMA, Federalism, Hugo, and 'Frisco. *Publius* 20 (3): 97–115.

Schuller, Mark. 2008. Deconstructing the Disaster after the Disaster: Conceptualizing Disaster Capitalism. In Nandini Gunewardena and Mark Schuller, eds., *Capitalizing on Catastrophe: Neoliberal Strategies in Disaster Reconstruction,* 17–27. Lanham, MD, AltaMira Press.

Schuller, Tom; Baron, Stephen; and Field, John. 2000. Social Capital: A Review and a Critique. In Stephen Baron, John Field, and Tom Schuller, eds., *Social Capital: Critical Perspectives,* 1–38. Oxford: Oxford University Press.

Scott, James C. 1998. *Seeing Like a State: How Certain Schemes to Improve the Human Condition Have Failed.* New Haven, CT: Yale University Press.

Seidensticker, Edward. 1991. *Tokyo Rising: The City since the Great Earthquake.* Cambridge, MA: Harvard University Press.

Sekikawa, Chihiro; Sakurai, Mayumi; and Song, Meiyu. 2006. Kōreisha shūgō jutaku ni kansuru kenkyū—Korekuteibu haujingu no jirei wo tōshite [Collective housing for seniors: An analysis of examples of such housing]. *Kyōto kyōiku daigaku kiyō* [Bulletin of Kyoto University of Education], no. 109:85–98.

Serra, Renata. 2001. Social Capital: Meaningful and Measurable at the State Level? *Economic and Political Weekly* 36 (8): 693–704.

————. 2004. "Putnam in India": Is Social Capital a Meaningful and Measurable Concept at the Indian State Level? In Dwaipayan Bhattacharyya, Niraja Gopal Jayal, Sudha Pai, and Bishnu N. Mohapatra, eds., *Interrogating Social Capital: The Indian Experience,* 259–295. New Delhi: Sage.

Shaji, K. A. 2008. Without Sight of Sea. *Tehelka* 19:18–19.

Sharma, Pravesh. 2005. Livelihood Strategies in Coastal Tamil Nadu: Case Study of a Tsunami Affected Village in Cuddalore District. Paper presented at Livelihoods Workshop, Chennai, 15 September.

Shaw, Rajib. 2006. Indian Ocean Tsunami and Aftermath: Need for Environment-Disaster Synergy in the Reconstruction Process. *Disaster Prevention and Management* 15 (1): 5–20.

Shaw, Rajib, and Goda, Katsuhiro. 2004. From Disaster to Sustainable Civil Society: The Kobe Experience. *Disasters* 28 (1): 16–40.

Sherman, Daniel. 2006. Not Here, Not There, Not Anywhere: The Federal, State and Local Politics of Low-Level Radioactive Waste Disposal in the United States, 1979–1999. Paper presented at the 2006 Northeastern Political Science Association Conference, Boston.

Sheth, Alpa; Sanyal, Snigdha; Jaiswal, Arvind; and Gandhi, Prathibha. 2006. Effects of the December 2004 Indian Ocean Tsunami on the Indian Mainland. *Earthquake Spectra* 22 (3): S435–S473.

Shibusawa, M. 1924. *A Description of the Damages Done by the Great Earthquake of Sept. 1, 1923 to the Electrical Installations in Japan.* Tokyo: Electrical Association of Japan.

Shrady, Nicholas. 2008. *The Last Day: Wrath, Ruin, and Reason in the Great Lisbon Earthquake of 1755.* New York: Viking.

Shrubsole, Dan. 1999. *Natural Disasters and Public Health Issues: A Review of the Literature with a Focus on the Recovery Period.* ICLR Research Paper Series 4. London: University of Western Ontario.

Siegel, David. 2009. Social Networks and Collective Action. *American Journal of Political Science* 53 (1): 122–138.

Silberbauer, George. 2003. Structural and Personal Social Processes in Disaster. *Australian Journal of Emergency Management* 18 (3): 29–36.

Simile, Catherine M. 1995. Disaster Settings and Mobilization for Contentious Collective Action: Case Studies of Hurricane Hugo and the Loma Prieta Earthquake. PhD diss., University of Delaware.

Simmel, Georg. (1908) 1950. *The Sociology of Georg Simmel.* Translated by Kurt Wolff. New York: Free Press.

Sinclair, Betsy; Hall, Thad; and Alvarez, R. Michael. 2009. Flooding the Vote: Hurricane Katrina and Voter Participation in New Orleans. Working paper 70, Voting Technology Project of Caltech.

Singer, Peter. 1972. Famine, Affluence, and Morality. *Philosophy and Public Affairs* 1:229–243.

Sirianni, Carmen. 2009. *Investing in Democracy: Engaging Citizens in Collaborative Governance.* Washington, DC: Brookings Institution.

Siromony, P. Michael Vetha. 2006. Critical Gaps in Disaster Governance. In C. Raj Kumar and D. K. Srivastava, eds., *Tsunami and Disaster Management: Law and Governance,* 183–200. Hong Kong: Thomson, Sweet and Maxwell.

Skocpol, Theda. 1979. *States and Social Revolutions.* Cambridge: Cambridge University Press.

Small, Mario Luis. 2009. *Unanticipated Gains: Origins of Network Inequality in Everyday Life.* New York: Oxford University Press.

Smethurst, Richard J. 1986. *Agricultural Development and Tenancy Disputes in Japan, 1870–1940.* Princeton, NJ: Princeton University Press.

Smith, Gavin. 2011. *Planning for Post-Disaster Recovery: A Review of the United States Disaster Assistance Framework.* Washington, DC: Island Press.

Sobel, Joel. 2002. Can We Trust Social Capital? *Journal of Economic Literature* 40:139–154.

Social Needs Education and Human Awareness, Law Trust and National Legal Services Authority. 2006. A Report of the Social Audit on Relief and Rehabilitation Interventions of Government of Tamil Nadu in Nagapattinam District, May 2005 to May 2006.

Solnit, Rebecca. 2009. *A Paradise Built in Hell: The Extraordinary Communities That Arise in Disaster.* New York: Viking.

Sorensen, Andre. 2007. Changing Governance of Shared Spaces: Machizukuri as Institutional Innovation. In Andre Sorensen and Carolin Funck, *Living Cities in Japan: Citizens' Movements, Machizukuri and Local Environments,* 56–90. London: Routledge.

South Asia Regional Knowledge Platform. 2005. Role of Panchayati Raj Institutions in Post-tsunami Reconstruction and Rehabilitation. Workshop Proceedings, 15 April.

Sridhar, Aarthi. 2005. *Statement on the CRZ Notification and Post-tsunami Rehabilitation in Tamil Nadu.* New Delhi: United Nations Development Programme.

Srinivas, M. N. 1987. *The Dominant Caste and Other Essays.* New Delhi: Oxford University Press.

Stallings, Robert, and Quarantelli, E. L. 1985. Emergent Citizen Groups and Emergency Management. *Public Administration Review* 45:93–100.

State Relief Commissioner, Government of Tamil Nadu. 2005. *Tiding over Tsunami.* Tamil Nadu: Government of India.

Stein, Robert; Dueñas-Osorio, Leonardo; and Subramanian, Devika. 2010. Who Evacuates When Hurricanes Approach? The Role of Risk, Information, and Location. *Social Science Quarterly* 91 (3): 816–834.

Steinberg, Ted. 2000. *Acts of God: The Unnatural History of Natural Disaster in America.* Oxford: Oxford University Press.

Stiglitz, Joseph E. 2000. Formal and Informal Institutions. In Partha Dasgupta and Ismail Serageldin, eds., *Social Capital: A Multifaceted Perspective,* 59–68. Washington, DC: World Bank.

Streeck, Wolfgang, and Thelen, Kathleen, eds. 2005. *Beyond Continuity: Institutional Change in Advanced Political Economies.* Oxford: Oxford University Press.

Suga, Masahiro. 2007. Atarashii komyuniti no keisei to tenkai [Forming and developing a new community]. In Masaki Urano, Jun Oyane, and Tadahiro Yoshikawa, eds., *Fukkō komyuniti ron nyūmon* [Introduction to theories on the reconstruction of communities], 98–100. Tokyo: Kōbundō.

Swaroop, Reddy. 1992. A Study of Long-Term Recovery of Three Communities in the Aftermath of Hurricane Hugo. PhD diss., Texas A&M University.

Sweet, Stephen. 1998. The Effect of a Natural Disaster on Social Cohesion: A Longitudinal Study. *International Journal of Mass Emergencies and Disasters* 16 (3): 321–331.

Syzerhans, Douglas. 2006. *Federal Disaster Programs and Hurricane Katrina.* New York: Nova Science Publishers.

Szreter, Simon. 2002. The State of Social Capital: Bringing Back in Power, Politics, and History. *Theory and Society* 31 (5): 573–621.

Szreter, Simon, and Woolcock, Michael. 2004. Health by Association? Social Capital, Social Theory, and the Political Economy of Public Health. *International Journal of Epidemiology* 33 (4): 650–667.

Taft-Morales, Maureen, and Margesson, Rhoda. 2010. *Haiti Earthquake: Crisis and Response.* Washington, DC: Congressional Research Service.

Taiheiyō Sensō Kenkyūkai [Pacific War Study Group]. 2003. Kantō Daishinsai [Great Kanto Earthquake]. Tokyo: Kawade Shobō.

Tajika, Eiji. 2000. Public Support for Livelihood Rebuilding. In Committee for Global Assessment of Earthquake Countermeasures, Hyogo Prefectural Government, ed., *Assessment Reports of the Global Assessment of Earthquake Countermeasures,* vol. 4, *Support of Disaster Victims,* 119–168. Hyogo Prefecture: Hyogo Prefectural Government.

Takahashi, Lois. 1998. *Homelessness, AIDS, and Stigmatization: The NIMBY Syndrome in the United States at the End of the Twentieth Century.* Oxford: Clarendon Press.

Takahashi, Masayuki. 2001. Kasetsu jūtaku nyūkyosha no jittai chōsa [Survey of actual conditions among temporary housing residents]. In Kobe Toshi Mondai Kenkyūjo [Kobe Institute of Urban Research], ed., *Shinsai chōsa no riron to jissen-shinsai higai, seikatsu saiken, sangyō fukkō, jūtaku, kenkō* [Theory and practice of the survey on earthquake—earthquake damage, life rebuilding, industry recovery, housings, and health]. Tokyo: Keiso Shobo.

Takasaki, Yoshito. 2010. Natural Disasters and Informal Risk Sharing against Illness: Networks vs. Groups. Working paper, Tsukuba University Economics Department.

———. 2011. Targeting Cyclone Relief within the Village: Kinship, Sharing, and Capture. *Economic Development and Cultural Change* 59 (2): 387–416.

Takashima, Masasuke, and Hayashi, Haruo. 1999. Denryoku shōhiryō jikeiretsu deita wo riyō shita fukkō jōkyō no teiryōteki haaku shuhō—Hanshin/Awaji Daishinsai heno tekiyō [Quantitative monitoring of recovery process using time series data of electric power consumption—an application to the Hanshin-Awaji Earthquake disaster], *Shizen saigai kagaku* [Science of natural disasters] 18 (3): 355–367.

Takemura, Masayuki. 2003. Kantō Daishinsai—Dai Tōkyōken no yure wo shiru [The Great Kanto Earthquake—learning about the quake of the Tokyo area]. Tokyo: Kajima.

Tamanoi, Mariko. 2009. Suffragist Women, Corrupt Officials, and Waste Control in Prewar Japan. *Journal of Asian Studies* 68 (3): 805–834.

Tanaka, Masaru. 2006. *Teito fukkō to seikatsu kūkan: Kantō Daishinsai no shigai chikeisei no ronri* [The revival of the Imperial City and its living spaces: The logic of rebuilding after the Kanto Earthquake]. Tokyo: Tokyo University Press.

Tanaka, Shigeyoshi. 2007. Sumtora Jishin to Komyuniti [Community and the Sumatra Earthquake]. In Masaki Urano, Jun Oyane, and Tadahiro Yoshikawa, eds., *Fukkō komyuniti ron nyūmon* [Introduction to theories on the reconstruction of communities], 235–244. Tokyo: Kōbundō.

Tandon, Rajesh, and Mohanty, Ranjita. 2000. *Civil Society and Governance: A Research Study in India.* New Delhi: Society for Participatory Research in Asia.

Tanida, Noritoshi. 1996. What Happened to Elderly People in the Great Hanshin Earthquake. *British Medical Journal* 313 (7065): 1133–1135.

Tarrow, Sidney. 1996. Making Social Science Work across Space and Time: A Critical Reflection on Robert Putnam's *Making Democracy Work. American Political Science Review* 90 (2): 389–397.

Tata Institute of Social Sciences. 2005. *The State and Civil Society in Disaster Response: An Analysis of the Tamil Nadu Tsunami Experience.* Mumbai: Tata Institute.

————. 2007. Case Study Follow-ups 2 Years after the Tsunami. Mumbai: Tata Institute.

Tatsuki, Shigeo. 2008. The Role of Civil Society for Long-Term Life Recovery from a Megadisaster. Paper presented at the 2008 annual meeting of the American Political Science Association, 28–31 August, Boston.

————. 2009. Social Capital and Community Governance: Evidence from a Study of the Kobe Earthquake. Paper presented at the Association for Asian Studies Annual conference, 26–29 March, Chicago.

————. 2010. The Effects of Empowered Social Capital during the Disaster Recovery Period. Paper presented at the annual meeting of the Association for Asian Studies, 25–28 March, Philadelphia.

Tatsuki, Shigeo, and Hayashi, Haruo. 2000. Family System Adjustment and Adaptive Reconstruction of Social Reality among the 1995 Earthquake Survivors. *International Journal of Japanese Sociology* 9:81–110.

————. 2002. Seven Critical Element Model of Life Recovery: General Linear Model Analyses of the 2001 Kobe Panel Survey Data. Paper presented at the second Workshop for Comparative Study on Urban Earthquake Disaster Management, 14–15 February, Kobe, Japan.

Tatsuki, Shigeo; Hayashi, Haruo; Yamori, Katsuya; Noda, Takashi; Tamura, Keiko; and Kimura, Reo. 2004. Hanshin Awaji Daishinsai hisaisha no chōkiteki na seikatsu fukkō katei no moderu ka to sono kensho: 2003 nen Hyogo ken Fukkō Chōsa Deta heno Kōzō Hōteishiki Moderingu (SEM) no Tekiyo [Model building and testing of long-term life recovery processes of the survivors of the 1995 Kobe earthquake: Structural equation Modeling (SEM) of the 2003 Hyogo Prefecture life recovery survey]. *Chiiki anzen gakkai ronbunshū* [Collected papers from the academic meeting on regional safety], 6:251–260.

————. 2005. Long-Term Life Recovery Processes of the Survivors of the 1995 Kobe Earthquake: Causal Modeling Analysis of the Hyogo Prefecture Life Recovery Panel Survey Data. Paper presented at the First International Conference on Urban Disaster Reduction, January 18–21, Kobe.

Taylor, Spencer. 2006. Insuring against Natural Catastrophe after Katrina. *Natural Resources and Environment Section of the American Bar Association,* Spring, 26–30.

Tedeschi, Gwendolyn Alexander. 2008. Overcoming Selection Bias in Microcredit Impact Assessments: A Case Study in Peru. *Journal of Development Studies* 44 (4): 504–518.

Teets, Jessica. 2009. Post-earthquake Relief and Reconstruction Efforts: The Emergence of Civil Society in China? *China Quarterly* 198 (June): 330–347.

Terry, Edith, and Hasegawa, Miharu. 1995. Kobe quake transforms Japanese into volunteers. *Christian Science Monitor,* 23 January.

Thakkar, Usha. 2004. Mohalla Committes of Mumbai. *Economic and Political Weekly* 7:580–586.

Tierney, Kathleen. 2007. From the Margins to the Mainstream? Disaster Research at the Crossroads. *Annual Review of Sociology* 33:503–525.

Tierney, Kathleen, and Goltz, James. 1997. Emergency Response: Lessons Learned from the Kobe Earthquake. Preliminary Paper 260, University of Delaware Disaster Research Center.

Tipton, Elise. 1991. *Japanese Police State: Tokkō in Interwar Japan*. Honolulu: University of Hawaii Press.

Tobin, Graham, and Montz, Burrell. 1997. *Natural Hazards: Explanation and Integration*. New York: Guilford Press.

Tocqueville, Alexis de. (1835) 2000. *Democracy in America*. Chicago: University of Chicago Press.

Tokyo Municipal Office. 1930. *Tokyo, Capital of Japan: Reconstruction Work*. Tokyo: Toppan.

Tōkyō Shi Kansakyoku, Tōkeika [Tokyo City Audit Department, Statistics Division]. 1936. *Senkyo tōkei* [Election statistics]. Tokyo: Tōkyō Shiyakusho [Tokyo Municipal Government].

Tomz, Michael, and Wittenberg, Jason. 1999. Interpreting and Presenting Statistical Results. Short course presented at the annual meeting of the American Political Science Association, September, Atlanta.

Tootle, Deborah. 2007. Disaster Recovery in Rural Communities: A Case Study of Southwest Louisiana. *Southern Rural Sociology* 22 (2): 6–27.

Tsuji, Katsuji. 2001. *Saigai katei to saisei katei: Hanshin-Awaji Daishinsai no shōjojishi* [The course of disaster and recovery: A short epic about the Hanshin Awaji Earthquake]. Kyoto: Kōyō Shobō.

Turner, Barry A. 1976. The Development of Disasters—a Sequence Model for the Analysis of the Origins of Disasters. *Sociological Review* 24:753–774.

Umeda, Atsuko. 2003. *Kochizu, gendaizu de aruku Meiji Taishō Tōkyō sanpo* [Strolling through Meiji and Taisho–era Tokyo with old and new maps]. Tokyo: Jinbunsha.

United Nations International Strategy for Disaster Reduction. 2005. *Hyogo Framework for Action 2005–2015: Building the Resilience of Nations and Communities to Disasters*. Geneva: UNISDR.

United Nations Team for Recovery Support. 2005. *Tsunami, One Year After: A Joint UN Report*—India. Chennai: United Nations.

United Nations Team for Tsunami Recovery Support. 2007. *Tsunami: India—Three Years After*. Chennai: United Nations.

United Nations, World Bank, and Asian Development Bank. 2006. *Tsunami—India: Two Years After*. Chennai: United Nations.

United States Government Accountability Office. 1991. *Federal, State, and Local Responses to Natural Disasters Need Improvement*. Washington, DC: USGAO.

———. 2006. *Barriers to Mental Health Services for Children Persist in Greater New Orleans, Although Federal Grants Are Helping to Address Them*. Washington, DC: USGAO. Link: http://www.gao.gov/new.items/d09563.pdf.

———. 2007. *Preliminary Information on Rebuilding Efforts in the Gulf Coast*. Washington, DC: USGAO. Link: http://www.gao.gov/new.items/d07809r.pdf.

———. 2008a. *FEMA Should More Fully Assess Organizations' Mass Care Capabilities and Update the Red Cross Role in Catastrophic Events*. Washington, DC: USGAO. Link: www.gao .gov/cgi-bin/getrpt?GAO-08-823.

———. 2008b. *Federal Efforts Help States Prepare for and Respond to Psychological Consequences, but FEMA's Crisis Counseling Program Needs Improvements*. Washington, DC: USGAO. Link: http://www.gao.gov/new.items/d0822.pdf.

United States Small Business Administration. 2006. *Entrepreneurship: The Foundation for Economic Renewal in the Gulf Coast Region*. Proceedings of the 11 April Conference, New Orleans. Washington, DC: USSBA.

Urano, Masaki; Oyane, Jun; and Yoshikawa, Tadahiro, eds. 2007. *Fukkō komyuniti ron nyūmon* [Introduction to theories on the reconstruction of communities]. Tokyo: Kōbundō.

Vale, Lawrence. 2006. Restoring Urban Viability. In Eugenie Birch and Susan Wachter, eds., *Rebuilding Urban Places after Disaster: Lessons from Hurricane Katrina*, 149–167. Philadelphia: University of Pennsylvania Press.

Vale, Lawrence, and Campanella, Thomas, eds. 2005. *The Resilient City: How Modern Cities Recover from Disaster.* New York: Oxford University Press.

Valelly, Richard M. 2004. What's Gone Right in the Study of What's Gone Wrong. *Chronicle of Higher Education* 50 (32): B6–B8.

van Biema, David, and Desmond, Edward W. 1995. When Kobe Died. *Time Magazine*, 30 January, 24.

Van Deth, Jan W. 2008. Measuring Social Capital. In Dario Castiglione, Jan W. van Deth, and Guglielmo Wolleb, eds., *The Handbook of Social Capital*, 150–176. New York: Oxford University Press.

Varney, James, and Carr, Martha. 2005. FEMA Drafting Trailer Park Map: Uptown, West Bank Sites on Initial List. *New Orleans Times-Picayune*, 26 October.

Varshney, Ashutosh. 2001. Ethnic Conflict and Civil Society: India and Beyond. *World Politics* 53 (3): 362–398.

Vaux, Tony, and Lund, Francie. 2003. Working Women and Security: Self Employed Women's Associations' Response to Crisis. *Journal of Human Development* 4 (2): 265–287.

Verba, Sidney, and Nie, N. H. 1972. *Participation in America.* New York: Harper and Row.

Vivekanandan, Shri V. 2005. From the Margins to Centre Stage: Consequences of Tsunami 2004 for the Fisher Folk of Tamil Nadu. Presentation to Planning Commission of India, 18 October.

Vogel, Steve. 1996. *Freer Markets, More Rules: Regulatory Reform in Advanced Industrial Countries.* Ithaca, NY: Cornell University Press.

Wallace, Tina. 1997. New Development Agendas: Changes in UK NGO Policies and Procedures. *Review of African Political Economy* 24 (71): 35–55.

Walsh, Edward J., and Warland, Rex H. 1983. Social Movement Involvement in the Wake of a Nuclear Accident: Activists and Free Riders in the TMI Area. *American Sociological Review* 48 (6): 764–780.

Warner, Coleman. 2006. Census Tallies Katrina Changes, but the Changing New Orleans Area Is a Moving Target. *New Orleans Times-Picayune*, 7 June.

Warner, Coleman, and Darce, Keith. 2006. Locals Not Waiting to Be Told What to Do. *New Orleans Times-Picayune*, 13 March.

Waugh, William. 2006. The Political Costs of Failure in the Katrina and Rita Disasters. *Annals of the American Academy of Political and Social Science* 604:10–25.

Webb, Gary; Tierney, Kathleen; and Dahlhamer, James. 2002. Predicting Long-Term Business Recovery from Disaster: A Comparison of the Loma Prieta Earthquake and Hurricane Andrew. *Environmental Hazards* 4 (1): 45–58.

Webb, Sheila J. 2009. Investing in Human Capital and Healthy Rebuilding in the Aftermath of Hurricane Katrina. In Robert Bullard and Beverly Wright, eds., *Race, Place, and Environmental Justice after Hurricane Katrina: Struggles to Rebuild, Reclaim, and Revitalize New Orleans and the Gulf Coast*, 139–152. Boulder, CO: Westview Press.

Weber, Max. (1904) 1958. *The Protestant Ethic and the Spirit of Capitalism.* New York: Charles Scribner's Sons.

Weil, Frederick. 2010. The Rise of Community Engagement after Katrina. In *The New Orleans*

Index at Five, 1–20. Washington, DC: Brookings Institution and Greater New Orleans Community Data Center.

Weil, Frederick; Shihadeh, Edward; and Lee, Matthew. 2006. The Burdens of Social Capital: How Socially-Involved People Dealt with Stress after Hurricane Katrina. Paper presented at annual meeting of the American Sociological Association, Montreal.

Weil, Rick. n.d. LSU Post-Katrina Studies of Community Resilience: Data Collection Methods and Results. Powerpoint presentation. Available at http://www.lsu.edu/fweil/Katrina Research.html.

West, Mark. 2005. *Law in Everyday Japan: Sex, Sumo, Suicide, and Statutes.* Chicago: University of Chicago Press.

Wetterberg, Anna. 2004. *Crisis, Social Ties, and Household Welfare: Testing Social Capital Theory with Evidence from Indonesia.* Washington, DC: World Bank.

Whelan, Robert, and Strong, Denise. 2009. In Robert Bullard and Beverly Wright, eds., *Race, Place, and Environmental Justice after Hurricane Katrina: Struggles to Rebuild, Reclaim, and Revitalize New Orleans and the Gulf Coast*, 183–203. Boulder, CO: Westview Press.

White, Connie; Plotnick, Linda; Kushma, Jane; Hiltz, Starr; and Turoff, Murray. 2009. An online social network for emergency management. *International Journal of Emergency Management* 6 (3–4): 369–382.

White, Halbert. 1980. A Heteroskedasticity-Consistent Covariance Matrix Estimator and a Direct Test for Heteroskedasticity. *Econometrica* 48:817–830.

Widestrom, Amy. 2008. Zoned Out: The Impact of Urban Renewal Policies on the Organizatonal Capacity of Voluntary Organizations in Inner-City Neighborhoods. Paper presented at the Policy History Conference, 29 May–1 June, St. Louis, MO.Wigand, Rolf; Crowston, Kevin; Sawyer, Steve; and Allbritton, Marcel. 2001. Information and Communication Technologies in the Real Estate Industry. Paper presented at Global Co-operation in the New Millennium the Ninth European Conference on Information Systems, Bled, Slovenia.

Williams, Jenny, and Sickles, Robin C. 2002. An Analysis of the Crime as Work Model: Evidence from the 1958 Philadelphia Birth Cohort Study. *Journal of Human Resources* 37 (3): 479–509.

Williamson, Thad. 2010. *Sprawl, Justice, and Citizenship: The Civic Costs of the American Way of Life.* New York: Oxford University Press.

Wilson, Charles. 2011. Five Years after Katrina, Teacher Tills Soil of Lower 9th Ward. *New York Times*, 15 January.

Wilson, Rick, and Stein, Robert. 2006. Katrina Evacuees in Houston: One Year Out. Working Paper, Rice University, Katrina Project.

Wood, Nathan; Burton, Christopher; and Cutter, Susan. 2010. Community Variations in Social Vulnerability to Cascadia-Related Tsunamis in the U.S. Pacific Northwest. *Natural Hazards* 52 (2): 369–389.

Woolcock, Michael. 2002. Social Capital in Theory and Practice: Reducing Poverty by Building Partnerships between States, Markets and Civil Society. In *Social Capital and Poverty Reduction: Which Role for Civil Society Organizations and the State?* 20–44. France: UNESCO.

Woolcock, Michael, and Narayan, Deepa. 2000. Social Capital: Implications for Development Theory, Research, and Policy. *World Bank Research Observer* 15 (2): 225–249.

Woolcock, Michael, and Radin, Elizabeth. 2008. A Relationship Approach to the Theory and Practices of Economic Development. In Dario Castiglione, Jan W. van Deth, and Guglielmo Wolleb, eds., *The Handbook of Social Capital*, 411–437. New York: Oxford University Press.

Wooldridge, Jeffrey. 2006. *Introductory Econometrics: A Modern Approach.* Mason, OH: Thomson Higher Education.

Worthington, Ian; Ram, Monder; and Jones, Trevor. 2006. Exploring Corporate Social Responsibility in the UK Asian Small Business Community. *Journal of Business Ethics* 67:201–217.

Wright, James; Rossi, Peter; Wright, Sonia; and Weber-Burdin, Eleanor. 1979. *After the Clean-Up: Long-Range Effects of Natural Disasters.* Beverly Hills, CA: Sage.

Wu, Jie Yang. 2003. A Comparative Study of Housing Reconstruction after Two Major Earthquakes: The 1994 Northridge Earthquake in the United States and the 1999 Chi-Chi Earthquake in Taiwan. PhD diss., Texas A&M University.

Xie, Yu, and Manski, Charles. 1989. The Logit Model and Response-Based Samples. *Sociological Methods and Research* 17:283–302.

Yamada, Misao. 1973. Keihin ni okeru toshi mondai no keihu: Kantō Daishinsai to Yokohama Fukkō [Tracing urban problems in Tokyo and Yokohama: Rebuilding Yokohama after the Great Kanto Earthquake] *Jinbun kenkyū* [Humanities research] 55:139–165.

Yamada, Shoji. 1993. Kantō Daishinsaiji no Chosenjin gyakusatsu sekinin no yukue [Tracing responsibility for the massacres of Koreans at the time of the Great Kanto Earthquake]. *Rekishi hyōron* [Historical review] 521:15–27.

Yamazaki, Masakazu. 1992. The Intellectual Community of the Showa Era. In Carol Gluck and Stephen Graubard, eds., *Showa: The Japan of Hirohito,* 245–264. New York: W. W. Norton.

Yasuda, Hiroshi. 1994. *Taishō demokurashī Shiron: Taishū minshu shugi taisei he no tenkei to genkai* [History of Taishō democracy: The shift to popular democratic system and its limitations]. Tokyo: Azekura Shobō.

Yasui, Etsuko. 2007. Community Vulnerability and Capacity in Post Disaster Recover: The Cases of Mano and Mikura Neighborhoods in the Wake of the 1995 Kobe Earthquake. PhD diss., University of British Columbia.

Yoshimune, Chie. 1999. Kobe Quake Victims Still Displaced. *Earth Island Journal,* Fall, 40.

Yoshimura, Akira. 2004. *Kantō Daishinsai* [The Great Kanto Earthquake]. Tokyo: Bungei Shunjū.

Yunus, Muhammad. 2008. *Creating a World without Poverty: Social Business and the Future of Capitalism.* New York: PublicAffairs.

Zandi, Mark; Cochrane, Steven; Ksiazkiweicz, Fillip; and Sweet, Ryan. 2006. Restarting the Economy. In Eugenie Birch and Susan Wachter, eds., *Rebuilding Urban Places after Disaster: Lessons from Hurricane Katrina,* 103–116. Philadelphia: University of Pennsylvania Press.

Zhao, Yandong. 2010. Social Networks and Reduction of Risk in Disasters: An Example of Wenchuan Earthquake. Paper presented at the International Conference on Economic Stress, Human Capital, and Families in Asia, 3–4 June, Singapore.

Zhao, Yandong, and Dalen, Kristin. 2006. Natural Disasters and Social Capital: A Study in Western China. Paper presented at the International Disaster Reduction Conference, 27 August–1 September, Davos, Switzerland.

Zook, Mathhew; Graham, Mark; Shelton, Taylor; and Gorman, Sean. 2010. Volunteered Geographic Information and Crowdsourcing Disaster Relief: A Case Study of the Haitian Earthquake. *World Medical and Health Policy* 2 (2): 9–33.

Index

Each year, natural disasters threaten the strength and stability of communities worldwide. Yet responses to the challenges of recovery vary greatly, often in ways that aren't explained by the magnitude of the catastrophe or the amount of aid provided by national governments or the international community. The difference between resilience and disrepair, Daniel P. Aldrich shows, lies in the depth of communities' social capital.

Building Resilience highlights the critical role of social capital in the ability of a community to withstand disaster and rebuild the infrastructure and ties that are at its foundation. Aldrich examines the post-disaster responses of four different communities—Tokyo following the 1923 earthquake, Kobe after the 1995 earthquake, Tamil Nadu after the 2004 Indian Ocean tsunami, and post-Katrina New Orleans—and finds that those with robust social networks were better able to coordinate recovery. In addition to quickly disseminating information and assistance, communities with an abundance of social capital were able to minimize the migration of people and resources out of the area.

With governments increasingly overstretched and natural disasters likely to increase in frequency and intensity, an understanding of what contributes to efficient reconstruction is more important than ever. *Building Resilience* underscores a critical component of an effective response.

"Why do some communities recover more quickly and fully than others? Using a comparative interdisciplinary approach and elegantly crafted research, Daniel P. Aldrich shows that social capital is the dominant force driving post-disaster recovery. *Building Resilience* is social science at its best, with rich implications that will prompt a paradigm shift in disaster planning." Arjen Boin, Utrecht University School of Governance

"Daniel P. Aldrich has drawn the lens back from the single event to reveal patterns of resilience—and roadblocks to recovery—in four different post-disaster contexts. *Building Resilience* offers a novel and compelling look at the darker side of social capital as it relates to post-disaster recovery." Emily Chamlee-Wright, Beloit College

Daniel P. Aldrich is associate professor of political science at Purdue University. He is the author of *Site Fights: Divisive Facilities and Civil Society in Japan and the West.*

ISBN-13: 978-0-226-01288-9
ISBN-10: 0-226-01288-3

THE UNIVERSITY OF CHICAGO PRESS
www.press.uchicago.edu